Documentary Graphic Novels

ism

Cultural Interactions
Studies in the Relationship between the Arts

Edited by J.B. Bullen

Volume 7

PETER LANG
Oxford · Bern · Berlin · Bruxelles · Frankfurt am Main · New York · Wien

Jeff Adams

Documentary Graphic Novels and Social Realism

PETER LANG
Oxford · Bern · Berlin · Bruxelles · Frankfurt am Main · New York · Wien

Bibliographic information published by Die Deutsche Bibliothek
Die Deutsche Bibliothek lists this publication in the Deutsche Nationalbibliografie; detailed bibliographic data is available on the Internet at ‹http://dnb.ddb.de›.

A catalogue record for this book is available from The British Library.

Library of Congress Cataloging-in-Publication Data:

Adams, Jeff, 1956-
Documentary graphic novels and social realism / Jeff Adams.
p. cm.
Includes bibliographical references.
ISBN 978-3-03-911362-0 (alk. paper)
1. Documentary comic books, strips, etc.--History and criticism. I. Title.
PN6714.A33 2008
741.5'355--dc22

2008036927

ISSN 1662-0364
ISBN 978-3-03911-362-0

Cover Image: detail from *Palestine* (p. 99), © Joe Sacco 2001, reproduced with kind permission of the author and Fantagraphics Books Inc.

Printed in Germany

Contents

Preface and Acknowledgements

This book has been developed from my PhD thesis 'Graphic Novels and Social Realism' (2003, University of Liverpool).

Material for this book was kindly and generously provided by Jaqueline Berndt, Jonathan Clements, Geoff Fenwick, Alan Gleason, Leonard Rifas, Jim Ottaviani, Joe Sacco, and Fred Schodt.

For their constructive criticism and encouragement I am indebted to Dennis Atkinson, Sarnath Banerjee, Fiona Candlin, Paul Dash, Diana Davies, Eric Fernie, Jonathan Harris, Shirley Brice Heath, Wendy Hyde, Ann MacPhee, Pam Meecham, Tara Page, and all my colleagues at Goldsmiths, University of London, who have assisted and supported me in the writing of this book.

Parts of this book have been developed from previously published works: "The Pedagogy of the Image Text: Nakazawa, Sebald and Spiegelman Recount Social Traumas" in *Discourse: Studies in the Cultural Politics of Education* 29.1 (2008): 37–52; "Troubled Places: Domestic Space in Graphic Novels" in *Our House: The Representation of Domestic Space in Modern Culture*, edited by Joanne Croft and Gerry Smyth, 161–174 (Amsterdam: Rodopi Press, 2006).

All efforts have been made to contact the copyright holders of all illustrations. Thanks to all of the publishers and authors who have given me the right to reproduce their works; Last Gasp, Project Gen and Fantagraphics Books were particularly helpful and generous in this respect. Special thanks to Joe Sacco for permitting the use of his work for the cover illustration, a detail from his Fantagraphics publication *Palestine* (detail p.99, © Joe Sacco 2001; reproduced with permission of Fantagraphics Books Inc.).

This book is dedicated to Wendy and Chrissi
for their love and support, and to Luca and Sonny
who were born during its creation.

Introduction

The desire of artists and authors to document social and political events, and the means by which they might do so, is an enduringly contentious subject. To explore this question the book examines a sample of contemporary documentaries in the graphic novel medium that give accounts of social crises. These novels are located and defined as part of a radical practice of realism, produced by artist-authors challenging orthodox mythologies.

The term graphic novel (sometimes referred to generically as 'image text'[1]) denotes the development of comic books for an audience interested in politics, current affairs and literature, and it is employed liberally in this book to allow for the inclusion of contemporary illustrated novels. The concept and classification of graphic novels have long been controversial, as is the way that they are situated in the field of cultural production, inextricably bound up as they are with the political context of state and society. The forms that documentary graphic novel authors use, and their appropriateness for creating narratives that explore conditions of social crises, are a central concern in this book; a fundamental question it asks is why some authors turn to graphic novel forms to deal with social/political catastrophes – and how appropriate the medium is for the documentary representation of these events.

The graphic novels used here conform to definitions (overtly or obliquely) of a critical social realism, in that they deal textually and visually with disruptive social or political events, and their various critical devices may be said to reveal something of the underlying social configurations. The term realism is frequently conflated with mimesis, or 'likeness' of depiction; in this book however, realism

1 Defined and analysed in Andreas Huyssen, *Present Pasts: Urban Palimpsests and the Politics of Memory* (Stanford, California: Stanford University Press, 2003).

refers to political critiques of beliefs and values, as opposed to the correspondence of depictions to (pre-existing) ideas about lifelike representations.

The authors referred to in this book examine the conditions of displaced and dispossessed people, and offer dramatic accounts of survival (or otherwise) in the face of overwhelming adversity. Seminal works that have explored such social upheaval are used as case studies, and through them theoretical and technical issues are discussed; these key works are Keiji Nakazawa's *Barefoot Gen*, Joe Sacco's *Palestine,* Marjane Satrapi's *Persepolis,* W.G. Sebald's *Emigrants,* and Art Spiegelman's *Maus.*[2]

Barefoot Gen is the first Japanese manga (comic book) to have been translated and republished in the West on a large scale, and is an autobiography of childhood in the aftermath of the atomic bombing of Hiroshima in 1945; *Palestine* documents Sacco's interviews with Palestinians, who recount their experience of life under occupation; *Persepolis* describes a young girl's experience of growing up in Iran under political revolution, and the effect upon young women of the nation's transformation into an authoritarian religious state, resulting in her exile in Europe; the illustrated novel *Emigrants* recounts the enduring suffering of generations as a consequence of the Holocaust and the wars in Europe, and is an image text work[3] that differs from the other graphic novels in that it is largely text-based, with a profusion of images liberally inserted throughout; *Maus* is an account of the author's parents surviving the Holocaust, and the subsequent fraught relationships between parent and son as his father recounts the traumatic narrative.

2 Keiji Nakazawa, *Barefoot Gen: Volume I, A Cartoon Story of Hiroshima* (San Francisco: Last Gasp, 2004); Joe Sacco, *Palestine* (Seattle: Fantagraphics Books, 2001); Marjane Satrapi, *Persepolis: The Story of Childhood* (London: Jonathan Cape, 2003); W.G. Sebald, *Austerlitz,* trans. Anthea Bell (London: Penguin, 2002); Sebald, W.G. *The Emigrants*, trans. Michael Hulse (London: Vintage, 2002); Art Spiegelman, *The Complete Maus* (London: Penguin, 2003).

3 Despite the more appropriate 'image text' name for Sebald's novels, for convenience and brevity his and all of the works discussed in this book are referred to as graphic novels.

All of these graphic novels have been produced in the post-war period, specifically during the last thirty years, but only since the late 1980s have they come to prominence in the West. Their period of publication coincides with the emergence of comic books for adults to read in mainstream publishing, largely a development in the west of the 'underground' comic publishing activities in Europe and the US in the 1960s and '70s, and from serialised manga in Japan. Each of the selected authors challenges dominant accounts of the events they depict, and they were all writing either of extreme social upheavals in which military and cultural institutions of the state were directly involved. The authors all employ autobiographic devices that serve to privilege narrative authenticity and to certify documentary truth, as they perceived it.

These autobiographical (or pseudo autobiographical) works give visual and textual accounts of some of the most catastrophic events of the twentieth century.[4] Their subject matter is explored in a broad political and historical context, but there is no assumption that the authors are politically neutral, or that they present an objective documentary of events. Why it is that these authors should choose to adopt this particular graphic novel format to represent extreme conditions of social crisis, which were of profound importance to them, is one of the questions that this book seeks to explore. First, however, it is necessary to examine the graphic novel medium that is so compelling for these authors.

4 All of which have been published in English; there have been good examples in many other languages. For example of Arab political comics are discussed at length in Allen Douglas and Malti-Douglas Fedwa, *Arab Comic Strips, Politics of an Emerging Mass Culture* (Bloomington and Indianapolis: Indiana University State Press, 1994).

The Graphic Novel: Definitions and Genealogies

There have been many debates held and distinctions made about the terms graphic novel, comic book, comics, comix, and image-text, and the evolution of graphic novels from comics and illustrated novels is by no means straightforward.[5] The late 1980s saw the term 'graphic novel' achieve widespread usage in the West. Gary Groth, co-publisher of Fantagraphics, a key publisher of graphic novels (*Palestine* in particular), when writing a summary of the development of graphic novels in 1988, described an important change in the reception of comic book works: '[…] there is a growing number of narrative cartoonists [Groth's footnote qualifies this term] who are bringing mature artistic values to the form and finding various degrees of acceptance from a literate public.'[6] Eric La Breque writes that *Maus*, because of its commercial success, is a key text in the genesis of the term.[7] He argues that its endurance in the best selling lists, especially in national newspapers like the *New York Times*, and its winning of the Pulitzer Prize, is significant for the status of graphic novels:

> It [*Maus*] is, for now, the consummate example of an emerging mode of self-expression, a new type of comics (or comix) narrative, a form that some do call "graphic novel". This new graphic literature, whatever it is termed, is obviously the direct descendent of superhero comics and the Sunday funnies, but like a child rebelling against its parents, it dispenses with the narrow conventions and existential confines of its elders. As with the underground comics of the 1960s, but to a perhaps even greater degree, the cartoonists are creating works that

5 For instance, see Art Spiegelman's dismissal of the graphic novel term in "Commix: An Idiosyncratic Historical and Aesthetic Overview," *Print* 42 (1988): 61–73; and also the discussion in Eric La Breque, "In Search of the Graphic Novel," *Print* 47 (1993): 21–35.

6 Gary Groth "Grown up comics: breakout from the underground," *Print* 42 (December 1998): 98.

7 La Breque, 21–35.

> chronicle their own experience and explore the great themes of existence. *Maus* couldn't exist in any other form.[8]

The extent to which graphic novels have been assimilated into mainstream commercial publishing may be demonstrated by the international success of *Maus,* and also by Chris Ware's *Jimmy Corrigan.*[9] The publication of Ware's novel in 2001 was something of a landmark in the UK, winning the Guardian First Book Award, despite being a graphic novel with an uncompromising narrative about familial dysfunction. As the British comic book author Raymond Briggs put it, when reviewing Ware's book: 'Now that *Jimmy Corrigan* has won the Guardian First Book Award, it can only mean that the strip cartoon had as long last become intellectually respectable.'[10]

A graphic novel can be thought of as an extended comic book that takes a sustained narrative throughout, in much the same way as a prose novel would do. Formally, graphic novels and comics may also usefully be defined as conforming to William Eisner's definition of sequential art; in this sequence is fundamental to the form – where images are arranged in order to denote the passage of time and/or space – and is the main vehicle for the generation of the narrative, giving the genre its particular and defining characteristics.[11] Graphic novel authors use a variety of formal devices and optical strategies integrated into their narrative structures, and the integration of imaging device, text and sequential narrative, unique to the medium, has a long history in both East and West. Most characteristic, and a precursor to the political realism of the novels under discussion here, are political cartoons; caricature and cartooning are well-established means of both the critique and dissemination of political events. The cartoons of James Gillray and George Cruikshank, for example,

8 La Breque, 21.

9 Chris Ware, *Jimmy Corrigan: The Smartest Kid on Earth* (London, Jonathan Cape, 2001).

10 Raymond Briggs, "The Genius of Jimmy Corrigan," *The Guardian*, December 8, 2001, Review Section, UK.

11 Will Eisner, *Comics and Sequential Art* (Florida: Poorhouse Press, 1985).

whose prints were widely distributed in urban centres in Britain during the late eighteenth and early nineteenth centuries, offer a precedent for graphic novelists who pay attention to the political history of the medium. Cruikshank's work has a particular significance for this book, especially his print *Massacre at St. Peter's* (figure 4.8), which depicts the violent dispersal by troops of a peaceful political protest in Manchester in 1819. This was considered by Sacco to be a formative source in his development as a political artist, influencing his work on *Palestine.*[12]

Historically, the first modern comic production is usually attributed to Rudolphe Töpffer in the mid-nineteenth century.[13] His *Essay on Physiognomy,* published in Geneva in 1845, was an analytical treatise that revealed something of the depth of the Western cultural investment in the drawn mark and its signifying process.[14] His singular contribution was to combine image and text within sequential frames using a caricature style of drawing. It is the combination of all four elements that mark out Töpffer's work, and made them appear like a modern comic book; his work greatly interested Spiegelman, and the formal devices that Töpffer employed influenced his *Maus.*

The historical relationship in the West between the comic strip and contemporary art is discussed thoroughly in Albert Boime's seminal essay on comics, 'The Comic Stripped and Ash Canned', a review of Judith O'Sullivan's book *The Art of the Comic Strip.*[15] As the *Art Journal* editor (who published it in 1972) put it: 'This essay began as a review but, as the reader will discover, developed into a critical book of the comic strip in American literature'.[16] Despite its disguise

12 Joe Sacco, interview with the author, September 1, 2000.

13 In particular, Spiegelman attributes this to Töpffer in "Commix: An Idiosyncratic Historical and Aesthetic Overview," 62.

14 Ellen Wiese, ed., *Enter the Comics: Rudolphe Töpffer's Essay on Physiognomy and the True Story of Monsieur Crépin* (Lincoln: University of Nebraska Press, 1965).

15 Albert Boime, "The Comic Stripped and Ash Canned: A Review Essay," review of *The Art of the Comic Strip* by Judith O'Sullivan, *The Art Journal,* 32/1, Fall 1972, 21–30.

16 Boime, 21.

as a review, the essay nevertheless presented one of the most incisive accounts of the development of the comic strip in the context of American art in the nineteenth and twentieth centuries. His survey and analysis has two important themes for comic book historiography: the first is the inclusion in his analysis of comics as a legitimate art form within the context of more orthodox art practices, such as painting and printmaking, and the second is his convincing case for an integration of the history of the American comic strip within the development of illustrated journalism and the mass newspaper medium. Boime traces the history of the American comic strip (which he was careful to distinguish from its European counterparts after the turn of the nineteenth/twentieth century) from the Civil War to the current day. In the process of doing so he highlights the presence of journalistic illustration and comic strip production as a formative experience for many prominent artists.

> 'While comics attained their maturity in the United States as a result of newspaper circulation, this unfoldment did not occur in isolation from other forms of journalistic art. It is related to the general evolution of illustrated journalism in America just prior to the Civil War, when publications like *Frank Leslie's Illustrated Newspaper* and *Harper's Weekly* hired reportorial artists to perform the work now done by the tabloid photographer. This practice quickly consolidated itself during the Civil War, and the art department soon became a necessary adjunct to most newspapers. These art departments offered aspiring young artists their primary professional outlet.'[17]

Boime, like Spiegelman, argues that the history of comics and modern art has parallels in modernist art practices that should not be ignored, citing an extensive set of examples to illustrate this point. Amongst them are artists fundamental to modernism, like Pablo Picasso and Marcel Duchamp, who used comics and caricature devices to facilitate their work.[18] He concludes that 'distortion for effect' is 'the fundamental contribution of caricature to modern art', and insists that the turn toward popular art forms in rejection of overused classicism by late nineteenth-century avant-garde artists was bound up with the

17 Boime, 21.

18 Especially in works like Picasso's *Dream and Lie of Franco*, Boime argues, 23.

development of comics in the same period.[19] The use of the visual vocabulary of caricature and comics by these artists established the prominence of these practices in the overall development of modernism and contemporary art. In particular, Boime cites the significance of Pop Art in the 1960s as an extension of these early modernist developments, where comic and caricature techniques were integral, and which in turn raised 'the status of the cartoon', as he put it.[20] He surveys the development of modern art in terms of the overlap with comic art, and gives numerous and often striking examples of how integrated these were; these include the 'speed lines' of the Futurists and the cartoon and visual abbreviations of Andy Warhol and Roy Lichtenstein, he even equates the forms in the abstract paintings of Mark Rothko and Barnett Newman to comic book frames, and points to the remarkable number of artists, like Feininger and Stuart Davis, who spent at least part of their careers specifically as comics or cartoon artists.[21]

Importantly, Boime argues that the content of comics was significant in terms of encapsulating (and constructing) cultural consciousness:

> what the comics have communicated since the First World War are the *fantasies* of "average men", [Boime is citing and contesting O'Sullivan's case here] and this removes it from the sphere of the mundane. Most strips are not about "average" human beings because their characters function in an entirely unreal universe, as remote from life as Hollywood musicals of a generation ago. […] Rather than reflect reality, they personify the fantasy ideals of the American majority.[22]

Here Boime touches on the limiting connotations of comic book/strip narratives, and simultaneously offers a causal relationship between comics and the notion of collective (US) consciousness, expressed as

19 Boime, 23.

20 Boime, 23.

21 Boime also considers the prevalence of onomatopoeic forms in comic books, especially in the work of George Herriman and his comic strip *Krazy Kat*. Boime, 24.

22 Boime, 24.

'fantasy'; he also examines the relationship between reality and that which is ideologically determined, an dilemma that haunts the recording and documenting of events in a popular medium. These connotations affect the work of many authors; Sacco, for example, when using the devices and motifs of war comics risks inadvertently replicating the nationalism and patriotism that they normally purvey.[23]

Underground Comics

The influence of underground comics, as many writers in the field such as Leonard Rifas and Roger Sabin have pointed out, was significant for the emergence of the adult readership of comics.[24] Many contemporary graphic artists owe a great deal to these comics ('comix', as they became known), particularly Sacco and Spiegelman, and this influence had a profound effect on adult-read comics generally. Underground artists virtually created this genre in the US from the precedents set much earlier by Harvey Kurtzman, creator of *MAD* comics in 1952. Spiegelman's formative years as a comic artist may be seen in the context of the US underground movement. Like many of these artists he looked back to the 1950s graphic work of Kurtzman, as a source for ideas. In Spiegelman's own history of comic production, one of his most emphatic statements concerns the realism of Kurtzman's comics:

> His war comics, published at the height of the Korean War, were realistic, compulsively researched, well-told tales that often had an anti-war bias remarkable for their time. Kurtzman is the single most important cartoonist in my personal pantheon, the reason I, and many cartoonists of my generation, became cartoonists in the first place. There was something genuinely subversive about his *MAD*.[25]

23 Joe Sacco, *Yahoo* (Seattle, Fantagraphics Books, 1991).

24 Leonard Rifas, correspondence to the author, January 21, 2002; and Roger Sabin, *Adult Comics: An Introduction* (London: Routledge, 1993), 36–37.

25 Art Spiegelman, "Commix: An Idiosyncratic Historical and Aesthetic Overview," 70–71.

Spiegelman and François Mouly founded and edited *RAW*, a sophisticated development of underground comix, which owed a great deal to *MAD* magazine. It was in *RAW* that *Maus* was first serialised, signifying its lineage from the comix era.

The contribution that underground artists made to the development of the documentary graphic novel can be expressed in psychoanalytical terms: 'The topicality of the underground comics – influenced largely by the example of *MAD* comics and Jules Feiffer – as well as their biting content, restores the comic strip's integrity by disclosing the repressed cravings behind the conventional idea in appropriate graphic images'.[26] As well as the concern of these artists to expose suppressed psychic imagery – and in this they shared the aspirations of generations of Dadaists and Surrealists – there is also the link with much earlier comic-strip artists and their concern with social issues.[27] Underground artists, typified by the radical, anti-establishment work of Robert Crumb, form an important platform for the new development of socially-oriented, adult-readership, serialised comics in the US and Europe. Additionally, the movement was also important for its reinforcing of the tradition of political criticism within the medium. Underground comics were one of the major cultural contexts for the development of documentary realist comics. Crumb's and Harvey Pekar's works offer precedents for realism through their highly idiosyncratic autobiographical serial cartoons that emerged coincident with the social phenomenon of 'youth culture' in the 1960s and 1970s.

Spiegelman's recognition of the underground was typical of comic artists and critics of his generation.[28] Sabin, for example, describes underground artists' practices as: 'a revolutionary break with the past', and explained that their lasting contribution to Western comics was to redefine the medium as suitable to convey issue-based

26 Boime, 24.

27 Boime, 24.

28 Gary Groth, "Art Spiegelman, Interview," *Comics Journal,* online archive, www.tjc.com/2 archives/i spiegelman.html (accessed January 1, 2002), 9.

themes.[29] Rather than merely a superficial, stylistic movement, Sabin saw the phenomenon as rooted in the post-war social and political shifts and events of the industrialised West:

> 'The underground is best understood as a product of the profound social divisions that racked the west in the 1960s and 1970s. These years are remembered for widespread protest at America's involvement in Vietnam, the emergence of civil rights and women's movements, and the 'May Events' in Paris. [...]. The underground comics both reflected and transmitted the counter-cultural message. [...], they were satirical *and* revolutionary.'[30]

Sabin recognises the fundamental changes in social conditions that were necessary for such comics to appear, and together with Spiegelman he provides an analysis of the fundamental ingredients of the new practices that were to prove potent for the emergence of the realist graphic novel. Underground comics were artworks rooted in the prevailing urban social political culture with a specificity of place and character, recording social events with an insistence upon detailed information garnered from personal experience and observation. The nature of that experience, in the case of underground artists like Crumb, took on an unorthodox appearance caused by his intense focus upon corporeal experience and social taboos. This was not unlike some of the Surrealist recordings of existence such as those of Louis Aragon in *Paris Peasant.*[31] This encapsulation of social experience, condensed and magnified by a myopic visual scrutiny of existence, typifies Crumb's work. As Spiegelman explains, referring to Crumb's *Self Loathing*:

> '[...] he was able to focus that hard on the non-events that make up most of everyday [...] my memory of it is that it he was able to inhabit every second of those non-events, so they weren't just a photostat of the same panel fifteen

29 Sabin, *Adult Comics,* 36.
30 Sabin, *Adult Comics,* 36.
31 Louis Aragon, *Paris Peasant*, trans. Simon Waston Tayor (London: Jonathan Cape, 1971).

times. He actually made it a project to observe what happens when nothing's happening.'[32]

Manga

Japanese comics have unique relationships between narrative and form, and their innovative and distinctive features have been to be very influential in the West, especially on 'experimental' graphic novelists like Spiegelman, and on the development of graphic novels generally.[33] Manga, as comics became known in Japan after the Second World War, developed in parallel to Western comic books, with an increasing stylistic interchange between East and West during the post-war period. This was the tradition within which Nakazawa's work developed.

Osamu Tezuka's success with *Astro Boy* represents the post war Japanese comic industry's exponential growth, and was indicative of Japan's position as one of the largest consumers of comics in the world in the post-war period. Frederick Schodt has demonstrated that in Japan there is a massive range of comic and graphic novel types matched by a correspondingly wide readership, with each section having its own specialist market.[34] The social status of some manga artists is often at film star celebrity level, and with its associated animé (cinematic animation), manga is a large and significant cultural formation within the country. Manga is also remarkable because of the scope of its readership, which has been claimed to straddle generations and class divisions.[35] The history of manga post-war has been described as starting with artists like Mizuki Shigeru who, having been disabled in the war, began to draw and work with picture-

32 Groth, "Art Spiegelman, Interview," 8.

33 Scott McCloud, *Understanding Comics* (New York: Harper Collins, 1994), 18–19, 80.

34 See Frederik L. Schodt, *Manga, Manga, The World of Japanese Comics* (New York: Kodansha International 1983).

35 Schodt, *Manga, Manga,* 15–16.

card shows.[36] Shunsuke Tsurumi argues that the picture-card show was a direct precursor for manga, and was also a means of dissent and resistance to what he describes as the 'Western cult of science', prevalent in the imposed entertainment culture of the US military occupation in the immediate years after Japan's surrender in 1945.[37] Tsurumi also claims that this theme was continued in the manga that succeeded picture-card shows when they became unfashionable after 1956. Manga also developed into a mass cultural phenomenon in relation to economic struggle, namely that poverty and scarcity in the immediate post war years forced people to use lending libraries, where manga was available, and use picture-card shows for social gatherings.[38]

Picture card shows comprised artists showing their sequences frame by frame on makeshift display boards, accompanied by a spoken narrative.[39] This practice was conditioned by post-war poverty, such as lack of paper, ink, printers, publishers etc., hence the medium's first appearances through libraries and street performance. Manga production increased in concert with the post-war Japanese economic boom, with manga comics and their associated film animations (animé) becoming widespread. Manga translations into English were made in the late 1970s, the first full-length series translation being *Barefoot Gen,* and subsequently manga publications and influence have become common in the West.[40].

The fundamental sequential characteristics of manga owe much to European and American comic strips, and most common conventions were adopted into manga during the first half of the twentieth century; for example, the marks that signify movement ('zip

36 Shunsuke Tsurumi, *A Cultural History of Postwar Japan 1945–1980.* (London and New York: Kegan Paul International, 1994) 37–38.

37 Tsurumi, 1–12.

38 Marilyn Ivy, "Formations of Mass Culture," in *Postwar Japan as History*, Andrew Gordon, ed. (Berkeley, Los Angeles and Oxford: University of California Press, 1993), 246.

39 Ivy, 62.

40 Paul Gravett, *Manga: Sixty Years of Japanese Comics* (London: Laurence King Publishing, 2004).

ribbons', curving parallel lines), contact (the 'star burst'), anger ('steaming' head) and fear (excessive perspiration). Manga artists developed culturally specific conventions that had a powerful influence on comic production in the West, and on graphic novels in particular.

In Japan manga is ubiquitous, and there are thousands of manga titles for every conceivable age and type of person. Manga is also used in schools and forms an important reading medium in everyday life, and when catching a tube or visiting a cafe in urban Japan one is likely to encounter many people, including adults, reading manga.[41] The serialised work of Osamu Tezuka is a prominent example of a manga artist who has been widely influential upon the development manga (including Nakazawa's work) and also upon the development of the graphic novel in the West, especially in terms of the formal properties of the medium.[42] This is discussed further in the chapter on visualisation methods.

Contextualising Graphic Novels

Making sense of graphic novels is necessarily a culturally conditioned socially reflexive process. As Martin Barker explains, understanding is not so much a decoding of language than a process of orientation.[43] Using the ideas of Voloshinov to develop his theory of ideology in relation to comic books, he argues that 'the first function of language is to establish social relations between human beings in society', with

41 Manga republished in the west has not been, however, necessarily been representative of Japanese manga. The comics and animé videos that are translated from Japanese for sale in the UK are often selected for an audience that is perceived by sections of the republishing industry as liking violent and pornographic subject matter. Rod Shaile, marketing manager at *Manga Entertainment,* London, interview with the author, February 22, 1996.

42 Gravett, *Manga.*

43 Martin Barker, *Comics: Ideology, power and the critics* (Manchester: Manchester University Press, 1989), 262–278.

comic books and graphic novels being expressions embedded in social language.[44]

Pursuing the primacy of social readings of art works, Raymond Williams argues that it is erroneous to study art works without reference to the society within which the art works were produced and also, significantly for this book, that it is equally inadequate to study society as if cultural production is merely the 'by-product' of societal functions. [45] He notes the complexity of social configurations, observing that society cannot be seen as an integral whole, in relation to which a work can be analysed. Rather he argues that art production is as much an integral part of society as any other component. Most of the sources and references used in this book are from authors and critics in whose work there is an emphasis on social production, where the objects of study are seen as material productions inextricably bound up with the political culture of state and society.

Ideological analysis of culture and the concept of hegemony is important for a discussion of the culture(s) in which the graphic novels are produced. Althusser's work on state institutions, for instance, particularly his willingness to look at the state beyond arbitrary private and public distinctions, is useful because so much comic production occurs on the margins of institutional practices, and is often subject to censorship. The forms of realism employed in the graphic novels studied in this book are directly related to the political and ethnic struggles that occur in each context, or, more accurately, the way they were *perceived* to occur by the authors. They all recognised larger political and cultural pressures that they felt compelled to resist and challenge, and it is in this act of visual/textual resistance that their realist strategies are developed and adapted. Boime argued, in 1972, that for all its apparent radicalism, the underground had failed to produce a 'genuine left-wing strip'. [46]

44 Barker, *Comics,* 265.

45 Raymond Williams, "The Analysis of Culture," in *Cultural Theory and Popular Culture*, ed. John Storey (New York and London: Harvester Wheatsheaf, 1994), 59.

46 Boime, 25.

Through the examples given, this book attempts to demonstrate that there are now works that constitute a radical practice.

Chapter 1: Social Realism: Historical and Political Contexts

Realism, in its critical, political forms, is the main theme of this chapter. There is an analysis of its political nineteenth-century origins and early twentieth-century applications, which is developed using the concept of a critical, social realism. This is modelled on the theories of art historians such as T.J. Clark, Linda Nochlin, and the political writings of Bertold Brecht and Georg Lukács on Marxist-based concepts of realism developed in the inter-war years of the 1930s.[1] They all share concepts of realism that can be defined primarily as political and critical practices that analyse social conditions, and it is these conditions that underpin the cultural events represented in artworks, and later in graphic novels. Key moments where these practices emerged in graphic novels are discussed, such as comics' censorship in the 1950s, underground comics, and political cartoon traditions. The principal question posed here is whether, and in what circumstances, graphic novel production can be considered a realist practice. If it can, then what kind of realism is evident and what, if any, are the precedents and conditions for such a realist practice?

All of the documentary graphic novels that form the focus of this book have been produced in response to events of extreme social upheaval, and this has fundamentally affected the form and the content of all of them. In the case of *Barefoot Gen,* Nakazawa experienced the Hiroshima events at first hand, although recording them retrospectively, many years later. In *Maus* Spiegelman gave an account of the Holocaust through his parents, with a secondary narrative about its consequences for succeeding generations. Sacco's response to the Middle East crisis is contemporary, produced in the immediate years after the research was carried out. The main foci for

1 Clark, *The Absolute Bourgeois*; Nochlin; Brecht, *Popularity and Realism.*

Nakazawa and Spiegelman were clearly historic World War II upheavals, which had legacies that affected US relations with existing states, and were produced at times of renewed tension over US foreign policies. The history and themes of anti-Semitism in post-war US politics, the establishment and maintenance of Israel, the Cold War and US trade and strategic relations with Japan were all significant factors in the production of these works, within the larger context of the global post-war expansion of US culture. These conditions affect *Persepolis* as well, but they tend to be overridden by Satrapi's experience of the Iranian revolution of 1989 and its rapid transformation into a religious fundamentalist state, and the ensuing war against Iraq. Concealed anti-Semitism in the post-war reconstruction of Europe informs much of Sebald's work, and *Austerlitz* and the *Emigrants* painstakingly reconstruct personal crises that have been overlain and neglected as modern European states emerged restructured.

The definitions of realism that are applicable to these works must also be appropriate for these specific circumstances. This is rendered problematic, but not necessarily insurmountable, by the transference of the terms from their nineteenth-century origins in Western literature, theatre and visual arts, to late twentieth century graphic novel practices. The problem is eased a little by the many precedents in these traditions for the sequencing of image and text, but as many writers in the field have pointed out (Sabin and Jaqueline Berndt in particular), comic books have too readily been located into traditional practices without due regard for their specific forms and conventions; modern comic books are principally a mass produced, sequential image/text form (with distinctive speech bubbles) that flourished in an industrial, post World War II urban context.[2] There are, however,

2 Roger Sabin, cited by Gary Goth in "Joe Sacco, Frontline Jounalist: Why Sacco went to Gorazde" *Comics Journal* online www.tjc.com/2_ws/i_sacco.html (accessed November 11, 2002); and Jaqueline Berndt, "What's art got to do with it? Observations on recent inter-relationships between manga and visual art," (paper presented at the Chelsea College of Art and the Japan Foundation symposium "Manga and Art: Visual Culture in Contemporary Japan," London College of Fashion, London, February 1, 2002).

clear political precedents for the form in eighteenth- and nineteenth-century practices. Examples include widely distributed political prints, such as Gillray's in England and Honoré Daumier's in France, illustrated serialised novels, and illustrated political critiques like those that occurred in the English satirical magazine *Punch*[3].

Realism is most commonly used in studies of Western literature of the nineteenth century to describe the practice of authors like Stendhal, Émile Zola and Gustave Flaubert in nineteenth-century France.[4] These analytical, politically-astute authors often referred to the contradictory rituals of class in contemporary society, and through a combination of melodrama and documentary established literary forms that may still be recognised in graphic novel narratives. As Nochlin has demonstrated, these authors and their practices (especially Zola and Charles Baudelaire) were closely allied to those of the graphic arts in this period, especially in terms of shared aims and ambitions.[5] Clark has exhaustively and convincingly demonstrated that there was a fundamental political relationship of all these literary and graphic practices to the revolutionary upheavals of the time, especially in the period between the 1848 Revolution and the Paris Commune of 1871.[6]

During this era in Western Europe there were many artists and writers influenced by socialism and working in similar styles, often collectively referred to as realists. Importantly, art historians, interested in revising the practices of art history itself, have made

3 Most famously the nineteenth-century caricatures of Sir John Tenniel.

4 Especially Stendhal, *Le Rouge et Le Noir* (London: Penguin, 1953); Émile Zola, *La Débacle* (London: Penguin, 1980); Gustave Flaubert, *Madame Bovary* (New York: Bantam Books, 1962).

5 Linda Nochlin, *Realism* (London: Penguin, 1990).

6 T.J. Clark, *The Absolute Bourgeois: Artists and Politics in France 1848–1851* (London: Thames and Hudson, 1999); Clark, T. J. *Image of the People: Gustave Courbet and the 1848 Revolution* (London: Thames and Hudson, 1999).

these artists their subject of study.[7] As Jonathan Harris has discussed in his historiography of radical art history, many key figures in the transformation of the practices and concerns of the discipline of art history were very active researching this field during the early 1970s to the early 1990s.[8] The results of this were in part a much greater emphasis on the political context of artworks, and the reappraisal of prominent historical moments of production. A further consequence of this is that art-historical concepts (realism included) that originated, or were modified, during the nineteenth century were significantly re-evaluated at the end of the twentieth. Just as it was shown that such concepts were rooted in the specific social conditions that prevailed at that time, so the rethinking of art-historical methodology was rooted in the specific political landscape of the late twentieth century.[9] The concept of realism used in this book is, however, necessarily a construction applicable to the particular graphic novels studied, despite the resemblance to former applications of the term.

At the same time as developing and promoting a social history of art that insists upon the importance of social conditions when assessing the reception of art works and practices in their social context, social historians of art warned against the application of general theories of cause and effect, arguing that the application of terms like realism are specific to the particular configuration of social conditions that prevail (hence 'social realism'), requiring each to be considered case by case. [10] Nevertheless, the term applied to contemporary graphic novels does resonate with definitions of realism that were rethought by art historians like Clark and Nochlin, and further analysis of these precedents follow.

7 Such as Griselda Pollock, "Modernity and the spaces of femininity," in *Art in Modern Culture*, eds. Frances Frascina, and Jonathan Harris (London: Phaidon, 1992).

8 Jonathan Harris, *The New Art History: A Critical Introduction* (London and New York: Routledge, 2001).

9 In particular the rethinking of Marxism after the failed French revolution of May1968, especially in the case of Clark, as Harris explains, 64.

10 Harris, *The New Art History,* 69.

Nineteenth-Century European Realism

The kinds of practices that became associated with realism in the nineteenth century vary in relation to overt political content. In the work of Stendhal, for instance, there was a powerful sense of the French 'body politic', and in *Le Rouge et le Noir* the romances were developed in the context of Republican revolutionary activity, with sub-plots exploring the nature of patriotism and sedition. Similar themes occurred in Gustave Courbet's painting, the allegorical *The Studio* (1851) for example, where the work was littered with allusions to popular prints, with socialists and political reformers set in pictorial contrast with reactionary figures of the period. The opacity of the allusions in both of theses cases – they both had to tread carefully in the heightened political tensions of their times – was brought about by their desire to avoid political censorship that may have prevented publication or exhibition of their work. In both literature and painting the forms that authors and artists selected were also modified by adherence to an emerging philosophy of realism, as illustrated by Courbet's correspondence on the subject.[11] Here he listed the contents of *The Studio* in considerable detail, displaying his evident concern with the meticulous, mimetic depiction that characterised so much realist painting in the nineteenth century.

The attention to the minutiae of selected themes from everyday, domestic existence was fundamentally linked to the political radicalism of the realism movements of this period. These were made explicit (within the rhetoric of the time) in Courbet's writing in his *Realist Manifesto* of 1855.[12] The use of pre-existing popular imagery (especially from prints), and the idea that artists can be agents of

11 Gustave Courbet, letter to Champfleury from "Gustave Courbet 1819–1877," exhibition catalogue, Grand Palais, Paris, 1854, 246–250; trans. by Francis Frascina, in "Texts A" Open University A316 course "Modern Art Practices and Debates," Milton Keynes: Open University, 1994, 17–18.

12 Gustave Courbet, "Realist Manifesto," in "Texts A" Open University A316 course "Modern Art Practices and Debates," Milton Keynes: Open University, 1994, 18; see also Gerstle Mack, *Gustave Courbet* (New York: Da Capo, 1951), 156.

political change (with all of the complications that this entails) were characteristic of realist practices of this era.[13] Courbet is often cited in both respects by modern and contemporary critics alike; examples of his political activism include his visual references to the organisation of figures from popular, widely available prints for the composition of paintings like his 1850 *Burial at Ornans*, and his painting of poor workers at their hard labour in the *Stonebreakers* (1849, figure 1.1). This work was in turn used for political ends by the anarchist philosopher Pierre-Joseph Proudhon in his 1865 *Du principe de l'art*,[14] supporting Courbet in his rendering of the working poor on a large scale in his paintings. The figures are depicted without sentiment, and Courbet goes to some lengths to emphasise their poverty and hardship. Furthermore, this was produced in a time of social crisis, in this case in relation to revolution and counter-revolution, with the artist consciously operating within the orbit of the political protagonists of the French State.[15]

Nochlin's description and analysis of realism in nineteenth-century European art focuses on artists' engagement with social and political issues; one of her primary definitions of realism is their willingness to locate their work in the realm of social engagement, to be politically orientated. She refers to Daumier, Courbet, Zola and Edouard Manet who:

> …were all involved in more or less serious encounters with the Establishment. The social engagement of Realism did not necessarily involve any overt statement of social aims or any outright protest against intolerable political conditions. But the mere intention 'to translate the appearances, the customs' of the time implied a significant involvement in the contemporary social situation and might thus constitute a threat to existing values and power structures as menacing as the throwing of a bomb.[16]

13 Clark, *Image of the People*, and Nochlin.
14 Nochlin, 258.
15 Clark, *Image of the People*, 116.
16 Nochlin, 50.

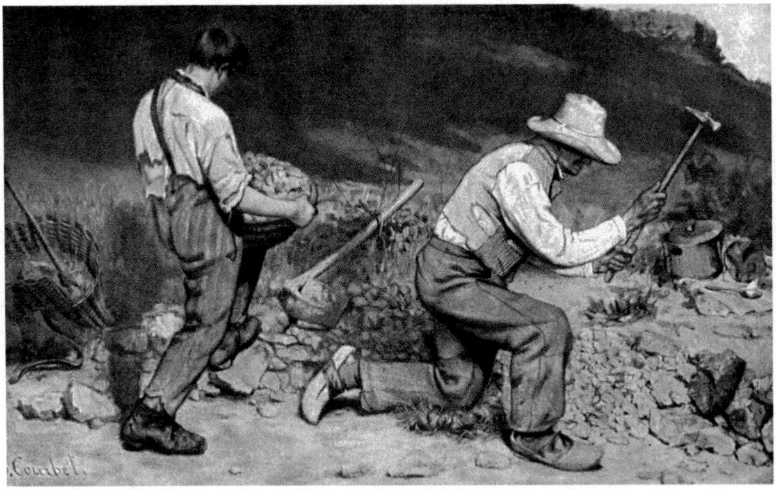

Figure 1.1. Gustave Courbet, *The Stonebreakers*, 1849–50

By way of example, Nochlin goes on to discuss the case of the police confiscation of Manet's lithograph of the *Execution of Emperor Maximilian* (1868), and the ensuing debate about the political nature of that work. Works that offered (or appeared to offer) a social critique are integral to Nochlin's definition of realism. Such critical stances, in the paintings and graphics of Courbet, Daumier and Manet, for example, and in the writings of authors like Zola, Baudelaire and Jules Antoine Castagnary dominate her accounts. Above all, it is in the encounters between the artists' practices and the control of the governing bourgeoisie that she defines realism:

> Born in the wake of the progressive upheaval of 1848 and reaching maturity in the period of social cynicism and political disillusionment following after it – the period of the Second Empire – the French realist movement in its dual character of protest against, yet expression of, a predominately bourgeois society, was eternally marked with a stamp of ambivalence.[17]

Nochlin offers further criteria for a realist practice; these revolve around notions of the *contemporary* and the *authentic*, informed by

17 Nochlin, 46.

nineteenth-century empiricism.[18] Authenticity, in the nineteenth-century realist meaning of the word, was to be found in knowledge gained from direct experience of the subject. For realists there was a political dimension to the idea of authenticity, for which selection of subject matter was crucial. Subjects that had hitherto been rejected on academic/political criteria were employed for their effectiveness in giving the appearance of authenticity, exemplified by works such as the *Stonebreakers*. In this painting meticulous attention was given to observed detail, as well as to the backbreaking and unrewarding nature of the tasks. Added to this is the large scale of the work, at a size normally reserved for historical or allegorical paintings. Jean-François Millet's paintings such as the *Winnower* (1848), *The Man with the Hoe* (1860–62) and *Gleaners* (1857)[19] offer similarly stark depictions of the realities of working life. Millet declared that his own familiarity of agricultural life was at the root of his desire to paint such subjects, and it is this contemporary experience that took precedence in determining the content of his work.[20] Nochlin associates these with the corresponding practices of science at this time, especially the detailed observation of natural phenomena.[21] She notes the preoccupation certain avant-garde painters of this era had with a contemporary subject matter of a particular type; as she explains, this new subject matter tended to focus on the poor and dispossessed within an increasingly bourgeois-controlled urban and rural environment:

> The Realists placed a positive value on the depiction of the low, the humble and the commonplace, the socially dispossessed or marginal as well as the more prosperous sectors of contemporary life. They turned for inspiration to the worker, the peasant, the laundress, the prostitute, to the middle-class or working-class café or *bal*, to the prosaic realm of the cotton broker or the modiste, to their own or their friends' foyers and gardens, viewing them frankly

18 Nochlin, 23–35.

19 In the National Gallery, London, Getty Center Los Angeles, and Museé d'Orsay, Paris, respectively.

20 http://www.getty.edu/art/gettyguide/artObjectDetails?artobj=879 Getty Center, (accessed 21 November, 2007).

21 Nochlin, 43.

> and candidly in all their misery, familiarity or banality. Courbet said that the goal of the Realist was to translate the customs, the ideas, the appearance of his own epoch in his art, and thus, the social dimension automatically acquired importance, whether the artist was a self-conscious political radical like Courbet himself, or an equally self-conscious, cynical anti-democrat like Jules or Edmond Goncourt. [22]

Paintings, engravings and sculptures of poverty, manual labour and death abound in this late nineteenth-century period, and became synonymous with the term 'Realist'.[23]

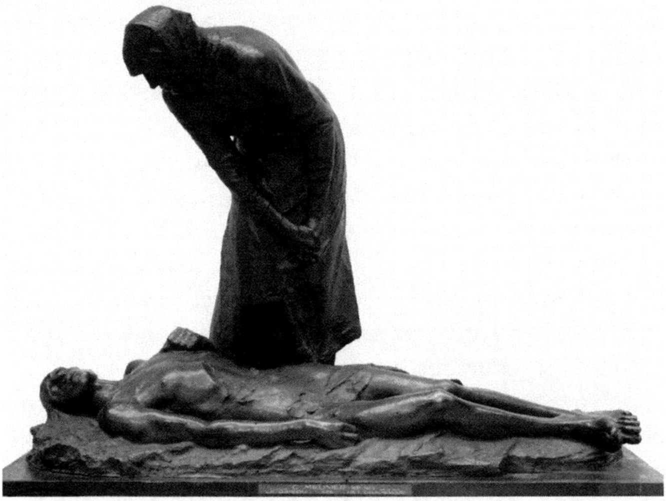

Figure 1.2. Constantin Meunier, *Firedamp Explosion* (Museum of Modern Art, Brussels, 1889)

Later in the century the Belgian sculptor Constantin Meunier's produced a body of work that exemplifies the political Realist's concerns at this time. His *Firedamp Explosion* sculpture (figure 1.2) is particularly relevant in this respect; its emotive narrative implies a

22 Nochlin, 34.
23 Nochlin, 34.

critique of the capitalist mining enterprise of the era with its disregard for the safety of its workers.

The work draws on academic precedents, especially those of a Renaissance Pietà, to critique an event from contemporary secular life.[24] Overt illustrations of working class political life, like fellow Belgian Eugene Laermans' painting *A Strike Evening*, of a mass of workers marching to join a strike, were part of the stock in trade of late nineteenth-century realist practices in Europe with the establishment of labour movements within the nation states of Western Europe. These particular practices were, stylistically at least, to inform the state art of Soviet Russia in the post-Lenin era, as Eric Hobsbawm has argued.[25] He designated Meunier's sculpture as a precedent from which the large-scale political art of Soviet Union artists drew their models. According to Hobsbawm, Meunier 'invented the international stereotype of the sculptured proletariat,' by which he means the heroic, ideal qualities with which he bestowed his sculptures.[26] Dignity in these works was acquired through references to the traditions of art academia, which includes the work of the French painter David, who also reused classical models in his works to add gravitas and monumentality to his subjects, which were often allegories for the revolution in which he was actively involved.[27] Drawing on these judiciously selected precedents Meunier developed a realist practice that was structured within the ideological parameters of a socialist society, and thereby provided the models from which Soviet artists like Vera Mukhina developed their monumental sculptures representing workers like *Worker and Collective Farm Girl* in the 1930s.

24 A Pietà is work that depicts Mary mourning the dead body of Jesus, most famously Michelangelo's marble Pieta (1499) in St Peter's, Rome.

25 Eric Hobsbawm, *Age of Empire 1875–14* (London: Penguin, 2001), 225.

26 Hobsbawm, *Age of Empire,* 225.

27 Examples of this are the paintings: "Oath of the Horatii" (Paris: Museé du Louvre, 1784) and "Death of Marat" (Brussels: Museé d'Art Ancien, 1793).

Twentieth-Century Political Realism

In the twentieth century the term realism has been ascribed to the Soviet Realist art under Stalin, from the late 1920s to the 1950s, as well as to German political art in the 1920s and early 1930s. [28] Once again the boundaries between high art and popular culture were blurred or even deliberately ignored. Artists and writers like John Heartfield and Bertolt Brecht pursued overtly political agendas, with the former's political illustrations for *AIZ* (the communist weekly Arbeiter-Illustrierte-Zeitung). Brecht frequently tested the principles upon which these political theories were founded and attempted to resist the tendency for ossified political dogma by calling for rapidly evolving and populist political activism.[29] In Brecht's Marxist theories of realism the artwork had to be demystifying in relation to the dominant political power, and utilise the forms of contemporary popular/mass culture, and through technical innovation resist the 'normalising' tendencies of the mass media.[30]

When art practices were put into the service of the State, and legitimised as such, in Stalin's Soviet Union of the 1930s, artists like Vera Mukhina were encouraged to reject those realist art forms noted for their specific and contingent characteristics, choosing instead a generalised idealism. This was more clearly the case when artists were preparing works for prominent public display, as Mukhina's large sculpture *Worker and Collective Farm Girl* for the Soviet Pavilion in the 1937 International Exhibition of Arts, Crafts and Sciences in Paris demonstrated. Such sculptures were designed to connote the ideology of a utopian state by drawing on past academic models that had, in

28 Paul Wood, "Realisms and Realities" in *Realism, Rationalism and Surrealism, Art Between the Wars,* eds. Bryony Fer, David Batchelor, and Paul Wood (London: Yale, Open University, 1993), 250–332.

29 Bertolt Brecht, "Popularity and Realism," in *Art in Theory*, eds. Charles Harrison and Paul Wood, (Oxford: Blackwells, 1993), 489–493.

30 In the sense that Noam Chomsky defined the mass media in *Necessary Illusions: Thought Control in Democratic Societies* (London: Pluto Press, 1993).

their own era, been put to a similar purpose. For Mukhina this meant referencing sculptures like the heroic foundry-worker sculptures of Meunier, that had in turn drawn on the Italian classical models of Michelangelo and Bernini.

Such idealism in the appearance of the human figure, embedded in the aesthetics of the Renaissance, is however, at variance with the individual specificity of the realism of contemporary German artists like Otto Dix and Georg Gross. Dix's realism depends upon the absence of the heroism associated with classical forms. As Paul Wood explains, there are sometimes overt criticisms in his work of the value of academic art and tradition, with direct political criticisms of the contemporary orthodox value placed upon aesthetics and art. [31] Dix's painting is very specific in its criticism and its depicted characters, and such specificity has been one of the defining characteristics of social realism in art since the mid-nineteenth century. This specificity was the opposite of the idealism of the twentieth-century incarnations of imperial, utopian idealism and classicism, as used by the State art of the Soviet Union or German Nazi art. Stalin, the Soviet president throughout the 1930s, instituted an official art that offered stylistic consistency which was determined incrementally through state interventions, such as the setting up of a single Artists' Union with compulsory membership in 1932.[32] The increase in state control was concurrent with greater instances of art works referencing a classical idiom, to which Mukhina's sculpture adhered. The critical reception in the Soviet Union of her sculpture was indicative of the ideological weight that such work had to support: 'an epoch-making work of art, expressing the content and the most advanced ideals and the tendencies of our age…World art has never seen popular images of such striking grandeur.'[33]

31 Wood, 292.

32 Wood, 321.

33 Soviet critic, M. Lifshits, quoted in Igor Golomstock, *Totalitarian Art* (London: Harper Collins, 1990), 132.

The debate surrounding realism resumed with vigour in the exchanges in the 1930s between writers of the Frankfurt School. This protracted discourse, notably involving Brecht, Georg Lukács, Theodor Adorno, Walter Benjamin and Ernst Bloch, centred around the problematic of establishing appropriate art forms for the visualisation of socialist principles and ideals.[34] This debate was further antagonised by the larger problematic of socialism itself in the Soviet Union under Stalin, and by the increasing dominance of 'expressionist' and abstract art in European modernism. Brecht's contribution, however, was significant in that it furthered the alliance between realism with social critique and commentary, linking realism with a socially engaged art. Such tendencies were already apparent in nineteenth-century realism, but Brecht's concept has the distinction of rejecting mimetic representation as a measure of realism, favouring instead the political position that the work represented. As exemplified by the photo-montages of John Heartfield, Brecht argued for a realism that should adapt and modify its forms to retain its modernity and its popular, mass appeal – 'Reality changes; in order to represent it modes of representation must also change.'[35] He demanded practices that constantly resisted attempts by the 'dominant order' to normalise and assimilate both popular and avant-garde art forms. Brecht did not offer any specific forms for this idea of realism, however. Rather, he cast his net wide in search of practices that most effectively offered a defence of socialism in the face of belligerent fascism in 1930s' Germany.

Lukács also discussed the concept of realism and expressionism in Marxist terms; for him the way to analyse art and aesthetics was in terms of the operation and effects of the experience of living in a capitalist system in semi-permanent crisis.[36] Importantly, these effects corresponded to configurations of the components that comprised capitalist society. Consequently he was strongly critical of art

34 Fredric Jameson, ed., *Aesthetics and Politics: The Key Texts of the Debate Within German Marxism* (London, Verso, 1998).

35 Brecht, "Popularity and Realism," 492.

36 Responding to Bloch's views in 1938 – in Jameson.

practices that failed to explore the underlying social class structures that maintained and curtailed the conditions for workers' exploitation:

> 'The modern literary schools of the imperialist era, from Naturalism to Surrealism which have followed each other in swift succession, all have one feature in common. They all take reality exactly as it manifests itself to the writer and the characters he creates. The form of this immediate manifestation changes as society changes. These changes, moreover, are both subjective and objective, depending on modifications in the reality of capitalism and also on the ways in which class struggle and changes in class structure produce different reflections on the surface of that reality. It is these changes above all that bring about the swift succession of literary schools together [...]. Both emotionally and intellectually they all remain frozen in their own immediacy; they fail to pierce the surface to discover the underlying essence, the real factors that relate their experiences to the hidden social forces that produce them [...].'[37]

Here Lukács criticises the numerous movements of modernist art as being fundamentally reactive to social pressures, without actually acknowledging these forces as such; as a consequence of which the movements could be characterised by styles rather than any incisive political insights. In accord with Brecht, despite their other disagreements on socialist art, he argues that realism must be an art form that above all recognises and offers a critique of social structures. Lukács also noted the importance of the society within which any realist practice might be produced, and observed that 'practice of every true realist demonstrates the importance of the overall objective social context and the "insistence on all-round knowledge" required to do it justice.'[38]

Like Lukács, Brecht's argument for realism was in part dependent upon his scepticism and rejection of certain modernist practices and paradigms. He was particularly vociferous in his critique of the notion of the avant-garde, essential to concepts of European modernism in the 1930s. He developed a concept of formalism in some depth, and used this to supplement and define his ideas about

37 Georg Lukács, "Realism in the Balance," in Jameson, 36–37.
38 Jameson, 33.

realism – 'a yard stick for dealing with such phenomena as the avant-garde.'[39] Brecht, using similar language to Lukács, described the shortcomings of certain avant-garde practices in terms of superficiality:

> *Naturalism* and a certain type of *anarchistic montage* can be confronted with their social effects, by demonstrating that they merely reflect the symptoms of the surface of things and not the deeper causal complexes of society. Whole tracts of literature which seem, judging by their form to be radical, can be shown to be purely reformist, merely formal efforts which supply solutions on paper. [40]

Brecht's demand for realism meant an art that, above all, overturned ideological dogmas and replaced them with a political challenge offered from the standpoint of working class experience. He argued for a continuously transforming reinvention of popular art forms to resist political normalisation. In a seminal article, *Popularity and Realism*, he called for a popular realism that was 'intelligible to the broad masses, adopting and enriching their forms of expression / assuming their standpoint, confirming and correcting it [...].'[41] From this patrician standpoint Brecht, like many theoreticians of realism before, saw popular art forms as central to a revivification of existing art forms, to enable a transforming socialist society and the enfranchisement of the working classes: 'the mass of producers who were for so long the object of politics must now become the subject of politics'.[42]

39 Bertolt Brecht, "On the Formalist Character of the Theory of Realism," in Jameson, 72.

40 Brecht, "On the Formalist Character of the Theory of Realism," in Jameson, 72.

41 Brecht, Bertolt "Popularity and Realism," 491.

42 Brecht, Bertolt "Popularity and Realism," 491.

The State and Graphic Novel Production

Although the realism of the artists discussed above, such as Courbet, Meunier and Heartfield, may be stylistically and culturally dissimilar, each was responsive to the dominant conditions prevailing in their respective nation states and polities. In the same way documentary graphic novels can be considered as examples of realism in the context of the forms of the states in which were created, and towards which they offered a critical commentary. In the post-war advance of global capitalism, cultural hegemonic structures – the dominant and prevailing ideology of a ruling group – has a great deal to do with the resultant form and content of artistic production, of which graphic novels of all types are but one manifestation.[43] For instance, Peter Novick's historiography of the recognition and acknowledgement of the Holocaust in the US, aligns it with contemporary events in Jewish-American relations, particularly the Cold War and the formation of Israel.[44] These ideological alignments contribute to the prominence of *Maus* in the period of its production and publication. In the same vein, the formation of the post-war Japanese nation-state and its relationship with the US during this period, first under direct occupation and then as a strategic ally in the Cold War, was critical for the reception of *Barefoot Gen* in the West.

The inconsistencies and incongruities within the ideological formations of the state seem to impinge on this too. The organisation and control of social groups by their selected representatives, ordered bureaucratically into a 'public sector', is common to all of the states in which the graphic novels considered here were produced. Often these states developed from models of European bourgeois and colonial nation-state formations that characterised nineteenth-century Europe. Their relationship to these forerunners has at times been crucial, and

43 Jameson.

44 Peter Novick, *The Holocaust and Collective Memory* (London: Bloomsbury, 1999); also, see Edward Said, *The Question of Palestine* (New York: Vintage Books, 1992).

historians like Hobsbawm have been quick to emphasise historical precedents in nation-state configurations that precipitated seemingly new crises in recent times.[45] The nation-state here is defined primarily as the ideological organisation of people who must subordinate community culture to a dominant organising power, a government, who attempt to control both ethnically and geographically.

The development of Israel bears out Hobsbawn's argument, with its foundation partly rooted in the failure of British rule in the aftermath of World War II, and its original structure relying, as Said has frequently pointed out, on nineteenth-century colonialism. According to Said this colonialism was characterised by the dominance of a particular ethnic group, and the translation of this into geographic regional control with expansionist aspirations, and its organisation of 'native' peoples.[46] He has also been emphatic about the legacy of colonialism distorting many Arab states, which continue to replicate repressive colonial state formations.[47] Sacco's Palestine project was particularly influenced by this perception of the effects of lingering colonialism.[48]

Most of the theorists of realism previously discussed are Marxist at root, in the sense that they were advocating or defending a socialist form of state organisation, although there are wide variations in their methods and the social structures that they considered appropriate. Marxist formulations of the social structure of the state privilege 'the material conditions of a society as the basis of its social structure and of human consciousness. The form of the State, therefore, emerges from the relations of production [...]', as Martin Carnoy (paraphrasing Karl Marx from the 1840s) put it[49]. Carnoy continues by explaining that for Marx the state could not be:

45 Eric Hobsbawm, *Age of Extremes: The Short Twentieth Century* (London: Penguin, 1994).

46 Edward Said, *The End of the Peace Process: Oslo and After* (London: Granta, 2000), p.110.

47 Said, *The End of the Peace Process*, 237.

48 Sacco, interview with the author.

49 Martin Carnoy, *The State and Political Theory* (New Jersey, USA and Guildford, Surrey: Princeton University Press, 1984), 46.

> the trustee of the society as a whole. Once he came to his formulation of capitalist society as a class society, dominated by the bourgeoisie, it necessarily followed that the State is the political expression of that dominance. Indeed, the State is an essential means of class domination in capitalist society. It is not above class struggles, but deeply engaged in them. Its intervention in the struggle is crucial, and that intervention is conditioned by the essential character of the State as a means of class domination.[50]

According to Carnoy, Marx's theory of a nation state could be classified into three fundamental categories: firstly a social structure based on material conditions, secondly a political expression of class structure, and thirdly as a repressive structure maintaining class control[51]. Later modifications of Marxist theory, adapting it to critique twentieth-century (and now twenty-first-century) state structures, have dwelt upon the problems with the way in which class control is transformed into state power, and thence maintained in capitalist states. The translation of ruling class ownership and control into state power is fraught and complex, and gives rise to many forms of state government, each of which raises 'questions of the form of the State and *why* it assumes different forms...'[52]

Difficulties with this translation of power at the level of the state may account for the very existence of some documentary graphic novels, especially Sacco's and Satrapi's work. Notwithstanding all of the difficulties with terms like 'class' in Marxist theory, the material conditions that determine the organisation of a state, and the problematic of cultural control and dominance have profoundly affected the production of the graphic novels studied here, and to an extent determine their realism; which is to say that it conditions the critical stance that each of them takes. Sharon Kinsella's work on the social production of manga demonstrates the relationship between the social status of manga artists and the broader culture of the state, and also attempts to deal with the complexities of class, albeit

50 Carnoy, 37. Here Marx is responding to, and rejecting, Hegel's thesis of the state.

51 Carnoy, 46–50.

52 Carnoy is quoting Miliband here; Carnoy, 51–52.

tentatively[53]. A striking example of this occurs in Nakazawa's work in *Barefoot Gen*. The theme of this work and the earlier *I Saw It* (the atomic bombing of Hiroshima in 1945) and their production as manga in the context of the Japanese post-war economic boom, are fundamentally related to the formation of the Japanese state and the changes it underwent in that period. Nakazawa's critique of militarism in pre- and post-war Japan, and with his condemnation of the US bombing offered pertinent criticism of both sides in that conflict, and therefore had a critical relationship to the post war state under US occupation and cultural dominance.

The Constitution of Japan was originally drafted under the auspices of New Dealers in the occupying US administration. [54] Its Western, socialist and democratic characteristics were obviously at odds with the wartime military ethics of Japanese imperialism (and later with US imperialism as well), and this dynamic of ideological conflict is reflected in Nakazawa's narrative, especially in the ambivalence of the children to the rapidly reforming state and government in the immediate post-war and post-bombing period, which is the focus of *Barefoot Gen*.[55]

Concepts of the 'state', as an agency or sponsor of cultural development, and as a purveyor of ideological nationalist identity, are important for the analysis of *Barefoot Gen* because of the competition for cultural hegemony between the US and Japan.[56] The gratuitous violence of the children depicted throughout the novel proved

53 Sharon Kinsella, *Adult Manga: Culture and Power in Contemporary Japanese Society* (ConsumAsiaN, 2000).

54 See J. M. Maki, "Direction and Theory in Constitutional Developments" in *The Constitution of Japan – Its First Twenty Years 1947–1967*, ed. Dan Fenno Henderson (Seattle and London: Uni. of Washington Press, 1968).

55 See Sharon Kinsella, "Change in Social Status, Form and Content of Manga 1986–1996" in *Japan Forum* 8 Part 1, 104–112, for a useful survey of the political development of manga.

56 Popular culture analysed in relation to the Japanese state is thoroughly discussed in Ivy, 239–58; see also S. Saito *Japan at the Summit: Japan's Role in the Western Alliance and Asian Pacific Co-operation* (London and New York: Routledge, 1991).

resistant to US sanitising of comics, as manifested in the 1950s' Comics' Code (Code of the Comics Magazine Association of America, Incorporated, 1954).[57] Judged by these standards *Barefoot Gen* is clearly inappropriate for a moral tale in terms of US legislation, despite such representations being unrestricted in Japanese manga. On the other hand the Japanese preservation of the Imperial Emperor immediately after the war is presented as an ideological difficulty in Nakazawa's narrative. His children continue their allegiance to their family, and hold this above their allegiance to the Emperor and State. This is a challenge in the novel to traditional Japanese nationalistic notions of the primacy of honouring the state, which remained a difficulty for many on the Right of Japanese politics during the novel's production and consumption. Similarly, the US military bombing of Hiroshima itself, and its cultural ramifications, is developed by Nakazawa in ways that did not make for easy assimilation to the dominant mythologies of either state.[58] The vast proliferation of rhetoric and myths surrounding the bombing, some of which are played out in *Barefoot Gen*, are dealt with in the novel with all their ambiguity and hypocrisy in evidence. The portrayal, legitimised by the Japanese State, of Japan as the ultimate victim, is not validated by Nakazawa anymore than is the US evaluation of itself and its actions as saviour of both Japan and the world.[59]

The vestiges of the US New Deal philosophies that re-emerged in post-war Japan enabled a publishing space for the pacifist sentiments of the *Barefoot Gen* narratives that would have been inconceivable had the military Japanese state prevailed. The New Deal ideology that underpinned the Japanese Constitution, drawn up

57 The Comics' Code is reproduced in Sabin, *Adult Comics,* 251–253; see also Amy Kiste Nyberg, "William Gaines and the Battle Over EC Comics," *Inks: Cartoon and Comic Art Studies*, February 1996, 3–15.

58 Roger Dingman, "Alliance in Crisis: The Lucky Dragon Incident and Japanese-American Relations, 1954–1955," in *The Great Powers in East Asia: 1953–1960*, eds. Warren I. Cohen and Iriye Akira (New York, 1990).

59 See Michael J. Hogan, ed., *Hiroshima in History and Memory* (New York: Cambridge University Press, 1996) for examples of the history of the battle to control the 'memory' of the Hiroshima bombing.

in the immediate aftermath of the war under US military occupation, was characterised by liberal sentiments with regard to freedom of speech and a pluralist democratic state. Manga would probably have developed very differently had Japan continued to be under direct control of the US State during the comics' censorship of the subsequent McCarthy era, as represented ideologically in the comics world by the 'self regulatory' Comics' Code.

Nakazawa's practices in *Barefoot Gen* had much in common with manga of its time, and this is indicative of it as a production specific to that society. The configuration of the state, both as national ideology, as political organisation and as institutional practice, had a determining effect on manga and therefore on Nakazawa's work. The adult readership of manga was already established in Japan, just as it withered in the West under the Comics' Code and the attraction of mass television. As Frederik Schodt has clearly demonstrated, this was in part due to the use of manga as a means of cultural subversion and resistance during the US occupation years.[60] Manga of this period would have attracted an adult indigenous readership that was able to read the Japanese text in comics and identify with the specific cultural signs that would have mystified the occupying US military. Nakazawa's *Barefoot Gen* may also be seen as following a tradition of resistance to orthodox power. Schodt explains how the artist Taro Yashima, for instance, created comics strips during the Second World War that were utilised as part of the US war-effort to prevent Japanese soldiers from fighting to the death, and also strips that showed 'that the Japanese were not savages or mindless slaves to their emperor, as the Western media often implied. […] an exposé of Japanese militarism and an account of how he and other dissidents had tried to oppose it before the war began.'[61]

As writers like Rifas have pointed out, Nakazawa's work also plotted a course between two opposing ideologies (Japanese and US), simultaneously scrutinising the mythologies of each, especially in terms of military justifications for war and bombing, with its attendant

60 Schodt, *Manga, Manga,* 61.
61 Schodt, 59.

stereotyping.[62] Figure 1.3 is an example of the Nakazawa's expression of anti-war sentiments, portrayed through a scene of considerable violence. Scenes like these were subject to pressures that would have led to publishing restrictions in both Japan and the US, had there not been active supporting groups to counter them. These influences, successful or not, indicate the way in which social configurations may have proscribed the reception of the images, which may in turn have affected their production. In the illustration Gen's father assaults school teachers with great violence. They have just falsely accused and punished his daughter for stealing, driven by their prejudice against her father's pacifism, and Nakazawa has the teachers conflate pacifism with sedition through their 'traitor' accusations. Scenes like these brought complaints of Nakazawa's (and the publisher's) lack of patriotism even thirty years later. Criticism from the Japanese political Right, for example, highlighted Nakazawa's resistance to the patriotic notion of the Japanese as victims at the hands of rampant US imperialism.[63] In the US, on the other hand, when it first appeared as *Gen of Hiroshima*, the scenes of violence created anxieties of an entirely different kind. An audience unused to stylised manga violence were distracted from the otherwise anti-militarist stance of the work.[64]

Within these differing cultural contexts reception could, as in the case of Nakazawa's work, affect the comic book's commercial assimilation adversely. The gratuitous theatrical repetition of the violence was characteristic of manga, although such distinctions were eroded over the course of the 1980s and 1990s as European and US comic books began to acquire more manga characteristics, as its popularity grew and translations became routine.

62 Leonard Rifas, "Globalizing Comic Books from Below: How Manga Came to America," (paper presented at *Big Apple Anime Fest* December, 21, 2001), 9; conference paper with minor additions by Rifas, sent to the author).

63 Alan Gleason, interview with the author December 20, 2001.

64 As Rifas points out, "Globalizing Comic Books from Below," 6–7.

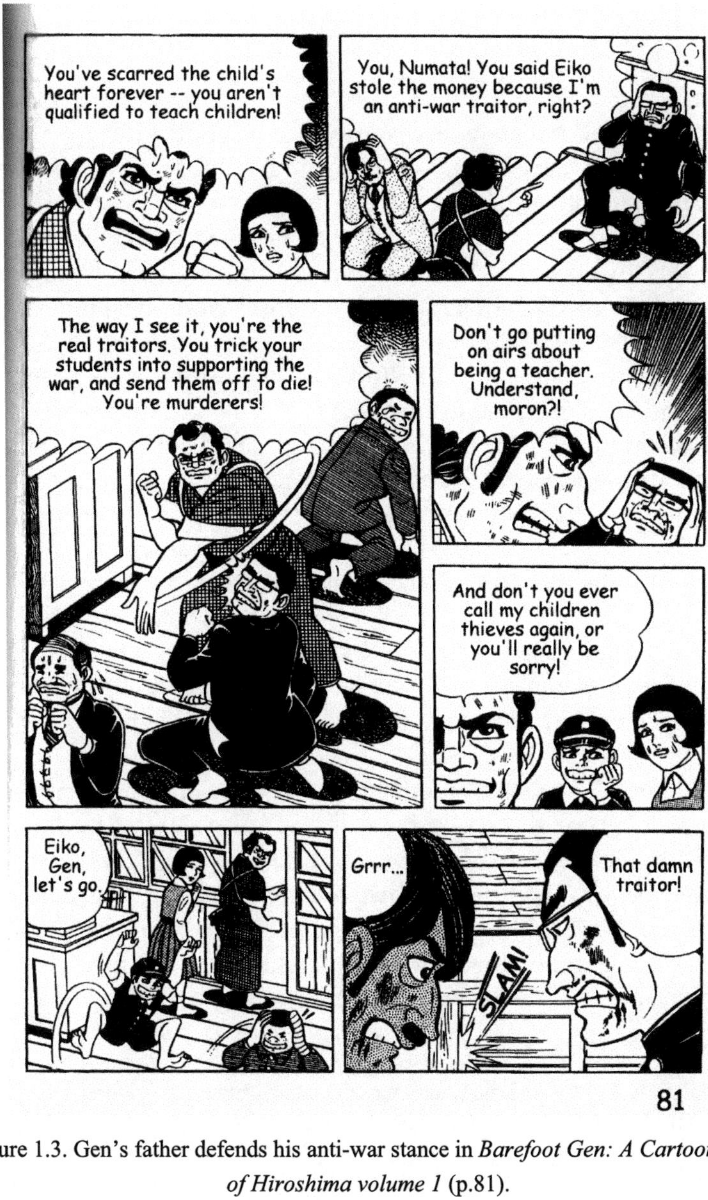

Figure 1.3. Gen's father defends his anti-war stance in *Barefoot Gen: A Cartoon Story of Hiroshima volume 1* (p.81).

Censorship

If the history of realism is necessarily one of political engagement, it is also one of censorship, whether in the form of the exhibition hanging committees that objected to the work of Courbet, or government oppression, such as the rise to power of the Nazis in the 1930s that forced John Heartfield out of Germany. Comic book production has always been subject to obstructive institutional and cultural mechanisms, and at times this has been manifest in the form of a repressive state apparatus (to coin Louis Althusser's term), like publishing and distribution constraints.[65] The key moments in the West occurred with the establishment of the Comics' Code in the USA in 1954 and its equivalent in the UK in the same year, and later the significant backlash against comics censorship that occurred later in the form of underground comix in the 1970s. Adroitness on the part of the artist in recognising the traps generated by these laws and associated societal myths, was clearly necessary in each case. Spiegelman, for instance, has on several occasions found himself the target of well-publicised criticism of his work, especially where that work transgressed ethical orthodoxies.[66]

The Comics' Code had a major effect on the content and readership of US comic production. It was a self-regulatory system developed by publishers principally to avert the possibility of legislation forcibly curtailing the content of comics. This threat was brought about by high profile media campaigns that targeted horror comics in particular, and successfully engendered the perception that such comics could be linked to anti-social and disturbed behaviour in young people. The imposition of regulatory codes in the US and the

65 Louis Althusser, "Ideology and the Ideological State Apparatuses," in Storey, 151–162.

66 The case of the kissing couple, Jew and Afro-Caribbean, that he drew for the cover of the *New Yorker* magazine being a case in point. See Barry Schwabsky, "Art Spiegelman: an exquisite sense of balance," *Art Press* 194, Sept. 1994, 27–32.

UK may partly account for low numbers of adult readers of comics in these countries. This is highlighted by comparison with Japan, where there was no equivalent regulation, and where adults read manga almost as readily as young people.

Publishers of comics, and horror comics in particular, developed a campaign of their own to resist the any imposed regulation on the content of their very popular comics. In the 1954 horror comics' publishers were forced to defend the macabre content of their productions. This marked one of the most significant conflicts between government and comic publishers, and was a measure of the extent to which the dominant social order felt threatened by the prevailing forms of comic production. William Gaines, proprietor of Entertaining Comics (EC), a large producer of horror comics, attempted to resist the imposition of censorship with his testimony on behalf of the publishers, set against the evidence of Frederic Wertham, as published in the 1954 *Seduction of the Innocent,* which was a key publication of this period making the case for the negative effects of the media, and comics in particular.[67] As both Barker and William Savage have demonstrated, Wertham's book caused (and reflected) the anxiety that was prevalent in powerful sections of US society at this time.[68] Its principal strategy was to link the increase in the number of comic books presenting horror and crime stories with the perceived rise in crime rates of young people, referred to at the time as juvenile delinquency. His strategy was premised on the idea that the association of media exposure (in this case comics) and behavioural patterns was relatively straightforward – unsuitable comic material will result in undesirable action, especially on the part of young people, the 'innocents'. As Barker explains, the social ills that were attributed to the practice of reading comics were wide-ranging, and

67 Frederic Wertham, *Seduction of the Innocent* (New York: Holt, Rinehart and Winston, 1954).

68 Martin Barker, *A Haunt of Fears, The Strange History of the Horror Comics Campaign* (London: Pluto Press, 1984), and William Savage, W. Jr. *Comic Books and America 1945–1954* (USA: University of Oklahoma Press. 1990).

largely unfocused.[69] Wertham assumed enough of a scholarly rhetoric to establish convincingly, to non-specialists and non-readers of comics at least, that the cause of these effects was to be found in horror and crime comics of the period; these supposed effects were aggravated by the public perception of rising levels of crime in teenagers.[70]

Amy Kiste Nyberg has explained how this was fuelled by the post-war decline in interest in Superhero stories, which resulted in attempts to attract and retain readers through elements of horror added to their crime and thriller comic books. The 'Senate Subcommittee to Investigate Juvenile Delinquency' began their investigations of the media industry – and comic books in particular – coincident with the publication of Wertham's book. Gaines' resistance to this brought him into direct conflict with the Committee and eventually forced the closure of his horror and crime comic book lines, as it did for most other comic publishers. Sabin and others have commented that this caused a major slump in the comics market, from which it took years or even decades for the comic book industry to recover.[71]

Gaines defended the case for horror comics at the Senate Subcommittee Hearings.[72] His unsuccessful defence was based on the premise that the commercially popular horror titles were under an attack driven by vested publishing interests. Citing 'do-gooders' attempts to constrain his comics publishing practices, he responded to his adversaries, including Wertham and rival publishers, by highlighting their own commercial activities:

> Comics are under fire…[…]. Due to the efforts of various 'do-gooder' groups, a large segment of the public is being led to believe that certain comic magazines cause juvenile delinquency, warp the minds of America's Youth and affect the development of the personalities of those who read them! Among these 'do-gooders' are: a psychiatrist [a reference to Wertham] who has made a

69 Barker, *A Haunt of Fears*, 65–70.
70 Barker, *A Haunt of Fears*, 65.
71 Sabin, *Adult Comics*.
72 Nyberg, 2–15.

> lucrative career of attacking comic magazines. Certain publishing companies who do not publish comics and would benefit by their demise [...].[73]

Rifas, however, has pointed out that Wertham's main contribution was to demonstrate that mass media productions like comics can affect behaviour adversely, and that this was prescient when considered in the light of subsequent media research.[74]

Gaines tried to combat the questions about the moral content of his stories head-on, by arguing that the stories could have a beneficial effect, referring to other contemporary psychiatric sources.[75] At the Hearings he defended a story that was condemned as inciting racial intolerance by claiming that, to the contrary, the comic dealt with racial stereotyping in a way that exposed prejudice rather than condoning it.[76] Tales of children killing their parents, like EC's 'The Orphan', dominated the hearings and made Gaines' position seem untenable. [77] Prior to the hearings Gaines had tried to turn the anti-comics tide by arguing that horror comic phobia stemmed from Communist anti-American sentiments, and that to object to comics was playing into the hands of 'Red Dupes'.[78] This took the form of a full-page advert in his horror titles and proclaimed that 'The group most anxious to destroy comics are the Communists!' Barker evaluates this claim by analysing the parallel British censorship campaign that was initially driven by Communist Party members (CP). This appeared in the form of 'A Bill to prevent the dissemination of certain pictorial publications harmful to children and

73 William M. Gaines, Jnr, editorial in *Shock Suspend Stories,* 18, EC Comics, 1954; Facsimile reproduced December 1996, USA, EC Comics, West Plains, MO: Gemstone Publishing.

74 Leonard Rifas "Fredric Wertham: Scientist," (paper presented at 1st Comic Arts Scholars' Conference in San Diego, USA, 1992).

75 Nyberg, 8.

76 Nyberg, 8.

77 Reproduced in full in Barker, *A Haunt of Fears*, 98–105. Detail of facsimile used in illustration from EC Comics *Shock Suspend Stories* 18, 4; See also "Cadillac Fever" in the same issue.

78 Barker, *A Haunt of Fears*, 7.

young persons'.[79] The key phrase in the very brief text referred to crime or horror comics that portrayed stories 'in such a way that the work as a whole would tend to corrupt a child or young person into whose hands it might fall'.[80] The involvement of CP members in the British campaign stemmed from an anti-American capitalist comics position adopted by the US and the British CP, and aimed at the imperialist ideology that they identified in war and superhero comics like *Captain America.* Barker describes the irony of the alliance between the reactionary press and the organised left that resulted in the later radical comic production being subject to legal restraint.[81]

In the US the 'Code of the Comics Magazine Association of America, Incorporated', was brought into effect as a self-regulatory code in October 1954, and sought extensive restrictions on the content of comic books, with much greater particularity than its British counterpart.[82] Many of its passages contained statements that were authoritarian to a degree that was disabling to comic books attempting to deal with almost any themes and issues that were not part of a politically conservative agenda. The representation of the state and government itself, for example, was tightly governed: 'Policemen, judges, government officials and respected institutions shall never be presented in such a way as to create disrespect for established authority.'[83] This statement alone would have prevented *Barefoot Gen, Maus*, *Palestine* or *Persepolis* attempting to raise the issue of state control, especially where this resulted in injustice, racism, nationalism or militarism. The Code also encouraged censorship from prejudicial standpoints; for example, the statement 'All characters shall be depicted in dress reasonably acceptable to society' assumed a homogeneous society where dress was standardised, and questions of

79 Reproduced in Barker, *A Haunt of Fears*, 16.

80 Barker, *A Haunt of Fears*, 16.

81 Barker, *A Haunt of Fears*, 16.

82 Reproduced in Sabin, *Adult Comics*, 251–253. The effects of the code are discussed in full in David Hajdu, *The Ten-Cent Plague: The Great Comic Book Scare and How It Changed America* (New York: Farrar, Straus and Giroux, 2008).

83 Sabin, *Adult Comics*, 251.

ethnicity, gender and class were simply not issues to be considered, much less explored in a comic book.[84] Similarly, the following requirement was based upon a mythology of social relations: 'Respect for parents, the moral code and for honourable behaviour shall be fostered. A sympathetic understanding of the problems of love is not a license for morbid distortion.'[85]

The Code could be seen as a case of a state 'apparatus', as Althusser would have described it, which sought to normalise social practices. All representations of behaviour that did not conform to the model expressed through the Code were thus positioned as aberrant. The arbiters of taste, and therefore the controllers of practices and behaviours, were also given freedom of interpretation, since the models of 'taste' and 'decency' were not explicit, only implied. As the opening statement of the 'General Standards' made clear: 'All elements or techniques not specifically mentioned herein, but which are contrary to the spirit and intent of the Code, and are considered violations of good taste or decency, shall be prohibited.'[86] The result of this intense institutional control, as David Hajdu has demonstrated, was anodyne comic production in the US, stalling the English language production of radical comics in the US and the UK until the emergence of underground comics in the late 1960s.[87]

This ideological repression obviously had profound effects on the form and content of mass-produced comics. The popularity of comics generally would probably have diminished in the subsequent period in the face of competing forms of popular culture such as television, as Sabin and others have argued. In the case of Japan, where manga was only subjected to ad hoc or ineffective censorship repression, the comic books assumed significantly different forms. The practices of Japanese manga artists like Osamu Tezuka, in the late 1950s and early 1960s for instance, would not have survived the publishing restrictions in force in the US and Britain. This context also

84 Sabin, *Adult Comics*, 252.
85 Sabin, *Adult Comics*, 253.
86 Sabin, *Adult Comics*, 252.
87 Hajdu, *The Ten Cent Plague*.

affected the output of the next generation of manga artists like Nakazawa, and to some extent accounted for the distinctness of the forms of manga in *Barefoot Gen.* This contrast is marked if *Barefoot Gen* is compared to Marvel comic-book publications, for example, that were popular in the US in the same period. In *Barefoot Gen* the stylised violence of children, the narratives of corrupt officials and the problems of unconditional patriotism were developed in a comics culture that was less fettered by repressive censorship and influenced – perhaps as a direct corollary of this – by an emerging and stable mass adult market for comics. The adult audiences for comics, barely materialised in the US and the UK in any comparable way. The documentary graphic novel, however, is a development coinciding with increased adult readership in the West, springing as it does from the adult underground movement and its emergent realism in the 1960s and '70s. Realism, in the context of these documentary graphic novels, is primarily a political critique, fundamentally determined by the context of its operation. It is the mechanism whereby an artist is able, often allegorically or metaphorically, to speak to an audience about power and their relationship to it. This context is created, and distorted, by overt state mechanisms like censorship, or covert ideological pressures. As works of documentary realism, novels like *Palestine* or *Persepolis*, similar to earlier realist works such as Meunier's *Firedamp Explosion*, have political meanings that operate within the specific social contexts of their time, such as resistance to an oppressive state, colonialism, religious practices and iconography, or racism. Realism in this sense is necessarily a contingent, critical and reactive practice.

Chapter 2: Documentary

The boundary between fiction and documentary is ill defined, and documentary is arguably dependent on fictional narrative structures; as Bill Nichols explains, it is the historical familiarity with the conventions of fiction that makes documentary intelligible, and conversely, fiction makes reference to documentary forms in order to legitimise its authority.[1] The dilemma between fiction and documentary is played out in the transformation of Nakazawa's main (autobiographic) character Keiji, as he is increasingly 'fictionalised' during the development of the novel, from its first manifestation as *I Saw It* to its later *Barefoot Gen* forms.[2] Fictionalised in this context means that Nakazawa imaginatively developed the underlying autobiographic narrative to widen its scope. In doing so he invented events and scenarios in which he, as Keiji, was not directly involved. Increasingly he was able to draw on his knowledge of the histories of the Second World War and of the atomic bombing gained over the subsequent years, in addition to his experience and memories as a survivor. As it became less 'factually' autobiographic – that is responding with less fidelity to his remembered experience, the more imaginative and fictionalised it necessarily became. Although fiction (as imaginative invention) may be contrasted with documentary (as the recording of fact), this straightforward opposition is rendered problematic in many instances, of which *Barefoot Gen* is one. This is because in *Barefoot Gen* Nakazawa's direct knowledge of events as a survivor is combined with his knowledge of other people's experience much more than in its forerunner *I Saw It*, giving the appearance of fictionalisation. Thus the scene of the raging father assaulting teachers (figure 1.3) may be a fiction (beyond personal experience) in relation

1 Bill Nichols, *Introduction to Documentary* (Indiana, USA: Indiana University Press, 2001), 1–5.

2 Keiji Nakazawa, *I Saw It* (EduComics, San Francisco, CA, 1982).

to Nakazawa's autobiography, but represents his knowledge of the factual (recorded) frustration of those victimised by excessive patriotism and militarism.

Nichols has made a detailed analysis of the documentary form in film, and made (qualified) categories within which it can be defined.[3] Applying this analysis to Barefoot Gen, the fiction/documentary contradiction could be rethought in terms of different modes of the documentary form. If the earlier versions could be classified as more 'expository' documentary, in that Nakazawa was inclined towards a didactic account of the events as he knew and experienced them, while the later versions give a more 'participatory' or even 'performative' mode of account, in Nichols' terms.[4] In these modes, especially the latter, others' accounts are given greater prominence, and greater liberties taken with the original autobiography. Thus the usually suppressed anger at Japanese institutional prejudices is actually played out in the narratives of *Barefoot Gen*, despite being constrained in the earlier version *I Saw It.* Spiegelman's *Maus* is a good example of a 'reflexive' documentary, since his mixture of biography and autobiography serves to question the documentary form itself, and gives rise to questions about subjectivity in his amassing of experiential evidence. *Palestine*, like *Barefoot Gen*, is created in a mode that conforms to 'participatory' form, where his role as narrator is dependent on his experience of the 'authentic' conditions of his subject. In this case Sacco participated at first hand in environment of his narrative, that of Palestinians living under military occupation.

Stella Bruzzi, however, argues that Nichol's categories are problematic because the overlaps between them are so ubiquitous that his whole classification system becomes redundant.[5] Instead she focuses on the relationship between event and representation, ac-

3 Bill Nichols, *Introduction to Documentary* (Indiana, USA: Indiana University Press, 2001).

4 Nichols, 102–138.

5 Stella Bruzzi, *New Documentary: A Critical Introduction* (London: Routledge, 2000).

knowledging the enduring issues that are problematic in this dialectic, such as truth, bias and subjectivity. If Nichol's categories can be applied to with some success to *Maus*, *Barefoot Gen* and *Palestine*, their application to *Persepolis* or to *Emigrants* reveals the limitations to which Bruzzi alerts us. *Emigrants,* for instance, is clearly literary fiction, derived from imaginative narratives, directed entirely by the author's will. Yet its relationship to historical events is also clear, since its 'autobiographical', narrative and photographic documentary style is firmly rooted in highly specific events. Despite Sacco's conspicuous visual innovations and his politically radical stance in *Palestine,* in documentary analyses like these his work appears more orthodox, less inclined to question the documentary form itself. That said, it is also significant that he makes no attempt to conceal the partisan subjectivity of his interviewees, and like Nakazawa he was willing to allow their accounts to stand even in the absence of corroborating evidence.

Each of the authors is primarily concerned with depicting a specific authenticity of lived experience. The selected graphic novels also have similarities in their narrative structures, all having a principal narrator who guides the reader. In *Barefoot Gen* and *Persepolis* narration is conducted via a semi-autobiographic character who is depicted participating directly in events. In *Palestine* Sacco depicts himself as a first-person narrator, with this author-as-narrator often relating accounts of others' experiences. Sacco's personal experiences were also included as a sub-narrative, as Spiegelman does in *Maus*. Like *Barefoot Gen* and *Palestine*, is also an autobiographical novel, but since it contains a biography (his father's) within an autobiography, it follows a variation on the single voice narrative structure.[6] Instead of using the novel to relate an entirely personal, secondary perspective on the Holocaust, Spiegelman uses his relationship with his father (a survivor) to depict events explicitly. Sebald switches from third person to first person narrator subtly with the same long paragraph, or even within one of his page-long sentences.

6 Art Spiegelman, foreword in Nakazawa, *Barefoot Gen, Vol. 1.*

These effects raise issues about memory, and the recovery, transmission and reception of knowledge and experience. Paul Ricoeur pursues these themes in his disquisition on memory and history[7]. He questions the whole notion of documentary by analysing such underlying concepts as remembering, recalling and imagining. His discussion of testimony is particularly relevant here, since he explores the idea of the 'autobiographical certification of a narrative', a concept which applies to all of the works studied in this book, and is at the heart of the matter in terms of the modes of documentary that the authors favour.[8]

Ricoeur places testimony and recounting at the problematic boundary of fiction and reality, where the testimony of the witness is called into question by the very act of narrating events; the act of creating a representation, even by the witness's recounting of direct experience, necessarily involves the socially acquired modes of narrative and memory recall. In terms of the latter, Ricoeur's analysis of the representational modes of memory include an extensive exploration of the images of memory, which is pertinent to an account of a graphic novelists' documentary methodology. For Ricoeur, central to the concept of the memory image is the idea of the 'presence of the absent'. In the phenomenological terms in which Ricoeur makes his analysis, this refers to the apparent presence of the past event or the reality in memory: the thing itself is gone, but the memory remains and seems to retain the presence of the originating moment.[9] This is where Ricoeur introduces the idea of the imagination, as a reconstructive mechanism within memory, and one that can generate the images of memory.

7 Paul Ricoeur, *Memory, History, Forgetting* (Chicago and London: The University of Chicago Press, 2006).

8 Ricoeur, 163.

9 Ricoeur, 44, for example; referred to numerous times throughout his book.

The graphic novelist is dealing with images literally, as opposed to the textual novelist's evocation of images, and this has consequences for the accounts that are presented. As documentaries they directly tackle the issue of 'presence of absence'; they involve a literal image creation, utilising all the artifices of the graphic artist – spatial illusions, formal mark making, cultural references to other visual practices etc, all of which conspire to recreate the presence of the event or moment that once was. This gives a paradoxical aspect to the idea of witness testimony and its relation to truth; in Satrapi's *Persepolis*, for instance, the seeming crudity of the graphic work – its graphic shortcuts such as caricature, lack of spatial information, restricted tonal gradation, exaggerated emotional responses – does not seem to negate the apparent verisimilitude of the documentary reconstruction. The novel's very artifice arguably reinforces the manifestation of the lost presence that seems to be fundamental to memory and documentary reconstruction. These ideas of testimony, images, presence and imagination are brought to the fore and developed case by case in the discussions about documentary graphic novels that follow, but first the concept of authenticity requires some explanation, particularly in its relation to documenting social crises that is the sine qua non of many of these novelists.

Authenticity

One of the chief problems that affects the recounting and retelling of experience, especially that of trauma and crisis, is that of authenticity. Cooper uses Nietzsche to explain the concept of authenticity in terms of the narrator's values being in accordance with the knowledge content of the material described.[10] Direct experience is not necessarily the most important attribute of the authentic documentary account, more the value of the information to the narrator, the belief in its veracity, and the imperative that drives its dissemination. The

10 David E. Cooper, *Authenticity and Learning: Nietzsche's Educational Philosophy* (London: Routledge and Kegan Paul, 1983), 2–6.

models of authenticity that Cooper identifies are those of correspondence and genesis, whereby the former is linked with 'likeness', and the latter by association with the original moment or event.[11] In the case of the image methods used by the authors under consideration here, the photographs or drawings with text imply both models, with the photographic image acting as the proof by correspondence (this is how it looked) and by genesis (it was created at that time). This appears to apply even where it is evident that neither condition has actually been met – as in the case of Nakazawa's fictionalised drama and Sebald's bogus use of photographs. When drawn images are produced from either primary or secondary sources, as in the case of Spiegelman's and Nakazawa's dominant practice, the authentic documenting of events is reinforced, but this time the concept of authentication is produced by the artist as witness, as opposed to the photo-chemical image as witness.

The pedagogical imperative that these graphic novels display is underpinned by specific and idiosyncratic visual documentary methods. As Swales has noted, Sebald's use of images, particularly photographs, have two principal ways of affecting us: 'They seem to be documentary material akin to a set of corroborative illustrations, and yet they also partake of and create a whole symbolic texture of evocative images.'[12] This comment is corroborated by Sebald's own observation that 'behind the illusions of the surface a dread inspiring depth is concealed. It is the metaphysical lining of reality, so to speak.',[13] which goes to the heart of the dilemma over the supposed boundary between fiction and documentary, and Sebald's probing of the divide between these paradigms. The 'metaphysical lining' may also be understood as the compelling narrative force that appears to authenticate the work. It is in this narrative imperative that the idea of

11 Cooper, 9.

12 Martin Swales, "Theoretical Reflections on the Work of W.G. Sebald," in *W.G. Sebald – A Critical Companion,* eds. J.J. Long and Anne Whitehead (Edinburgh: Edinburgh University Press, 2006), 27.

13 W.G. Sebald and Jan Pieter Tripp, *Unrecounted,* trans. Michael Hamburger (London: Penguin, 2005), 87–88.

the authentic is encapsulated, and helps to confer upon these works validity.

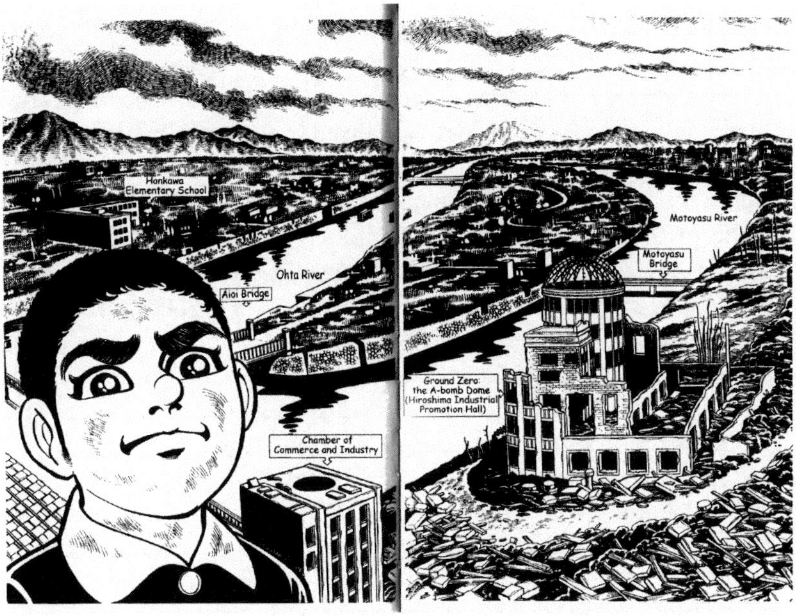

Figure 2.1. Pages showing the devastation of Hiroshima. The scene is based on contemporary news photographs in Keiji Nakazawa's *Barefoot Gen, Volume 2, The Day After* (San Francisco: Last Gasp, 2004), pp. 7–8.

Nakazawa's accumulated memories of others' accounts and, importantly, others' images in *Barefoot Gen* became an important feature of his documentary technique, integrating familiar images, usually drawn from newspapers, prints and photographs, that were produced in response to the bombing and its aftermath, into his work. As can be seen in his rendering of an aerial view of the devastation of Hiroshima shortly after the bombing, with his own face superimposed upon it, the background is drawn from a freely available news photograph (figure 2.1). Nakazawa here literally inscribes his visual narrative upon photographs, and one is forced to reconsider the original image within the new narrative context.

These methods of memory reconstruction and visualisation are fundamental to the documentary graphic novel as a procedure. Nakazawa shares Sebald's predilection for the detailed documentation of personal, specific and individualised calamity, and uses very specific sequential devices to imbue his image texts with foreboding and despair. In common with many Japanese manga artist-authors, he uses the method identified by McCloud as 'aspect to aspect,' a frame transition device, in his scenes of disaster, in preference to the more common image transition 'action to action'.[14] The latter would not allow the reader to dwell on the aspects of a scene, engendering moments of reflection and deliberation – necessary for the horrific moments of recollection associated with traumatic memory. Figure 3.10 shows the first moments of Gen encountering a soldier suffering from radiation sickness after the radioactive fallout from the Hiroshima bomb. The 'aspect to aspect' transition, where all of the panels on the page follow a sequence determined by the visual path of the onlooker, focus on different aspects of the room, which together build a picture of the squalor and the suffering.[15] There is no text after the initial single 'gasp' from Gen as he looks into the room for the first time. In the last two frames on the page the focus is on a single foot in two stages of progressive close-up, the final image using a cropped and enlarged section of the previous one. This text-free sequence emphasises the horror that has resulted from the victim's family's prejudice against radiation sickness, which was thought by many at the time to be contagious. The narrative subsequently dwells on the relatives' unwillingness to enter the room to tend to the sick person, and their consequent enlistment of Gen to do this 'risky' work for them. Gleason, one of the translators of *Barefoot Gen*, points out that Nakazawa may have had a specifically Japanese agenda behind the scenes depicting Gen battling against adversity in this way:

14 McCloud, 74.
15 McCloud, 74.

> The character of Gen is sort of an exaggerated version of himself – Gen is an unbelievably perky character the whole time. A sort of little superhero because Nakazawa thought that it would be good for the youth of Japan to see this larger than life young hero their age who would overcome these horrendous obstacles.[16]

In his interest in the way that prejudice functions to bring about personalised calamity, Nakazawa's intention is pedagogical, to inform a new generation about the prejudice and patriotism, which led to the camouflage of social catastrophes of monumental proportions. Spiegelman's pedagogic contribution is similarly aimed at subsequent generations, since the very transmission of this 'unutterable' knowledge of the Holocaust clearly has its own traumatic effects. Spiegelman's father's memories of the Nazi's forced labour camps are made available through the narration of his experiences, each packed with a specificity of events. These recollections are in turn translated by and through Spiegelman's drawing, creating a number of steps of mediation. Each of these stages transforms the original experiential event, a process that Spiegelman had obviously considered carefully. Spiegelman is, however, acutely aware of the vagaries of memory: 'Ultimately, the source for the information is often a memory which, by the nature of how one narrates one's life, has elements that aren't verifiable'.[17] In terms of the authentic recreation of experience, Spiegelman compares *Maus*, interestingly, with the work of Steven Spielberg's film *Schindler's List*. This is a film that, like *Maus*, attempts to portray the Holocaust through a specific, biographical realism. For Spiegelman, however, the film transgresses certain boundaries that he implies *Maus* had observed:

> … it feels no compunction, this film, about representing dramatically things better let lie, like shower sequences, or… whatever. It dramatizes them for cheap thrills, no matter what else is claimed for the movie. […] I say that as one

16 Alan Gleason, interview with the author.

17 Barry Schwabsky, "Art Spiegelman: an exquisite sense of balance," *Art Press* 194 (1994): 29–30.

enters this territory, one inherits a legacy that requires an exquisite sense of balance in order not to transgress against the ghosts of the past.[18]

Spiegelman was wary of over dramatising his father's experience, and affirmation of his 'sense of balance' came in the form of comments from Holocaust survivors who reviewed *Maus*. Spiegelman highlights one in particular, made by his cousin Lolek: 'He said that the book really shocked him because it was all so accurate. I count that as the best review that I could have gotten, because he was there'.[19] This suggests that authenticity lay at the heart of Spiegelman's values in his production of *Maus*. Authenticity is best measured, as far as Spiegelman is concerned, by those who actually experienced that which he had only imagined; this is seen by his audience as verifying the truth of the account. As Berman says of Spiegelman's research:

a good part of that understanding was based on exhaustive primary research. To supplement his interviews with his father, Spiegelman spoke to other camp survivors and their children. As well, he read hundreds of histories, biographies, and memoirs, and visited Auschwitz and Birkenhau.[20]

For Spiegelman this concept of the truth of the work was brought about by the evidence of research in combination with a perception of honesty on the part of the author. The veracity of his research was crucial for his project, and represents a pedagogic impulse, a desire to inform others truthfully, despite all of the contradictions and ambiguities of the concept of truth in relation to past traumas.

These graphic novels represent an emerging way of representing social chaos and trauma, and do so in a number of innovative ways. They employ the means of popular and commodity culture, and yet seem to remain resistant to it; they adopt the visual detritus of that culture, assembling images and photographs that have in themselves little value, and yet produce effects of considerable profundity; they are often ambiguous in their sequence and juxtaposition of image with

18 Schwabsky, 29.
19 Avis Berman, "The Maus That Roared," *Art News* 92 (May 1993): 64.
20 Berman, 64.

narrative, but manage to reference moments of great importance and gravity, and authenticity is achieved by seemingly inauthentic means. If this is all in the context of the twenty-first-century cultural desire for memory, as Andreas Huyssen suggests, then these novels may represent a significant development towards a visually orientated documentary of traumatic memory, predicated on authenticity and truthfulness.[21]

Wilms explores the ideas of primary memory and truth in relation to the initial experience of sustained violence and its subsequent translation 'into the 'secondary memory' of something like a national consciousness'.[22] In reference to Sebald's work he points to a fundamental difficulty with the dissemination of narratives based on traumatic memory:

> In trauma, witnessing unwillingly collapses. The witness cannot fully register the truth or scope of an experience as it occurs owing to its overwhelming intensity. Traumatic history is thus history that is not owned in its entirety.[23]

To deal with this traumatic history, contemporary authors like those cited here, have developed the graphic novel medium in combination with their highly specific narratives. This seems to have the effect of imbuing authenticity into the recounting of the traumatic experience, notwithstanding the artifices of their methods. The recounting of memory in this manner also helps to deal with Wilms question, about the fate of 'truth' within traumatic experience (unmediated knowledge in his terms), if this rests primarily with those who witnessed it. The problem arises when others' subsequent attempts to turn that experience into knowledge seem false or inadequate.[24] The authors discussed in this study here have all attempted to challenge this directly by assuming the position of visual witness, despite sometimes

21 Andreas Huyssen, *Present Pasts: Urban Palimpsests and the Politics of Memory* (Stanford, California: Stanford University Press, 2003).

22 Wifried Wilms "Tabbo and Repression in W.G. Sebald's 'On the Natural History of Destruction," in Long and Whitehead, 178.

23 Wilms, 181.

24 Wilms, 175–176.

feigning actual experience within seemingly empirical accounts. In the manner of a recreation of primary experience, these graphic novels comprise a complex network of references, allusions and ambiguities that offer a surprising degree of experiential realism, greatly facilitating their recounting of trauma. Testimony to the effectiveness of this medium is the increasing number of artist-authors who have chosen to employ the graphic novel when attending to events of great social magnitude. Sacco's determination to disseminate narratives from Palestine and the Balkans war, and Satrapi's autobiography of an Iranian childhood under the gendered oppression of religious law are examples of this trend, as is one variation of the report of the commission into the 9/11 New York disasters, which has taken a graphic novel format.[25]

Radical Methods, Radical Forms

The emergence of the documentary graphic novel in the latter stages of the twentieth century has been accompanied by a pedagogic impulse, a desire to document traumatic incidents from the past for a contemporary audience. In this way the works constitute a visual pedagogy, a means by which the contemporary audience may come to know, or to vicariously experience, past events by means of narratives that are generated by the juxtaposition of image with text. They also critique the very genres – biography, documentary – that they appear to simulate. This critique occurs most strikingly at the level of the medium itself, so that great horror is conveyed through caricature or cartooning, for example, or where personal trauma is suggested by bogus picture-postcard photography, or when 'original' photographs are reproduced by hand drawn copies. By doing so each of the authors

25 Sid Jacobson and Ernie Colon, "Story of a Momentous Day," in *The Illustrated 9/11 Commission Report* (UK: Viking, The Times, timesonline.co.uk/books, 2006).

has attempted to locate their works beyond the reification that commodity cultures present. Yet, paradoxically, each novel overtly uses the visual tropes of commodity culture; the specificity of their accounts, in terms of visual method as well as narrative, is perhaps the most significant resistance that they offer to those aspects of commodification that reduce historical memory to mythologized entertainment. This ambiguous resistance to commodity culture, albeit temporary and contingent, is a quality that appears to be sought and shared by each of these authors.

If these graphic novels can be said to comprise a visual pedagogy of crises, there are a number of methods that the authors employ to focus and emphasise the veracity of their medium. They operate principally through the sequential relationship between images and an associated text, framed by temporal juxtaposition – narratives of the past located within the present. By these means their project emerges: the transmission and dissemination of experientially derived (albeit partial and fragmented) traumatic historical societal events. The sequential graphic novel, as a medium for recounting societal or collective memory (as defined by the widespread acquisition of knowledge of social events), appears to facilitate the ways in which we come to experience, and to know, traumatic history. Evidence for this can be found in each of the selected examples, where the subject matter is of such magnitude that it can be thought of as beyond representation, or 'unutterable' as Judith Butler has described it.[26] It is significant that these authors have nonetheless attempted to document these events, and have chosen the graphic novel form to do so.

An important reason for this may lie, paradoxically, in the lack of a finite resolution, and equivocation, that arises from the juxtaposition of image narrative with text narrative. Ambiguity becomes a quality that is mobilised by the artist-authors in pursuit of the unutterable. In other words, it may be the case that the dissemination of knowledge of specific traumatic events may be rendered more effective through the confounding of any unitary, fixed meaning; ambiguity and

26 Judith Butler, *Precarious Life: The Power of Mourning and Violence* (New York: Verso, 2004).

obliqueness may be a vital constituent of these representations, and examples of this occur throughout their works; for instance, Sacco's painstaking hand copying of photographs rather than merely reproducing them in their original form, and Sebald's practice of arranging of images that only have a tenuous connection to the initial experience, aided by text narratives that refer indirectly to the intended event.

Realism as Radical Form

A further question, central to the debates about realism, is the question of form and its relationship to content: does the creation of a radical, documentary text demand a radical form? Or rather, does a radical narrative necessitate a radical form? The concepts of 'new', 'innovative' and 'modern', part of the vocabulary of modernist accounts, have been abundant in reviews of graphic novels. Artists' perceptions of themselves often conform to the formalist model of an avant-garde, progressing by the technical developments of their medium.[27] The parallel with twentieth-century Western modernist practices has been further endorsed by the self-conscious references in graphic novels to new developments in other media; these have often been to film and cinematic devices, utilised frequently by artists like Sacco and Nakazawa. Contemporary graphic novel authors have used lens-based effects depicted with a wide repertoire of graphic techniques, which serve to remind the audience of the *act* of reading the sequences. These innovations are necessarily both temporary and contingent, in that they quickly cease to be innovations as imitations proliferate.

In recent years graphic novel authors have employed many seemingly unfamiliar visual devices. For instance, the vast re-

27 This is clear enough from the many interviews with comic/graphic artists in the popular comic press; Jonathan Clements, "Otomatic Exposure," interview with Kutsuhiro Otomo in *Manga Mania* 37, Manga Publishing Ltd., UK, August 1996, 6–9, is a good example.

publication and distribution of manga in the West has enabled the introduction of conventions that were commonplace in manga but not elsewhere. This is illustrated effectively by McCloud's analysis of the pictorial conventions used in manga, where he shows that in manga a bubble coming out of a nose signifies sleep, or a nose bleed signifies lust, for instance; these may be completely incomprehensible – a signification breakdown – without a working knowledge of the visual codes applicable to manga in a Japanese context.[28] Unfamiliar signifiers for time and space, when they occur either in a translated manga or in a Western graphic novel appropriation of it, can be initially disruptive to the reading of a page. These have, however, become compelling because of their cultural difference and their novelty; the way that a reader unwittingly learns the characteristics of a particular convention is demonstrated more easily where graphic artists take particular devices to extremes. When this occurs it is momentarily easier to recognise the familiar rendered as unfamiliar, a reminder once again that all marks are subject (usually tacitly) to interpretation prior to recognition, evidence that the pathway from signifier to signified is not natural or predetermined; like any code the resulting sign is determined by a socially conditioned response. More familiar to Western readers, and therefore less easy to notice, are the marks that curve through the air following an arm or a leg that denote movement, known as 'zip ribbons'; easily assimilated and therefore overlooked, but just as conventional, in the sense of being determined by an agreed set of signs, and therefore relatively arbitrary.[29] A similar effect is found in 'thought balloons', where the balloons contain no text but act as a further frame to contain another image. To read these as 'movement' and 'thought' respectively is by no means natural or straightforward, but entirely conventional.

The French Situationists' comic pages that were produced in the 1970s demonstrate their awareness of the political potential of disrupting these conventions, especially the agreement between image

28 McCloud, 131.

29 'Relatively' arbitrary because zip ribbons can arguably be founded upon afterimages created by moving objects leaving momentary retinal traces.

and text. Steef Davidson notes the importance of this comic-book technique to the Situationists:

> The Situationists were the first politically motivated group to make use of photographs with 'balloons', and to adapt the texts of existing comic strips. They called this technique 'detournement' (diversion), and defined it as follows: ''Diversion' is the recycling of existing artistic elements in a new context which lends them a totally new meaning.' This idea was not a new one in artistic thought, but the Situationists adopted it because they recognised the value of the comic strip as a mass medium.[30]

In one Situationist example, a comic book page has been appropriated, and the original narrative, concerned with fashion, display and assignation, has been transformed to one of political debate.[31] The juxtaposition of the two paradigms is particularly disorientating in its innovation, with a Marxist discussion of commodification overlaying an image of romantic social interaction.[32]

Political Impact

For theorists like Roland Barthes, 'political speech' is that which avoids the reduction into myth and deception by those with power; he uses the example of timber cutter in 'Myth Today', who speaks 'politically' when he expresses directly his knowledge of cutting timber, emphasising the relation of truth to direct experience, in this case of labour, as opposed to the institutionalised governmental rhetoric that substitutes for political speech.[33] 'If myth is de-politicised speech, there is at least one type of speech that is the opposite of myth: that which *remains* political.'[34]. The question that arises from this is: can documentary graphic novels, created in a

30 Steef Davidson, *The Penguin Book of Political Comics* (Middlesex, England, Penguin, 1982) 62.

31 Davidson, 59.

32 Davidson, 58–59, his translation.

33 Roland Barthes, *Mythologies* (London: Paladin, 1973), 117–174.

34 Barthes, *Mythologies,* 158.

medium that is inherently reproducible in conception, act as a vehicle for this kind of direct 'political speech'? If so, can they demystify sufficiently to change political behaviour?

Leonard Rifas, a publisher of *Barefoot Gen* in the US, when asked about the political impact of comic books, remarked: '…comic book stories themselves have no "political impact," except through the people who take inspiration or encouragement from them, and then do things differently, especially through activist organizations.'[35] Although seeming to dismiss the idea, this may be interpreted as endorsing the effectiveness of comic books in facilitating political change. The change in behaviour that Rifas describes may be read as a definition of the political process in its most fundamental form, as opposed to the highly ritualised politics of official state political parties, and therefore an argument *for* 'political impact'. Either way, he was providing evidence that documentary graphic novels may encourage political protest that in turn helps to bring about social change. It is possible to argue that the determination of a cultural artefact's political engagement – and its effectiveness – is to determine its recognition as such by people who might be in a position to effect change, like political organisations, pressure groups, other artists etc. Rifas, though, cautions against relying on the mainstream press solely as a measure of effectiveness:

> In the case of *All-Atomic Comics*, my comic about nuclear power, the fact that I sold so many copies to grateful activist organizations who used them in campaigns which helped stop new nuclear power plant construction has left me feeling obliged to testify that protest does work (sometimes, under certain conditions, given the requisite amount of luck, somewhat,) and, by extension (but without satisfying proof,) that protest comics can be effective.'[36]

The mainstream press, defined by large circulations and therefore widely available, may nevertheless help to establish whether the reception of a documentary graphic novel ever goes beyond a specialist audience. Using the mainstream press as a calibration of

35 Leonard Rifas, correspondence to the author, December 21, 2001.
36 Rifas, correspondence to the author, December 21, 2001.

effect – that the exposure there enables its entry into the consciousness of a wider community – is reasonable as long as the evidence is handled with caution. In the case of *Barefoot Gen*, for example, it might involve simplistically deducing that its association with the anti-nuclear movement, and the latter's successful activities in reducing the growth of nuclear power in the US, were cause and effect; can it be said that the publication of *Barefoot Gen* ipso facto furthered that change? Yet whilst it may not be possible conclusively to prove the political effectiveness of graphic novels, it is possible to present circumstantial evidence that corroborates a case for it. The next chapter examines *Persepolis*, *Barefoot Gen*, and *Jimmy Corrigan* and the effectiveness of their political realism, through their documentaries of children within traumatic social crises.

Chapter 3: Depicting Childhood in Times of Crisis

Satrapi's *Persepolis*

Marjane Satrapi's documentary realism in *Persepolis* is distinctive for a number of reasons, principally its focus on the experience of girls and young women under religious revolutionary conditions and war, and offers a contrast to the more common focus on male experience. It has a spare, simplified drawing style and explores the significant themes of religion and politics, with their effects upon a girl's developing worldviews. *Persepolis* has stylistic and thematic similarities to Nakazawa's *Barefoot Gen,* in particular the experience of children negotiating the imposition of colossal social pressures.

Satrapi's narrative in *Persepolis* is fundamentally structured on two levels, one dealing with the minutiae of childhood and adolescence, and the other with the political configurations of pre and post-revolutionary Iran. The latter is further contextualised within the politics of the wider Middle East and colonialism, whilst the former is recounted and explored using domestic childhood events as nodal points in the narrative. This creates a tension between the everyday, utilitarian moments, which have acquired significance for the growing child, and the larger societal forces that reshaped the lives of the Iranian populace. The chapters are organised and titled with childhood and family themes that are markers of change or growth, such as 'The Cigarette' (about taking up smoking), or 'The Wine' (about family parties). The alternation between the domestic and the political experience has the effect of a dynamic contextualisation of the particular within the general, prevailing political situation. This narrative device persists throughout *Persepolis*, and enables a reading of Iranian and Middle Eastern politics through the eyes of Satrapi herself as a child, in the form of the child protagonist, Marjane.[1]

The Marjane of the novels is of course a child, although the novel was written many years later by the adult Satrapi, and this retrospective view is important to bear in mind, as it is with *Barefoot Gen*, since the acculturation of Satrapi into Iranian and later European society, and the issues surrounding her immigrant status inevitably determine the shape of the final narrative. As Satrapi herself explains: 'A simple question that for everyone is a one-word answer to "Where do you come from?" […] For an Iranian, it's a one-hour explanation: "I am Iranian but, I am Iranian but…" '.[2] Such an profound degree of internal speculation over these issues affects the shape of her narrative, all the more so given that her readers are largely the very same Europeans/Americans for whom she perceives the need to express detailed explanations of her nationality.

Disciplinary Gendering

Gender construction, through the Iranian government's disciplinary patriarchy, forms one of the dominant accounts in *Persepolis*. The forced wearing of a veil when on public view is an example of this disciplinary regime that Satrapi explores. It should come as no surprise that the veil looms large in Satrapi's childhood recollections; in the first image of *Persepolis* she depicts herself at ten years old wearing a veil, and the following pages depict conflicts with the state that this enforcement brought about for women. These opening pages make visual contrasts between the former secular society and the new fundamentalist state that had taken its place, and Satrapi represents these opposing configurations through contrasting images (figure 3.1).

1 'Marjane' is used when referring to the character in the novel, "Satrapi" when referring to the author.

2 Annie Tully, "An Interview with Marjane Satrapi," *Bookslut*, October 2004, http://www.bookslut.com/features/2004_10_003261.php (accessed November 30, 2007).

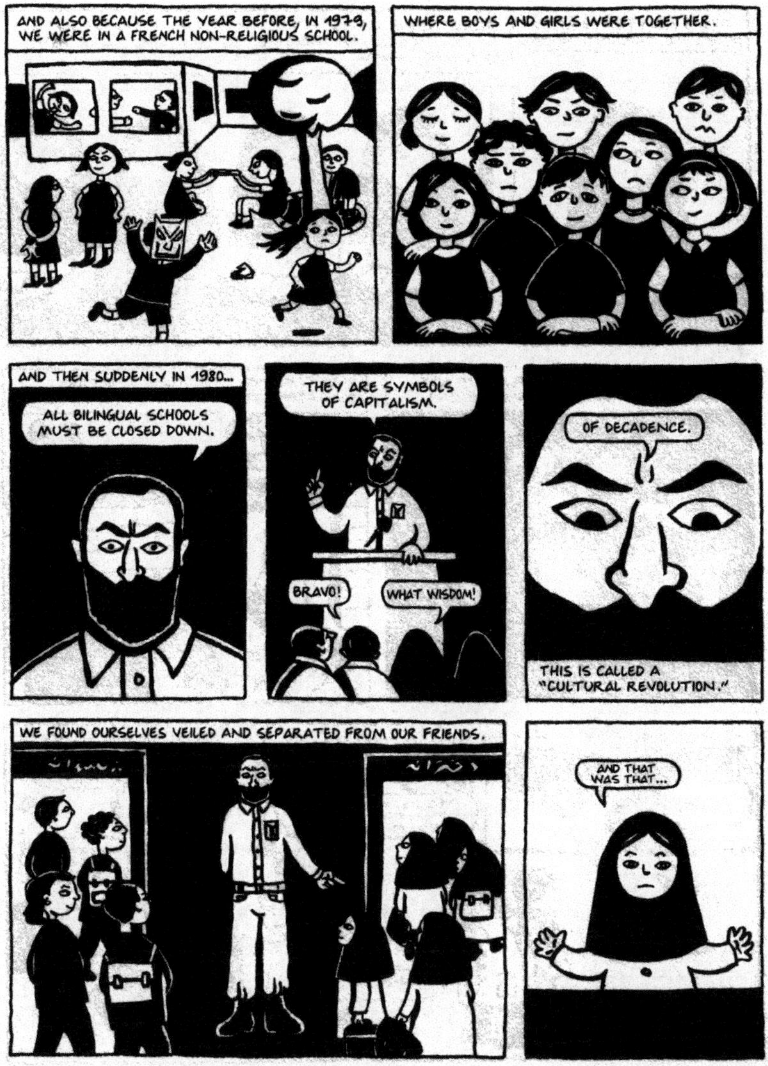

Figure 3.1. The gendered segregation of children under the fundamentalist government. From *Persepolis: The Story of Childhood* by Marjane Satrapi, translated by Mattias Ripa & Blake Ferris, translation copyright © 2003 by L'Association, Paris, France (p.4). Used by permission of Pantheon Books, a division of Random House, Inc.

Firstly she depicts the children grouped as a class in mixed sex rows, as if for a class photograph, whilst in the penultimate frame of the same page she has an image of the children segregated by a frowning and bearded soldier. He directs with his finger and a sidelong glance the girls, now veiled, into one classroom door, the boys into another. Satrapi follows this with depictions of women's street demonstrations against the enforced wearing of a veil, this time using her characteristic solid block shading of the figures to offer a visual contrast that reflects their opposing political viewpoints. In this instance the groups of figures are also overlapped and ranged against each other on opposite sides of the image, and the flattening out of the picture plane caused by the absence of tonal modelling, in combination with the occluded groups of people, make reference to design features of medieval drawing styles.[3] This is an association that Satrapi encourages with her restricted use of tone, detail and spatial depiction, which combine to limit the illusionist verisimilitude of work.

In terms of narrative, the references early on in *Persepolis* to secular pre-revolutionary times draw out through contrast the oppressive characteristics of the fundamentalist government, and upon women in particular. In this respect Satrapi's work has similarities to Margaret Atwood's, *Handmaid's Tale.* Atwood's protagonist Offred's reflects upon her former life's freedoms, cherishing her former name, and in doing so emphasises the cloistered and enslaved life that she must now endure.[4] Throughout *Persepolis* Marjane is depicted having discussions with a series of adult characters, debating the suppression of political opposition and the potential enslavement of women under the new laws of the state; in this manner she mirrors Atwood's device of exploring the politics of oppression through Offred's clandestine meetings with her owner, the Captain. In *Persepolis,* the authority figures with which Marjane is engaged in dialogue are in some cases

3 Such as those characteristic of Byzantine and Persian miniature paintings.

4 Margaret Atwood, *The Handmaid's Tale* (London: Virago Press, 1986). Atwood makes allusion to the similarities between religious fundamentalist American politics and those of Iran in her postscript.

overtly imaginary (God and Karl Marx), while in others they are relatives or family associates who are ideologically opposed to the government – uncle Anoosh in particular. These characters provide a platform for Satrapi to deliberate the issues that she perceives to be of paramount importance to the cultural transformation of Iran, which would eventually lead to her exile.

Judith Butler discusses the idea of power as subjugation acting through and upon the body, important to analyses of gender production through 'disciplinary regimes'.[5] The enforced wearing of a veil is an example of this, as is the girl Marjane's recognition of the way that her body will be put at the service of a husband through the production of children, again making similarities with Atwood's story. Satrapi chooses a narrative moment to express this anxiety as one that coincides with references to the Iranian state closure of the universities in 1980, a device that enables her to depict Marjane contrasting her secular and personal ambitions (scientist, liberated woman) with the threat of being denied education, and enslavement to husband and parenting children; as she remarks (depicted in bed dreaming of possible futures): 'Misery! At the age that Marie Curie first went to France to study, I'll probably have ten children…'.[6]

As Butler argues, analysing subjection is in part 'an account of the way regulatory power maintains subjects in subordination by producing and exploiting the demand for continuity, visibility and place'. Satrapi's narrative describes the specificities of this exploitation, and this is particularly evident in her illustrations of men and women's dress, showing the visible but subtle signs of subjugation in the details of clothing that conform to the fundamentalist tenets of the régime (figure 3.2). Women demonstrate their resistance by 'letting a few strands of hair show', and men by shaving.[7]

5 Judith Butler, *The Psychic Life of Power* (Stanford: Stanford University Press, 1997), 85.
6 Satrapi, *Persepolis*, 73.
7 Satrapi, *Persepolis*, 75.

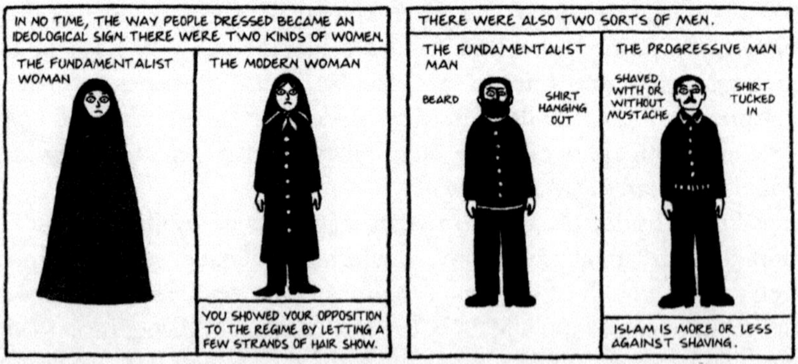

Figure 3.2. Subtle signs of resistance through dress. From *Persepolis: The Story of Childhood* by Marjane Satrapi, translated by Mattias Ripa & Blake Ferris, translation copyright © 2003 by L'Association, Paris, France (detail p.75). Used by permission of Pantheon Books, a division of Random House, Inc.

Later such indiscretions are met with violence, in a series of frames about the suppression of a demonstration against the imposition of wearing a veil.[8] Satrapi's depiction of these women has her characteristic simplifications of form: the drawn figures are mostly all black without tonal variation, or occasionally white, again without tonal delineation. The characters are stylised, too, in the sense that they are drawn to conform to repeated wave patterns across the frames, as in the example of men wielding sticks, and figures are copied and repeated side by side, emphasising the anonymity created by conformity on the part of the police who are perpetrating the violence. This stylistic device of simply drawn, undifferentiated characters helps to emphasise the demand for conformity of which Butler speaks. Frequently the agents of oppression are depicted in this way, and the peoples' resistance is similarly minimal in terms of features or detail in her drawing. This minimalist caricature offers a metaphor for the absence of opportunities for resistance to a pervasive state control that erases individuation and pursues homogeneity,

8 Satrapi, *Persepolis*, 76.

which penetrates to intimate and personal levels of the subject's daily routine.

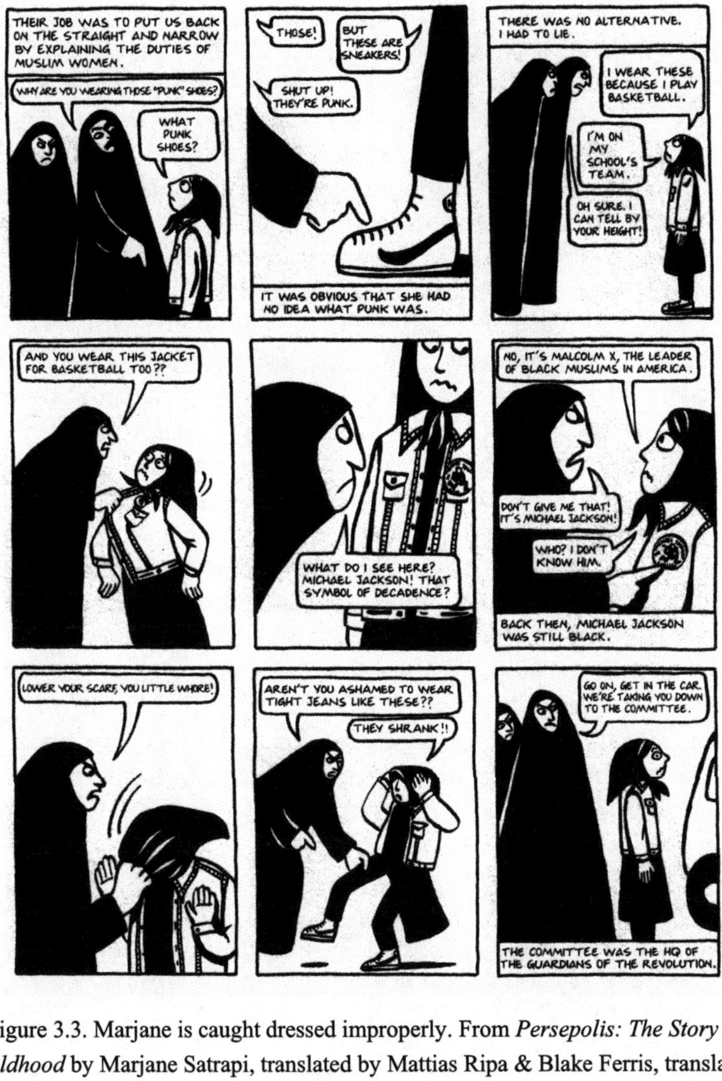

Figure 3.3. Marjane is caught dressed improperly. From *Persepolis: The Story of Childhood* by Marjane Satrapi, translated by Mattias Ripa & Blake Ferris, translation copyright © 2003 by L'Association, Paris, France (p.133). Used by permission of Pantheon Books, a division of Random House, Inc.

The effects of this upon young women in adolescence is shown in *Persepolis* when Marjane encounters women 'Guardians of the Revolution' enforcing girls' dress on the streets of Tehran.[9] Once again the Guardians are undifferentiated, apart from slight differences in stance and angry expressions. Marjane is caught wearing badges (of the US pop star Michael Jackson), a denim jacket and 'punk' shoes (figure 3.3). Her visual display of resistance leads to temporary detention where she protests, then lies and pleads for her release. The stark black and white page displays depicting menacing agents of state violence are reminiscent of Spiegelman's *Maus*, which Satrapi readily acknowledges as a source for *Persepolis*.[10]

Her resistance steadily weakens in the face of the war with Iraq, when the bombing of Tehran induces an outbreak of patriotic sentiments. Although many restrictions are imposed upon their lives, the possibility of an even greater destructive enemy temporarily unites the family. This is short lived, however, as the realisation dawns that the Iranian government is perpetuating the war in order to garner jingoistic support. In one scene her girlfriend from next door, Baba-Levy, is killed along with her family when their house is destroyed in an air strike.[11] Marjane finds the bracelet of her friend in the debris, in a series of frames that Satrapi constructs to indicate unspeakable distress (figure 3.4). To accomplish this she draws the scene with minimal detail, eschewing action and melodrama. Once again Satrapi changes the 'pace' of reading by increasing and regularising the frames, directing the focus of the reader upon Marjane in a two close-ups, the second showing her face in her hands, with the final frame depicted blank (in black), apart from the narrator's voice in the

9 An AFP report noted the setting up of women-only police stations in Tehran, presumably to deal with just the kind of offences to which Satrapi is alluding. *Iran in Focus*, "Iran to launch police stations for women in capital: report," http://www.iranfocus.com/modules/news/index.php?storytopic=6 (accessed December 11, 2007). Satrapi, *Persepolis*, 132–133.

10 Marjane Satrapi, "On Writing *Persepolis*", interview with Pantheon staff, http://www.randomhouse.com/pantheon/graphicnovels/satrapi2.html (accessed December 11, 2007).

11 Satrapi, *Persepolis*, 141–142.

caption box underneath. This is a scene reminiscent of Gen's distress at discovering the bones of his family in the remains of his house after the Hiroshima destruction,[12] and both authors are careful to draw our attention unadulterated to the suffering of children in war.

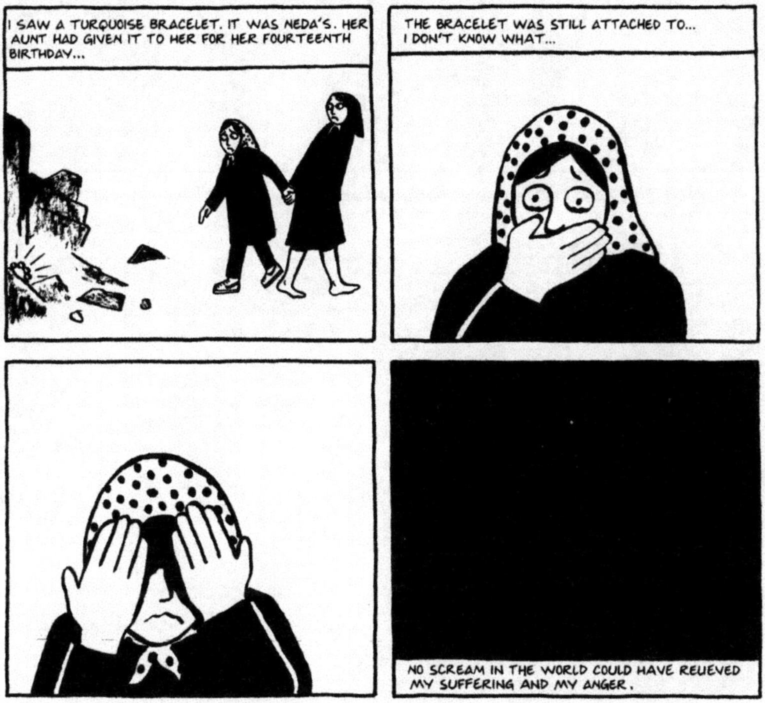

Figure 3.4. Marjane is horrified to discover her friend and neighbour has been killed in a bombing raid From *Persepolis: The Story of Childhood* by Marjane Satrapi, translated by Mattias Ripa & Blake Ferris, translation copyright © 2003 by L'Association, Paris, France (detail p.142). Used by permission of Pantheon Books, a division of Random House, Inc.

12 Nakazawa, *Barefoot Gen, Vol. 2*, 181–188.

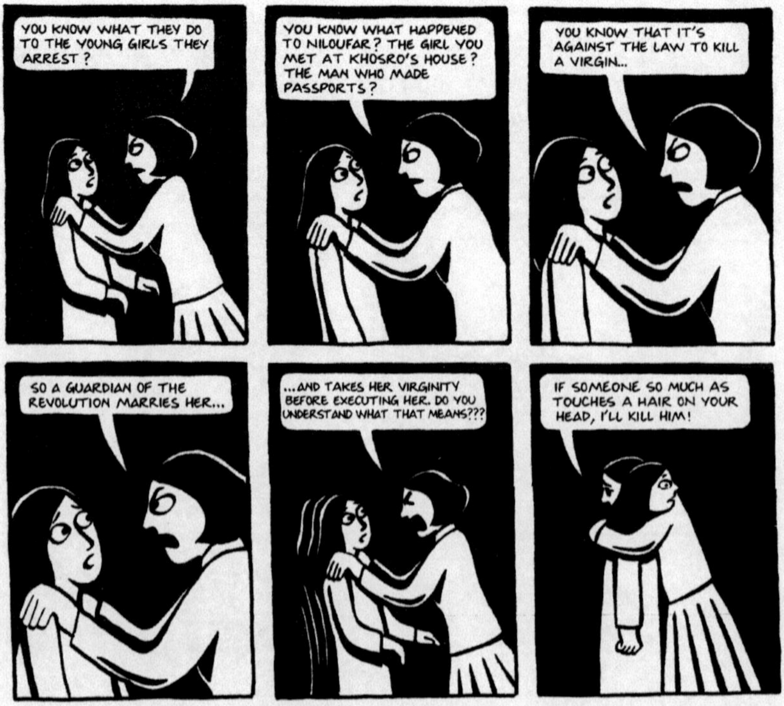

Figure 3.5. A heated debate between mother and daughter. From *Persepolis: The Story of Childhood* by Marjane Satrapi, translated by Mattias Ripa & Blake Ferris, translation copyright © 2003 by L'Association, Paris, France (detail, p.145). Used by permission of Pantheon Books, a division of Random House, Inc.

The full weight of the gendered oppression is brought to bear upon Marjane's female acquaintance Niloufer, who is raped and murdered for being a communist and an associate of a maker of false passports. The rape is signified by the payment of a dowry to Niloufer's parents, since the prison guards responsible believe that by marrying her (hence the token dowry payment which the 'husband' is obliged to pay) they legitimise the rape and the murder, since it is 'against the law to kill a virgin'.[13] Satrapi implies that the patriarchal and oppressive government, which covertly wants Niloufer executed for being a communist dissenter, endorses all of this. The rape, the dowry and the execution are the subject of a lecture from mother to daughter in a series of six panels (figure 3.5) which have a remarkable economy of image: almost identical drawings of the shocked Marjane are repeated no less that five times in succession, with the mother's face and pose repeated four times; the only concession to dramatic verisimilitude being the gradual enlargement of the figures over the four frames, as Satrapi closes in upon the pair.

Children and State Oppression

Satrapi's political realism is emphasised through street scenes with children. Marjane is often depicted debating the emerging state oppression with other children, and in one instance they try to outdo each other by mimicking the torture to which they hear others are subjected (figure 3.6). Interestingly, Satrapi takes an unorthodox view here, in that she depicts the children knowingly and willingly subjecting each other to a variety of cruelties. Butler's theories of subjection are pertinent here, as she explains how power constructs the oppressed subject:

> Subjection is, literally, the *making* of the subject, the principle of regulation according to which a subject is formulated or produced. Such subjugation is a kind of power that not only unilaterally *acts on* a given individual as a form of domination, but also *activates* or forms the subject.[14]

The images of Marjane and her friends engaged in the imitation of torture with her friends, are examples of power in the form of violent bodily oppression constructing the young subjects. They play-out and mimic the dominant mode of clandestine control and subjugation, and are unwittingly 'activated' as subjects formed within the oppression

13 As Satrapi has her mother saying: Satrapi, *Persepolis*, 145.
14 Butler, *The Psychic Life of Power*, 84.

that is signified by the torturers. Yet, since this is at an early stage of the fundamentalist regime, there is a moment of redemption for Marjane, as she recognises the play torture for what it is, an expression of the 'diabolical feeling of power', as she expresses it in the novel.[15]

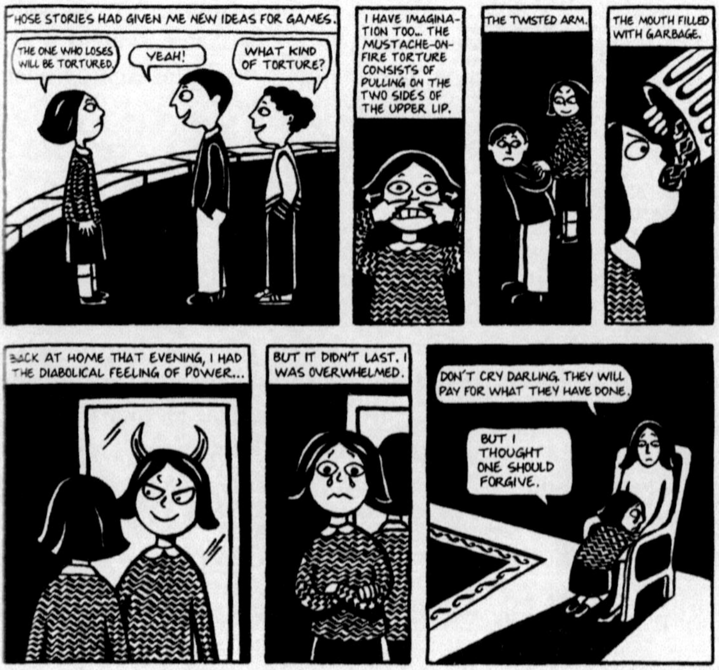

Figure 3.6. Children re-enact torture. From *Persepolis: The Story of Childhood* by Marjane Satrapi, translated by Mattias Ripa & Blake Ferris, translation copyright © 2003 by L'Association, Paris, France (detail p.53). Used by permission of Pantheon Books, a division of Random House, Inc.

One dominant figure in Satrapi's recollection is her Uncle Anoosh, whose role is to provide a political narration for the reader, via his bedside stories to Marjane. She represents this political history

15 Satrapi, *Persepolis*, 53.

through Anoosh's tales in various guises, such as love stories, and each is depicted in her distinctive high-contrast, black and white style.[16] Anoosh has returned after a period of imprisonment and exile, punishments for his involvement in political opposition. The narrative voice Satrapi provides for Anoosh creates a radical political dialogue that contextualises the events in terms of her view of the oppressive character of the government, with torture, imprisonment and disappearance as dominant themes. Satrapi employs the same device that she uses in the torture scenes, whereby the political events are discussed and contested by the adults and then re-enacted by the children. For example, snippets of political analysis are given in the conversation between her father, Eby, and Anoosh, and then acted out by the children in the street, with a discussion about the difficulties of living under a religious regime, and the possibilities of escape and exile in the West.[17] By using this narrative device Satrapi provides a voice for Marjane to reflect on these events and debates, in this example by the feelings of friendship that she has for boy whose parents are making him leave. The constant referencing of the political and its effects upon the personal is repeated throughout *Persepolis*.

The gradual increase in political and social oppression that occurs throughout *Persepolis* culminates in Anoosh's arrest and imprisonment.[18] Satrapi creates a dramatic scene where Marjane is the only one able to visit him in jail. These images are rendered in even simpler, starker contrasts (figure 3.7), and mix her intense personal emotions of loss and injustice, which are heightened further by the accounts of his death, resulting in her rejection of God. The scene in the prison cell is restricted to one full page, and four of the six regular frames are half-length portrait views of Anoosh with the girl on his knee, with limited dialogue – only Anoosh speaks in each frame with a single speech balloon. The composition of these frames is reminiscent of Mary Cassatt's mother and child paintings, and

16 Satrapi, *Persepolis*, 58.
17 Satrapi, *Persepolis*, 62–63.
18 Satrapi, *Persepolis*, 68–69.

therefore connotes the parent/child intimacies that she popularised in her work, and its subsequent reproductions.[19] The only visual details of the forms of either figure are the patterning of the girl's dress and the man's hair. The background wall is an undifferentiated blanket black with a white bed upon which they sit. This simplicity and regularity is broken on the following page with Anoosh's death retold in a single image of a photo-newspaper report of his execution. The intensity of emotion that the girl experiences is revealed by a single frame covering an entire page, acting as a literal expansion of her explosive distress at this point.

Given her predilection for the narrative cycles of the personal with the political, Satrapi exploits this nodal point, which visually represents her crisis, with a lead into a political context though the star-shaped text box, warning her to run to the basement (like a voice-over from an a different but immanent scene in a film), and a small dialogue box in the bottom corner: 'it was the beginning of the war'.[20] Turning the page reveals that this is not simply a reference to the personal war that she has just depicted between herself and God, but also to the new war with Iraq that had just erupted.

The upheaval of war bringing children together is a theme that both Satrapi and Nakazawa pursue. Just as in *Barefoot Gen* the boy with his mother and sister are forced to endure a disastrously pernicious family situation when they appeal for accommodation as refugees from Hiroshima, so Marjane has to accommodate refugee children in her apartment, and experience the difficulties of relationships in this configuration.[21] The two children and their family are subject to abuse as refugees from the south of the country, as part of the influx of people into Tehran escaping the war zone.[22] At first Marjane considers the refugee children to be troublesome, but as she witness the prejudice to which they are subjected, she becomes compassionate towards them.

19 Mary Cassatt, French painter and printer (1844–1926).
20 Satrapi, *Persepolis*, 71.
21 Nakazawa, *Barefoot Gen, Vol. 3.*
22 Satrapi, *Persepolis*, 91–93.

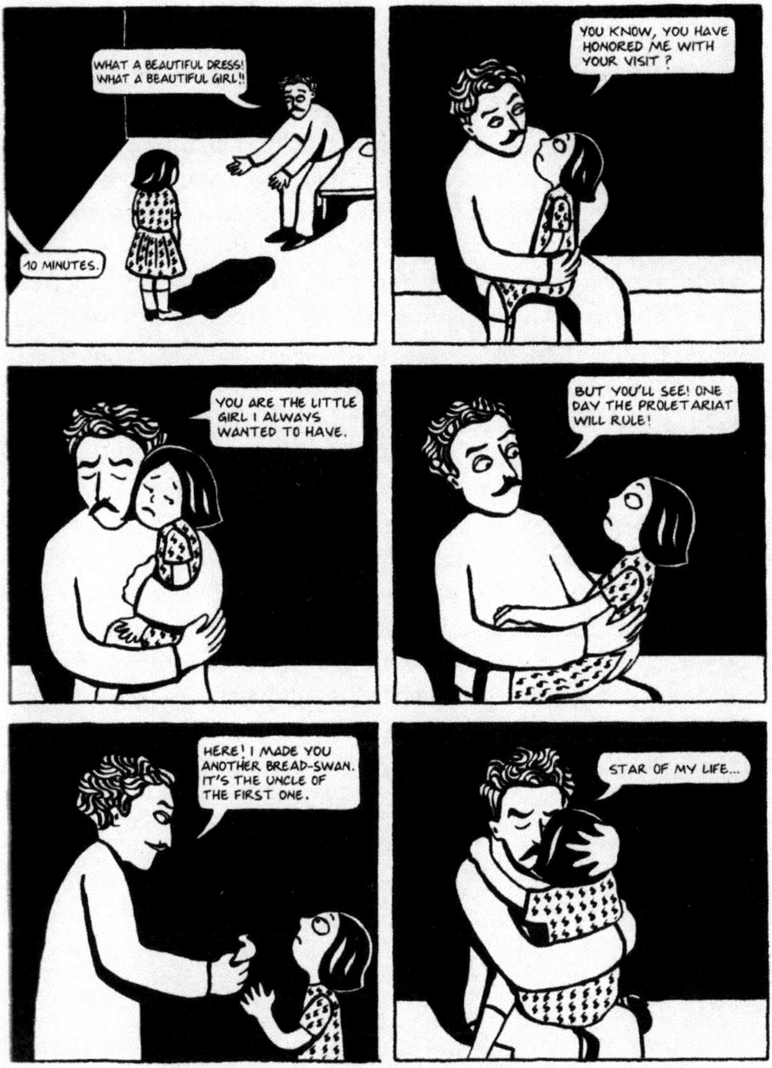

Figure 3.7. Uncle Anoosh is sentenced to death and Marjane is his last visitor, From *Persepolis: The Story of Childhood* by Marjane Satrapi, translated by Mattias Ripa & Blake Ferris, translation copyright © 2003 by L'Association, Paris, France (detail p. 69). Used by permission of Pantheon Books, a division of Random House, Inc.

In Gen's experience, the prejudice against him as a refugee himself stems from the family within which he has to stay, and leads to allegations of stealing. In both cases the trauma of being a refugee is exacerbated by the abuse to be endured, which is itself a sign of the poverty, of insufficient resources having to be shared.

The children in both novels find that the classroom becomes an ideological battleground, in which their family loyalties force them to participate. Like Gen, Marjane has several conflicts with her teachers, and one in particular leads to the possibility of being reported to higher authorities, which in this heavily policed state would have serious consequences, hence her parents' decision to send her into exile. Her refutation of her teachers' comments on political prisoners leads to complaints about her conduct;[23] Satrapi's depiction of parental interventions at the school, like those of Nakazawa in which Gen's father protests the treatment of his child, creates a platform for the author to engage in political dialogue on the effects of the imposition of nationalistic and religious ideology upon the children. All of this, as both Satrapi and Nakazawa make clear, is a result of militarism and nationalism, the antithesis of a progressive society, ideals of which are offered throughout both *Barefoot Gen* and *Persepolis*, principally through the mouthpieces of the children's parents in their opposition to the war.

23 Satrapi, *Persepolis*, 144.

Surviving the Atomic Bombing in Nakazawa's *Barefoot Gen*

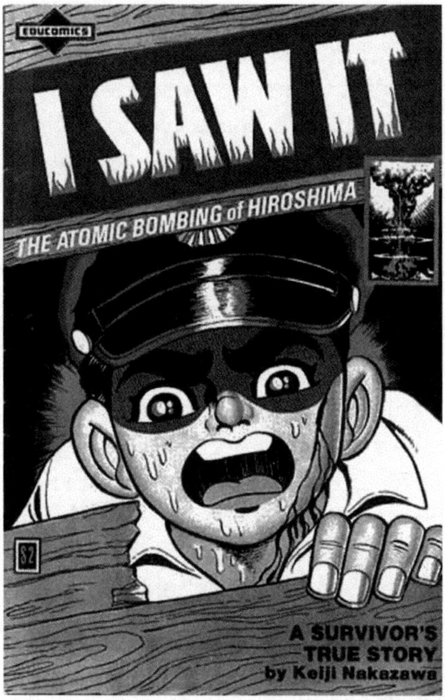

Figure 3.8. The cover of Nakazawa's *I Saw It* when translated and republished in the USA (1980–82). © Keiji Nakazawa; translation Project Gen; reproduced with permission of EduComics and Project Gen.

Writers on manga have acknowledged *Barefoot Gen's* importance and its significance as a key moment in post-war comic production. Paul Gravett, Roger Sabin and Frederik Schodt, for instance, all attribute a significant role to *Barefoot Gen* in the post-war development of manga.[24] Spiegelman was instrumental in assisting the republication

24 Paul Gravett, *Manga*; Roger Sabin, *Comics, Comix and Graphic Novels* (London: Phaidon, 1996) 217 and 229; Schodt, *Manga, Manga.*

of Barefoot Gen in the US, lending his support in the form of a foreword for the republished English language editions, hence positioning *Barefoot Gen* as an important work in the development of graphic novel realism in the West.

Barefoot Gen was originally written and published as *Hadashi no Gen,* a black and white manga in Japan during 1972/3, as weekly instalments in a boy's magazine, bound together in quarterly editions.[25] This was preceded by Nakazawa's much shorter, and more factually autobiographical manga, known as *Ore wa Mita,* translated and republished in the US by EduComics in 1982 as *I Saw It* (figure 3.8). In this earlier manga Nakazawa is known by his real name Keiji, and the narrative is concerned with the events of his childhood in the days and weeks leading up to the atomic bombing of Hiroshima, and his survival of the bombing itself with the loss of his father, brother and sister; his pregnant mother survives and almost immediately gives birth to his sister. The rest of the narrative concerns Keiji's schooling and his later attempts to get work as an illustrator, all within the context of the aftermath of the bombing and the city's recovery. He concludes with events from later in his life: his apprenticeship as a manga artist, his marriage, the death of his mother and his leaving Hiroshima to work in Tokyo. The whole tale is narrated in the first person, as Keiji recalls events from the standpoint of some twenty years later as a young man. The latter part of the tale is concerned with Nakazawa's rage about the radiation illness that contributed to his mother's death and about the negative effect of the bombing on his own and his mother's life.

In *Barefoot Gen* the first part of this basic narrative is maintained, but greatly extended and modified.[26] Nakazawa dispenses entirely with the later parts of his life, and focuses instead on the events in the days before and after the bomb. In addition, he creates many sub-narratives that show, in much greater depth, how domestic life was affected by militarism, radiation sickness and the American

25 Frederik L. Schodt, interview with the author, February 7, 2002.

26 This refers to the scope of the English translated versions; the Japanese original ran for much longer and contains many more volumes with greater scope.

occupation of Japan. At the end of the lengthy series (four novel-length parts in the English translation) Nakazawa, now known as Gen, is still depicted as a young boy grieving over the death of his baby sister.

The main historical events that shape the narratives in *Barefoot Gen* are the cultural imperialism and military expansionism of the pre-war Japanese government, the atomic bombing of Hiroshima (August 6, 1945), and the immediate post-war US occupation of Japan (1945–52). All of these are critiqued by Nakazawa through his experience as a child, and it is the effects of this colossal national and global events upon children in first hand accounts that makes his documentary manga distinctive.

One of the fundamental changes to the Japanese State that this military occupation brought about was the drawing up of a 'New Deal' influenced Constitution. Japan's post-war cultural history bears many hallmarks of the brief yet powerful jurisdiction of the US, and its Constitution represented the attempted imposition of a Western cultural hegemony. These wide ranging and globally traumatic changes form the wider context for the production of *Barefoot Gen*, and also for many other literary and artistic practices, like the novels of Kazuo Ishiguro, whose discourse on the rejections of militarism by the Japanese post-war generation makes a parallel to Nakazawa's graphic work, through its critique of Japanese society.[27] Like Satrapi, Nakazawa keeps his narrative within the tight confines of the local children and their parents, and it is from within this highly specific viewpoint that he is able to develop his larger political discourse.

Nakazawa's mother is a prominent character in *Barefoot Gen*, and her relationship to the child Gen is maintained as a strong bond throughout the novel. This reflects Nakazawa's commitment to an anti-war message, since she came to personify for him the suffering that such disasters confer upon civilians. The events following her death profoundly affected Nakazawa, and may have provided the impetus for the realisation of the whole *Gen* project. Nakazawa, as

27 See in particular Kazuo Ishiguro, *An Artist of the Floating World* (London: Faber and Faber, 1986).

Gleason explains, found himself embroiled in an ideological confrontation, when US Atomic Bomb Casualty Committee (ABCC) claimed her body for an autopsy to investigate the effects of the atomic bomb:

> Apparently they took away his mother's body and analysed it, did whatever they wanted to do with it, cremated it and just sent the ashes back. He was angered, horrified and appalled by this treatment of her. He then and there vowed that he would write something about it, he wouldn't forget it and he would tell the world – so he did.'[28]

As well as his grievances with the US ABCC, Nakazawa also took issue with the Japanese patriotism promoted during the war. The novel's realism, in its harshness of the depiction of repression from militarist Japan and the US army, brought objections from both sides.

The Translation and Republication of Barefoot Gen.

Project Gen was a pacifist group formed in Tokyo to translate and promote Nakazawa's work into English, and later many other languages. Gleason is a founder member, and explains that Project Gen hoped that Nakazawa's work would help disseminate an anti-nuclear war message in Japan, the US, and eventually throughout the world:

> […] in 1976, some Japanese participated in a 'transcontinental walk for peace and justice' organized by the US Peace Movement that was meant to coincide with the American Bicentennial. There was a fresh coming together of Japanese and American Peace activists, and they discussed Hiroshima. Some of the Japanese happened to have copies of this comic book and said 'it's all in here'. American people were impressed and moved by the comic and said 'why don't you have this translated?'[29]

These books were the first full-length translations of a manga series from Japanese into English to be published in the West, making

28 Gleason, interview with the author, December 20, 2001.
29 Gleason, interview with the author.

Project Gen 'pioneers in Japanese/English comic translation'.[30] Project Gen, allied as it was to the wider international peace movement that grew in response to the Hiroshima and Nagasaki bombings, developed a unique form of representation for their objections to the nuclear arms race and nuclear war though the *Barefoot Gen* translations. As Gleason points out: 'It set an example for the fact that cartoons could be used to describe horrific factual events'.[31] Once translated *Barefoot Gen* found its first support for publication from the War Resistors' League and an audience amongst peace activists, but not among the wider population. The impetus for the translation and republication in the West came with the growing concern with the possibility of nuclear war as a result of the Cold War: '… it was really from the '80s to the '90s, during the time when the 'nuclear freeze' movement was very big, that *Gen* was cited most as a graphic depiction of the reality of nuclear war.'[32]

Leonard Rifas was the publisher who initially brought Nakazawa's work to the West, by republishing *Hadashi no Gen* in serial form as *Gen of Hiroshima.*[33] Rifas had founded EduComics, a publisher of radical comic books on a range of socialist and environmentalist topics. His reasons for republishing Gen were based on his conviction that it was vital for people in the US: 'as citizens of the leading nuclear superpower, to be able to imagine in greater detail what nuclear weapons actually do.'[34] He argues that *Gen* was especially significant for the protest movement because it presented a challenge to the orthodoxy (in radical thinking) of the Hiroshima bombing being visited upon innocent civilians and children, without abandoning the concept of the event as an atrocity perpetrated by the US:

30 Gleason, interview with the author.

31 Gleason, interview with the author.

32 Gleason, interview with the author.

33 Keiji Nakazawa, *Gen of Hiroshima 1* (San Francisco, CA: EduComics, January 1980), and *Gen of Hiroshima 2*, (San Francisco, CA: EduComics, April 1981).

34 Rifas, "Globalizing Comic Books from Below," 1–2.

> 'Nakazawa does not depict the men, women and children of Hiroshima as passive, innocent victims, but as full participants in a cruel, violent world, in which the Japanese government had started the war, enacted racist and imperialist policies, crushed dissent and encouraged a fanatical willingness to fight to the death, despite their apparent defeat.'[35]

Rifas found that his outlets for radical comics were limited and reducing at the time that he was attempting to promote *Gen of Hiroshima*, and the underground comics market was waning. In a conversation with Tezuka, he lamented loss of comic books as a major medium for popular consumption; in addition, there were difficulties with the graphic translation of manga that entailed considerable expense, such as graphic reversal and re-lettering. This culminated in Rifas making aesthetic interventions that were later to become commonplace in the republication of manga in the west, principal amongst them being the introduction of colour and shading, to: 'make it look more familiar to American comics fans, who are used to either four-color comics, or black and white comics with a full range of gray tones.'[36] Still *Gen of Hiroshima* did not sell well enough for Rifas to get beyond issue two, and shortly after this New Society Publishers began republishing the work as *Barefoot Gen*, printing the story in graphic novel format, with smaller pages and in thicker volumes. Rifas' subsequent republication of the earlier (and less violent), shorter and more directly autobiographic *I Saw It* was more successful, however.

Gen and Wartime Realism

It is important to recognise that, at its first appearances in the West, *Barefoot Gen* not only presented serious information in an unusual comic book format, but that it also used visual codes that presented a challenge to the traditional means of representing children in a narrative. Nakazawa uses a simplified method of depiction that was

35 Rifas, "Globalizing Comic Books from Below," 7.
36 Rifas, "Globalizing Comic Books from Below," 9–10.

unfamiliar for western comic-book readers, making the points of reference to contemporary and traditional practice hard for the reader to locate, and offending some readers as well. His use of violence between family members and between children is frequent and exaggerated, albeit in a caricatured way. Nakazawa was firmly embedded in the manga practices where stylised violence between children was not uncommon, and was keen to emphasise the brutalisation of people, including children, in the chaos of war. The effect of Nakazawa's methods on the peace movement and a wider audience, however, was negative, as Gleason makes clear:

> Where Nakazawa got criticised in the US is where he had a lot of family violence: father slapping sons, children biting fingers off of the enemy... Our major audience for so many years were people in the peace movement, and they had particular sensibilities towards any type of violence, domestic or political. The *Gen* series was criticised by quite a few people in America who liked its message but didn't like all this gratuitous personal violence. They didn't want to read it to their kids or have their kids read it for that reason. When I reported this to the author he got rather defensive and said well 'this was the way that it was, we weren't a bunch of little pacifists running around, we were ordinary kids with ordinary problems, and besides, it was wartime.'[37]

Nakazawa is here defending his choice of narrative events through a desire for a form of realism. From the point of view of style and medium Nakazawa's work was unfamiliar and unexpected, causing difficulties for its assimilation by the activists in the anti-nuclear and peace movements. It did, however, achieve increasing recognition by other graphic artists, who may have recognised its potential for social realism. Since underground comix artists were keen to experiment with the medium and had no qualms about explicit violence, some were receptive to the realism that *Barefoot Gen* presented. Spiegelman for instance, was sufficiently impressed with its production and political effectiveness that he chose to write the foreword for the translated novel.[38] *Maus*, his own autobiographical war narrative, is clearly indebted to *Barefoot Gen* in its forms, narratives and themes.

37 Gleason, interview with the author.

38 Spiegelman, foreword in *Barefoot Gen, Vol. 1.*

Gleason argues that the novel was received by different audiences in different ways: one that drew inspiration form an anti-nuclear war perspective, another for its innovations as a documentary graphic novel.[39] This latter group maintained its interest in, and drew inspiration from Nakazawa after its impact as an anti-bomb work had subsided.

The depictions of violence in *Barefoot Gen* can be seen as part of a wider realism, which represents civilian suffering during war and occupation as well as that of soldiers. One key difference between Nakazawa's work and many mainstream war comic books is Nakazawa's ability to overturn the typical interests of artists and publishers of the genre. Rather than glorify the military aspects of the war, he instead develops the virtue of resistance to militarism and nationalism. Rifas summarised this on the rear cover of his publication of *Gen of Hiroshima*:

> Opposition to war is encouraged by showing how a government can trick people into supporting policies which leave them impoverished or dead, […] Racist ideas about enemy people are lies that the government tells to incite and cover up atrocities, […] It is heroic to refuse to support war.[40]

This is a statement of the significant characteristics that distinguish this work from traditional accounts of war in comic book form. Nakazawa's realism relocated the focus of action, heroism, suffering and control to the civilian population rather than the military. Heroism is an important concept in the hegemonic processes of patriotism, and Nakazawa, like Heartfield in his critique of the Nazis in the 1930s, exposed the contradictions of militarism that state and mass media was required to conceal. The prevalence of hunger throughout *Barefoot Gen* is a good indicator of its wartime realism, especially amongst children, a subject that is often omitted from war stories.[41]

39 Gleason, interview with the author.

40 Rifas, "Globalizing Comic Books from Below," 12, 33.

41 Rifas, "Globalizing Comic Books from Below," 23 (with additions in made by Rifas, February 2002).

Nakazawa, like Satrapi, utilises the school institution to stage the ideological struggle between state ideology and political resistance. Here it is useful to explore Althusser's notion of subject 'recognition', constructed through 'ritual', an idea which is central to his concept of the ideological construction of the subject through the state[42]. The Japanese citizen as an ideological subject within the pre-war militaristic hegemony of Japan is manifest in the overtly patriotic rituals of school assemblies with their militaristic songs and demonstrations of allegiance to the Emperor (figure 3.9). Gen and his sister are depicted suffering greatly at school at the hands of their teachers, mostly as a consequence of their father's lacking of patriotism, tantamount to being a traitor. Gen's family encounter these entrenched ideas at every turn prior to the atomic bombing, and much of their suffering is as a result of their unwillingness to conform to these dominant ways of thinking.

Nakazawa's device to reveal the interpolation of individuals as subjects is to make Gen and his family aware of these ideological structures in a way that may have been impossible at the time (as in figure 1.3, for example). They have sensibilities and reactions that run counter to their friends and fellow pupils, which are also contrary to their 'correct' recognition of themselves as subjects constructed by the rituals of the state through the school. Gen's father is the main character in the novel to question and challenge, often physically, the ideological conditioning of his fellow citizens. The mundane and domestic rituals that Gen and his family have to practise, which are principally to support imperialist ambitions, may be seen as complying with Althusser's theory of embedding subjects in the ideological recognition of themselves, to 'interpolate concrete individuals as concrete subjects'.[43]

42 Althusser, 151–162.
43 Althusser, 157.

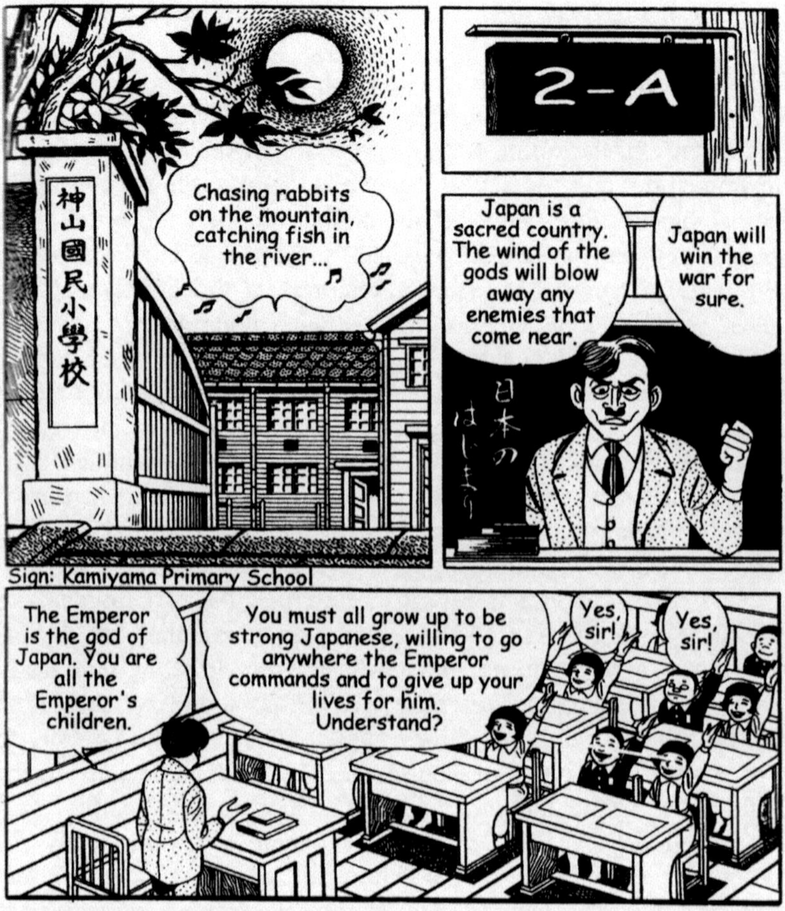

Figure 3.9. Depiction of popular support for militarism in *Barefoot Gen, Volume I, A Cartoon Story of Hiroshima* (p.51, detail). © Keiji Nakazawa 2005; translation Project Gen; reproduced with permission of Last Gasp of San Francisco.

Koji, Gen's brother, for instance, is forced to participate in patriotic military duties that he and his father see as futile and likely to prolong the war.[44]

44 Nakazawa, *Barefoot Gen, vol. 1*, 112 and 223.

Edward Said's analysis of imperialism highlights correlations of intolerance and racism that occur in this kind of social and ideological structure. The root causes of imperialism, for Said, 'are to be found less in tangible material wants than in the uneasy tensions of societies distorted by class division, with their reflection in distorted ideas...'[45] He makes the case that we should look to the collective, imaginative life of the state that enables imperialist ideas to become commonplace, then 'naturalised', and eventually become acceptable. Nakazawa repeatedly explores these social mechanisms and the expression of commonplace ideas, often in the form of classroom instruction to the children; an example of this is when the pupils are exhorted to 'give up your lives for him [the Emperor]', which is received with enthusiasm (figure 3.9). Gen's family are not 'ordinary', but are structured as *different*, in not being susceptible to the conditioning to which everyone else around them is shown to succumb. By speaking from the present back to the past, as Nakazawa does through the character of Gen's father, he is able to portray the limitations of the ideas that informed militarism and patriotism. These mini-narratives may be seen as representing a critique of the past from Nakazawa's present; as such they reveal ideological structures, extrapolated from events in his autobiographical history, which would probably have been obscured at the time.

Barefoot Gen was produced by Nakazawa and Project Gen as an animated film (animé) in 1983.[46] It is largely a de-politicisation of the manga, where events that cast Japanese society in militaristic or aggressive light are played down.[47] Rifas notes this ideological manipulation, pointing to the absence of 'bad' characters like the boy Ryukichi, who torments Gen in the manga. Presumably this editing took place to prevent the representation of Japanese society as anything other than the victims of the US bombing – and thereby

45 Edward W. Said, *Culture and Imperialism* (London: Chatto and Windus, 1993), 10–11.

46 Streamline Videos, "Barefoot Gen," Orion Home Video, 1995 (re-released 2002 as a DVD).

47 Rifas, "Globalizing Comic Books from Below," 17, and footnote 102.

reducing the political critique of the militarism that Nakazawa presents in the manga. A web display of the animé *Barefoot Gen* similarly presents the work as a display of grotesque and melodramatic scenes, by extracting individual frames rather than whole pages.[48] Any sense of narrative, and with it political critique, is lost by this process; the display recreates *Barefoot Gen* as a kind of special-effect horror. Nakazawa's critical realism is demonstrably dependent upon its medium as a graphic novel, and the effectiveness of such critical, social realism is also context specific. In the case of *Barefoot Gen*, the social position that Nakazawa personally occupied in relation to the bombing, as a victim, and the development of the Japanese state in the intervening period, provides that context. Graphic novel production has been at the interface of Japanese/US cultural relations throughout this period, and Nakazawa's novel is a key work of the post-war era in this respect. It offers a political critique of the Hiroshima bombing from a social position that was itself being reconstructed during the same period – that of a manga artist during the boom years of manga and of Japanese economic success.

Anxious Children: Astro Boy, Adolf and Barefoot Gen

As many writers on manga have pointed out, Tezuka's work has been extremely significant to the development of manga and graphic novels.[49] His *Astro Boy* manga ran throughout the 1950s, exploring narrative themes of social rejection and assimilation, as the robot boy attempts to acquire human social behaviour and values. This influenced the narrative content and structure of manga, and *Barefoot Gen* in particular.

48 "The Black Moon: Art, Anime, and Japanese Culture," http://www.theblackmoon.com/BarefootGen/bomb.html (accessed December 3 2007).

49 Gravett, *Manga*, for example.

Astro Boy is one of the most enduring manga. It was a long running (17 years) manga series from 1951, and then serialised on TV from 1963; it became the first animated manga cartoon to appear on prime TV viewing time. Yukio Kondo points out that *Astro Boy* and *Iron Man*, (serialised on TV at the same time) became heroes in post-war Japan because they encapsulated ideas about Japanese national post-war identity as a heroic and technologically advanced nation.[50] Kondo claims that the rise in popularity of science fiction was largely due to government and media corporations attempting to avoid direct accusations of jingoism.[51] If, however, such popular tales as *Iron Man* and *Battleship Yamato* are but thinly-veiled nationalism, Kondo argues that *Astro Boy*, in its manga form (as opposed to the animated TV version), is far more sophisticated in its attempts to illustrate the uncertainties of identity, nationalism and ethnicity.[52] In this sense *Astro Boy* offered a precedent for the issues raised in *Barefoot Gen*, since Tezuka depicts *Astro Boy* as having difficulty being assimilated into society because of his robot status, and as having difficulties accepting his own supernatural powers.

Astro Boy is frequently ostracised because his robot condition does not allow him to die and this prevents him from being truly human, as a consequence of which others discriminate against him. Similarly, Gen is rejected as a traitor because of his father's anti-militarism, then as a friend of a Korean who is subjected to racism, and later as a victim of radiation after the atomic bomb blast.[53] Nakazawa explores the extensive ostracism of radiation victims that took place in the aftermath of the Hiroshima bombing: when Gen begins to lose his hair after exposure to the radiation from the bomb, he too is frequently a source of derision and fear for other children, and adults too. In the case of the ill Japanese soldier neglected by his family, this reaches an extreme point, when a child of the family asks

50 Kondo, "The Agony of Astro Boy."
51 Kondo, "The Agony of Astro Boy."
52 Kondo, "The Agony of Astro Boy."
53 Nakazawa, *Barefoot Gen, vol. 1,* 60.

Gen to murder his sick uncle for payment.[54] Nakazawa repeatedly cast Gen into such roles of social conflict, as Tezuka did with the manga version of *Astro Boy*. Just as *Astro Boy* was Tezuka's 'magnum opus' so the extended *Barefoot Gen* proved to be for Nakazawa.[55]

Tezuka became disillusioned with the TV series that he was producing, and believed that *Astro Boy* was increasingly becoming a simplistic character; losing the social complexities that he explored in the manga. In a final act of self-sacrifice that ended the TV series in 1966, *Astro Boy* destroyes himself in the sun, an ending that, according to Kondo, Tezuka particularly disliked.[56] This was mainly because of its association with the self-sacrifice ideology that underpinned (and prolonged) the war in 1944–45, and its blatant nationalistic symbolism. This transformation of *Astro Boy* may be indicative of the increasing power of TV corporations over manga, and Tezuka's corresponding loss of control.[57]

Nakazawa and Tezuka represent manga artists who explore such issues with uncompromising social realism. Tezuka's *Adolf* is an example of a manga that comprises many of the characteristics that have made the form so influential in the West.[58] It deals primarily with the militarism and nationalism in Japan and Germany leading up to the Second World War through a detective-thriller type of narrative. *Adolf* is an integrated graphic narrative dealing head on with the imposition of racism and nationalism upon children, exposing Japanese militarism and Aryan supremacist practices through the resistance to ethnic assimilation by his child protagonists. The sense of complacency, always a danger with a well-worn topic such as the cruelty and excesses of the Nazis, is avoided by means of Tezuka's

54 Keiji Nakazawa, *Barefoot Gen, Life After the Bomb, Volume 3* (San Francisco: Last Gasp, 2005), 33.

55 Yukio Kondo, "The Agony of Astro Boy: curating the first Osamu Tezuka exhibition at the Tokyo Museum of Modern Art," symposium paper at *Manga and Art: Visual Culture in Contemporary Japan*, London College of Fashion, London W1, February 1, 2002.

56 Kondo, "The Agony of Astro Boy."

57 Kondo, "The Agony of Astro Boy."

58 Osamu Tezuka, *Adolf: An Exile in Japan*; (Canada: Cadence Books, 1996).

extensive graphic repertoire, underpinned by historical references selected for their poignancy.

Problematic Depictions: Gen and the Violence of War

In the solicited reviews for *I Saw It*, writers discussed its representation of the bombing of Hiroshima and the way that created a vicarious experience of suffering:

> 'The personal experience of the author makes the Hiroshima bomb real to me. Not only the blast, but the devastating aftermath illustrates our future. This book will inspire people to work for a world without nuclear weapons. The artwork, pace of the story and personal viewpoint give an intimacy that is stunning.'[59]

These reviews were produced at a time of tension over nuclear arms between the US and the Soviet Union. The election of Ronald Reagan resulted in Nakazawa's work being received with as much attention given to the contemporary potential for nuclear disaster as it was to the catastrophe of the 1945 bombing. Its perceived prescience at this time stemmed from this Cold War anxiety and the increasing prominence of Japan, economically and culturally, as a competitor and an ambivalent strategic ally of the West. The reviewers were also writing about the new appearance in the US of manga, with its new and, at the time, not entirely explicable visual conventions. With Nakazawa's exaggerated depiction of events, in combination with an unrelenting realism of the effects of the bomb, it's possible to read the reviews as wonder tainted with anxiety and revulsion.

The depiction of children in violent and horrific situations, often perpetrating violence themselves, was, according to Leonard Rifas, a significant factor in the 'failure' of both his Gen publications (in terms of sales), and he made a detailed analysis of the reasons for it. Arguing that a comic book could be a vehicle for social issues, he considered added warnings on the covers and not recommending its

59 Joyce Farmer, in Rifas, "Globalizing Comic Books from Below," footnote, 65.

sale to children.[60] The translators of Project Gen, who had initiated the whole *Barefoot Gen* publication, also confirmed the idea that the gratuitous familial violence in Nakazawa's narrative was a major factor in the unwillingness of the various protest groups to make more use of *Barefoot Gen*:

> 'I recognize there is a tendency to romanticize victims, but I think it was largely the violence that turned them off, and more than that, the general cartooneyness of the style. Peace activists, serious folks by inclination, would be just the sort of people to view comics as too low-brow a medium for conveying serious truths. And the commix audience … was the reverse – no problem with cartooneyness and violence, but not given to indulging in portrayals of harsh reality.'[61]

The visual signifiers of violent actions are usually 'speed lines' around the bodies and limbs to denote rapid movement, with puffs or cloud-like squiggles to indicate light impact, with sharper outward radiating lines for harsh impact. These are common conventions in cartoons and comic books in manga and the West, but the frequency of their occurrence, coupled with Nakazawa's tendency to represent quarrels and disagreements by the metaphor of physical violence, is a distinctive characteristic of his work; in one instance Gen is beaten, tied and hung by the waist by his father as a punishment.[62] Compared to other Japanese manga, however, the work seems less unusual in this respect. Tezuka's *Adolf*, for example, has as many scenes of physical violence and used similar conventions to depict it.[63]

The context of the documentary realism of the topic, with the frequent involvement of children in the depictions of violence, had a negative effect on the US readers. In the still wider context of a new translation for Western audiences unfamiliar with the metaphoric use of physical violence in Japanese manga, these early reactions are less

60 Rifas, "Globalizing Comic Books from Below," 7.

61 Rifas, "Globalizing Comic Books from Below," 26; also, Alan Gleason to Leonard Rifas, correspondence October 22, 2001.

62 Nakazawa, *Barefoot Gen, Vol. 1*, 236.

63 Osamu Tezuka, *Adolf: An Exile in Japan*, (Canada: Cadence Books Graphic Novel, 1996), 66–69, for example.

surprising. The comparative success later of *I Saw It*, which, as Rifas points out, had significantly fewer frames of this nature, does seem to be accounted for by its lack of stylised violence.[64] The graphic comics artist Jim Ottaviani, however, put these difficulties with *Barefoot Gen* down to formal and stylistic problems with Nakazawa's work:

> At the time *Gen* first appeared over here I don't think the comics' audience was ready to accept the conventional manga-form of storytelling. Couple this with the subject matter and people were likely to dismiss *Gen* (unfairly, I think) as either a polemic aimed at children or an inappropriate format for a serious subject. [...] He's clear in his storytelling, sincere in his intent, and has an important story to tell. But there's little subtlety to his work, and in many places he's clumsy. And I think this undercuts the story he's trying to tell – when all the gestures are broadly drawn and the characters seem to be shouting more often than not, it's hard to connect with the emotions.[65]

Ottiviani's experience of the formal conventions of comics and graphic art clearly informed this insight. The idea of levels of competence, separate from the content, is a concept that has characterised the histories of Western art. The naivety of Nakazawa's art, as Ottiviani describes it, was seen as a negative factor in relation to his narrative content. The effectiveness of Nakazawa's narrative, however, may be located in its very idiosyncratic and repetitive visual realisation. Just as the *hibakusha* paintings (art work by untrained atomic bomb victims) take naïve stylistic liberties with pictorial conventions without losing their narrative force, so Nakazawa's autobiographic conception is expressed through its specific naïve form as well as its content. His direct 'political speech' is as least in part due to his disregard of conventions, albeit through alleged incompetence. In this respect Sartapi's work has much in common, but the much later publication of her work, by some twenty years, appears to have reached a public more willing to accept a crude, simplified style as a positive feature of the work.

Gleason's comment above about the 'cartooneyness' of *Barefoot Gen* is also revealing. This is a characteristic of manga too (less so in

64 Rifas, "Globalizing Comic Books from Below," 14.

65 Jim Ottaviani (2001) correspondence with Jeff Adams, March 7, 2002.

the past few years as manga styles have become widespread in the West), that was difficult for Western readers to assimilate until familiar with the conventions. In *Adolf*, for example, Tezuka's characters are drawn in a variety of reduced and simplified forms. The rapidly changing methods of depiction in Tezuka's work, with caricatured simplifications and extreme physical actions, are more akin to newspaper cartoon strips in the West. Such techniques were largely absent from the comic books of well-known mainstream Western artists, such as Jack Kirby the creator of Marvel Comic characters like the *Fantastic Four*, or Hergé the artist of *Tintin*, for example.[66] Although many artists since then have acquired this tendency for greater variety of styles for the same character in a single narrative (the Hernandez brothers being a conspicuous example of this with *Love and Rockets*), in the early days of manga in the West the variety and extreme action may have been read as inconsistency. [67]

Some of the difficulties in the early publication of *Barefoot Gen* may be attributed to this assimilation of the unusual formal conventions of Nakazawa's manga in the signifying process. The cultural conditioning that permitted Kirby and Hergé's conventions to be read seamlessly in the West made the variations and seeming inconsistencies in manga conventions impenetrable, at least at first. The signs for aggression and despair in *Barefoot Gen* may have led to 'aberrant decoding', to use Roland Barthes' term, whereby the signifying marks are attached by the readers to a different, unintended set of concepts.[68] This may have been caused by Nakazawa's use of unusually simplified cartoon forms, as well as the manga conventions of stylised violence. These characteristics could only be re-coded and more readily assimilated with the great increase in manga availability in the 1990s in the West. Although critics, and other professional

66 For example: Hergé, *The Adventures of Tintin in the Land of the Soviets*, (San Francisco: Last Gasp, 2003).

67 Hernandez, Gilbert and Jaime *Love and Rockets* (Seattle, USA. Fantagraphics Books, 1981–1995).

68 Roland Barthes, *Image, Music, Text* (Glasgow: Fontana, 1990).

comic artists, like Ottaviani, questioned Nakazawa's competence as a graphic artist and his ability to depict social crises with a limited repertoire of graphic motifs, this should not be seen as compromising his realism.[69] Like the realist works described earlier, a socially demystifying work signifies more in political terms than one measured by technical capability.

The Visualisation of the Hiroshima bombing

The panoramic depiction in *Barefoot Gen* of the devastation of Hiroshima after the bombing (figure 2.1) relies on US news and military aerial photographs. By locating the drawing of the child Gen's face within a well-known view of the destroyed city, Nakazawa creates a visual reminder of the human cost of the act of bombing. In his analysis of the nuclear bombings of Hiroshima and Nagasaki, Eric Hobsbawm asserts that:

> In the longer run democratic governments failed to resist the temptation of saving their own citizens' lives by treating those of enemy countries as totally expendable. The dropping of the atom bomb on Hiroshima and Nagasaki in 1945 was not justified as indispensable for victory, which was by then absolutely certain, but as a means of saving American soldiers' lives. But perhaps the thought that it would prevent America's ally the USSR from establishing a claim to a major part in Japan's defeat was not absent from the minds of the US government either.[70]

On August 13, 1945, one week after the Hiroshima bombing and only three days after that of Nagasaki, *The Stars and Stripes'* front page (a US military newspaper) carried images of the bombings in two sequenced photographs under the title 'One-Two Punch'. [71] As well as the boxing analogy, the captions refer to the 'mighty atom bomb'

69 Gleason, interview with the author.

70 Eric Hobsbawm, *Age of Extremes,* 27.

71 Times Publishing Company Ltd. *Stars and Stripes, Daily newspaper of the U.S. Forces in the European Theater*, vol. 5, no. 240, August 13, 1945, London edition, 1 and 8.

and the ‘potent new weapon’. The language is clearly partisan, consistent with the general war reportage of this Forces newspaper. Such were the visual/linguistic codes that were used in the initial reception of the bombings in the West, and which Nakazawa challenged by his retelling with the alternative conventions and visual codes in *Barefoot Gen*.

Despite the attempts of the wartime US government to describe the bombings in the familiar terms of military victory and military might, the social anxiety that followed was to have a profound impact on US culture, generated by the extremely effective, instant and near total civilian as well as military destruction that the bombs wrought. As Novick notes: ‘Hiroshima had a much greater impact on Americans that did the Holocaust [in 1945]’[72] Michael J. Hogan’s work on the cultural memories of the Hiroshima bombing draws interesting conclusions about the visualisation of the event; he explains that the immediate post-war censorship on publication of the sufferings – imposed by the US administration until 1952 – was endorsed by both sides.[73] The US controlled Japanese government and media corporations were by and large amenable to the silence surrounding the numerous victims of the two nuclear bombings, and special assistance only began with the end of the occupation. The US ensured press censorship on the massive civilian casualties and their enduring suffering. This was not surprising, since to admit to this would have been tantamount to acknowledging committing war atrocities on non-combatants.

More surprising, perhaps, was the initial reluctance by Japanese people to accept the scale and the consequences of the disaster for civilians. According to Hogan, this was related to the social difficulties of accepting defeat and the disastrous state in which the war had left a subjugated Japan. The hibakusha, as the victims of the bombs were known, were seen as visible signs of the wretchedness of Japan and rapidly became stigmatised as such. It wasn’t until after the occupation that the Japanese incorporated the victims into the peace

72 Novick.
73 Hogan, 126–129.

movement and changed the status of the hibakusha to that of innocent sufferers. Hogan demonstrated that this censorship and silence during the occupation years delayed the visualisation of the event in terms of popular consciousness.[74] Many of the images, ideas and concepts that now commonly inform this visualisation didn't reach publication until many years after the event(s), and much may have been lost.[75]

Some of the most effective images, in terms of their popularity and commercial reproduction, that appeared immediately after the occupation, were a series of drawings by Toshi and Iri Maruki who witnessed the suffering caused by the bombing. Hogan explains that part of their rationale for producing the works was fear of the total absence of visual records, so draconian was the censorship on such images.[76] Many other witnesses (often themselves traumatised) and survivors turned to drawing and painting, and the publication of many of their works by the Japan Broadcasting Corporation (NHK) in 1977 revealed an abundance of works of this kind.[77] *Barefoot Gen* shares stylistic characteristics with some of these works, and the abrupt 'cartoonish', superficially 'naïve' drawing techniques that characterise *Barefoot Gen* may be related to the numerous NHK depictions of the hibakusha by mostly untrained artists. Nakazawa's depiction of the vilification of the hibakusha in *Barefoot Gen,* may be seen in the context of a re-conceptualisation of the illnesses of the victims, an attempt to visualise a formally taboo subject.[78] This rejection is perpetrated by children just as much as adults in Nakazawa's accounts.

Nakazawa's narrative in figure 3.10 (discussed in chapter two) deals with the rejection of a soldier by his family because of his radiation sickness and his burns, which they believe to be contagious.

74 Hogan, 128.

75 Hogan, 127 (esp. footnote 12).

76 Hogan.

77 Japan Broadcasting Corporation (NHK) *Unforgettable Fire: Pictures Drawn by Atomic Bomb Survivors* (New York, NHK, 1977).

78 Nakazawa, *Barefoot Gen Vol.3*, 80–81.

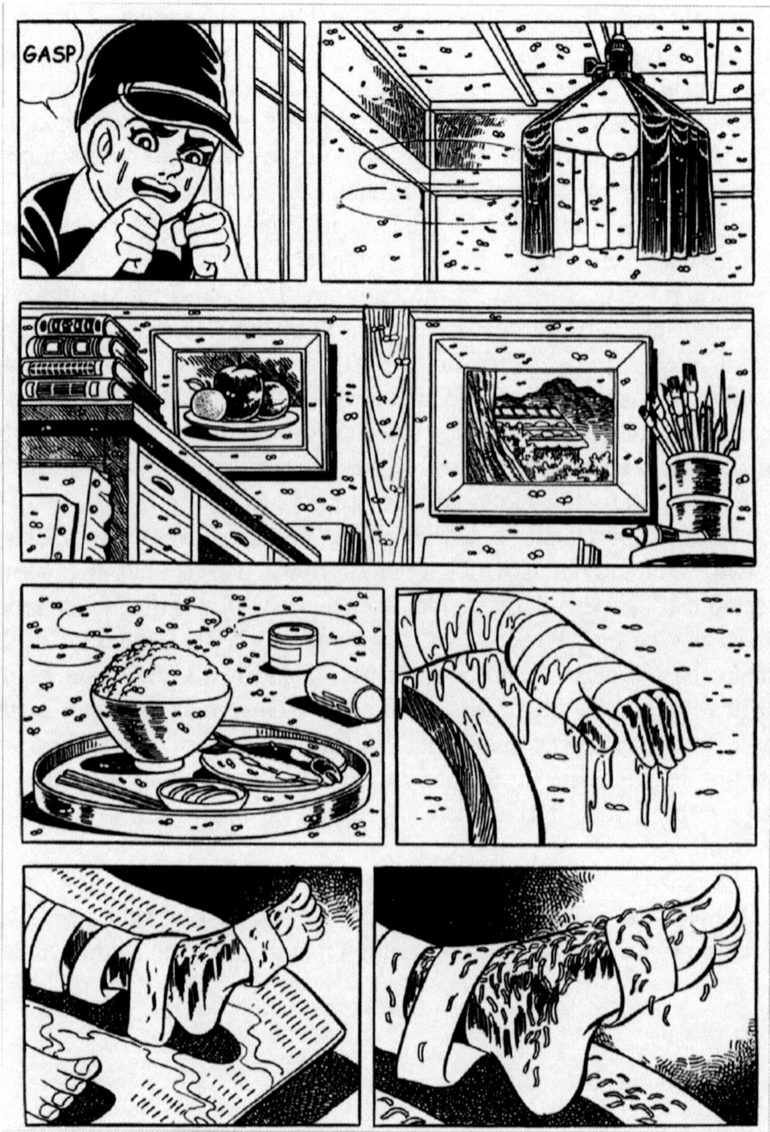

Figure 3.10. Gen is confronted with radiation sickness in Nakazawa's *Barefoot Gen, Volume 3, Life After the Bomb* (p. 23). © Keiji Nakazawa 2005; translation Project Gen; reproduced with permission of Last Gasp of San Francisco.

Consequently he is confined to a bedroom unattended, where he is infested with maggots and exudes the stench of rotting flesh. Gen is depicted repeatedly trying to help rehabilitate the man and resist the myths surrounding his illness. The victim is depicted in a room infested with flies, and he invokes repulsion and fear in his relatives, especially the children, who fear stigmatisation by association with the feared 'disease.' The aerial views, as if the viewer were one of these flies on the ceiling, lay bare the entire room, confronting the reader with the suffering. It is difficult for the reader to seek respite visually, and therefore avoid the enormity of the episode. The aerial viewpoints of the body, and the frame-by-frame depiction of the removal of the maggots are graphic and literal in their detail, and make a stark contrast with the concept of a 'cartoon' (when defined in the Western sense as comical or sentimental, vis-à-vis Disney productions, to which *Barefoot Gen* also bears stylistic resemblance).

Using different views of the room with each frame the viewer is allowed to 'tour' a scene, understanding many visual aspects without any 'time' passing. The visualisation of the room take place incrementally, with views reminiscent of an eye scanning a room and then focusing in on a key point: the horror of the discovery of the maggot-eaten foot in *Barefoot Gen*. Nakazawa next uses a double frame from the same viewpoint, concluding the sequence with a 'double take' of the foot, closing in and enlarging it. This effect simulates the reaction of shock on the part of the narrator, as Gen 'realises' the enormity of the scene. The sense of time is created by the absence of other narrative events, in conjunction with a heightened visualisation through framed views of the scene. This is a distinctive form of the medium that Nakazawa exploited, like many manga artists before and since, appropriately for such a dramatic moment as this. He enhances the specificity of the scene and thereby avoids the generalising tendencies of many contemporary war comics.

Representing Time and Psychological States

Time can be signified in graphic novels through individual frames, where a moment in time is indicated by a frame enclosing an image.

Frames can still signify the passage of time even when blank, like the device of adding empty (and sometimes diminishing) frames to the end of a sequence of images to signify that time continues, the equivalent of the cinematic device of fade out.[79] Natsume describes this in linguistic terms, where the frames can be likened to punctuation, controlling rhythm and tempo. He argues that frames are used extensively in manga to act as metaphors for time related events: the breakdown of consciousness of time and confusion, for instance. In these cases frames may be overlaid or merged, sometimes occluding images beneath, or containing seemingly abstract marks designed to signify temporary states of mind like confusion, for instance. There is a good example of 'psychological' time in Nakazawa's page of the moment of the atomic bomb explosion (figure 3.11). The first three frames are all a single moment, with time suspended. Time gradually accelerates back to 'normal' pace as we read to the bottom of the page, as the surviving boy begins to comprehend the event.

The vocabulary of manga routinely includes psychological states, readily understood as such once the visual vocabulary of manga has been assimilated by the reader; for example, Gen's state of shock after regaining consciousness after the explosion is indicated is by the ellipse (dots) in the thought bubble. Such indicators of metal processes are a feature of comic books, which create 'a rich sense of psychological time, heightened by the sheer physical effect of turning the page'.[80] This physical process of turning itself generates a (temporal) sense of anticipation, initiated by the visual delay that occurs before the next page is revealed. The thick, heavy compilation books in which weekly serialised manga is printed make the physical act or holding and turning more apparent in Japan than is usually the case in the West.

79 Natsume, "The Structure of Manga Expression."
80 Natsume, "The Structure of Manga Expression."

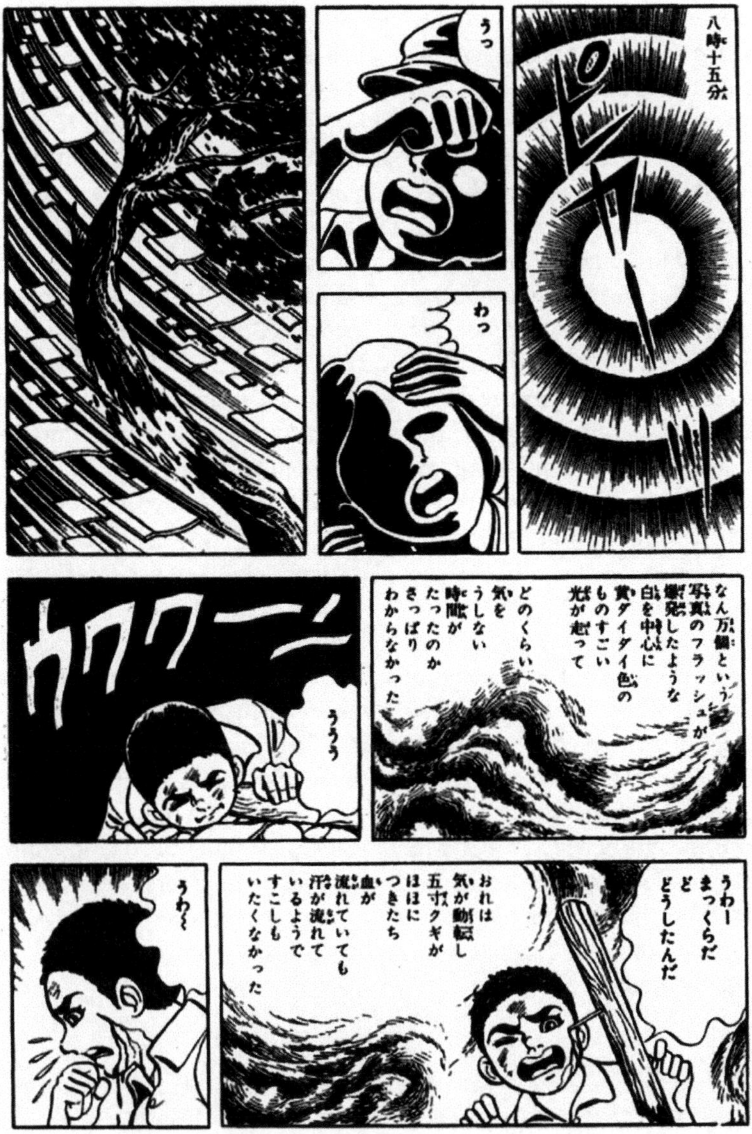

Figure 3.11. A crucial page of the story, from the original Japanese black and white manga. Reading order right to left. *Ore Wa Mita* (*I Saw It,* 1972–73, p.241) © Keiji Nakazawa 1973; reproduced with permission of Project Gen.

As Spiegelman points out, frames that simply show a shining sun occur often in *Barefoot Gen*, and act as double visual metaphor within the pictorial page displays (figure 3.12).[81] The sun may appear drawn as a white circle, in a narrow cell inserted at intervals into the narrative; its significance stems from its shared characteristics with the initial explosion and the frequent 'flashbacks' (literally) to it. All events in the child's world revolve around this single moment, conceptualised and represented by a bright shining object in the sky.

The complex evolution of manga from the specific cultural context of post-war Japan, with traditional and contemporary art, politics and Western mass media all playing a part, have resulted in distinctive formal properties of manga. Fusanosuke Natsume defines manga as the interaction of picture/word/frame, where each of these components is essential for manga to function, and this interaction frequently involves a blurring of the boundaries between picture and word through operations like onomatopoeia.[82] By this Natsume is referring to features like those described as 'sound-effects' (often abbreviated to SFX), where the (imagined) voiced sound of the word with its image as a written word are closely inter-linked, and the reader of a word-image is expected to recognise this interplay. Katakana characters are used in sound effects, which are the set of phonetic written Japanese characters that are also used to denote words of foreign origin and for scientific terms. Nakazawa uses Katakana in the lettering across the key frame depicting the exploding bomb in figure 3.11. Manga artists often play with these conventions, for example by the visual distortion of katakana letters to indicate the timbre of the sound. Sound effects are often used in ways that underline the importance of the relationship between visual and onomatopoeic signifiers.

81 Spiegelman, foreword in *Barefoot Gen, Vol.1,* v–viii.

82 Fusanosuke Natsume, "The Structure of Manga Expression," (paper presented at the symposium "Manga and Art: Visual Culture in Contemporary Japan," Chelsea College of Art and the Japan Foundation, London College of Fashion, London, 1 January 2002).

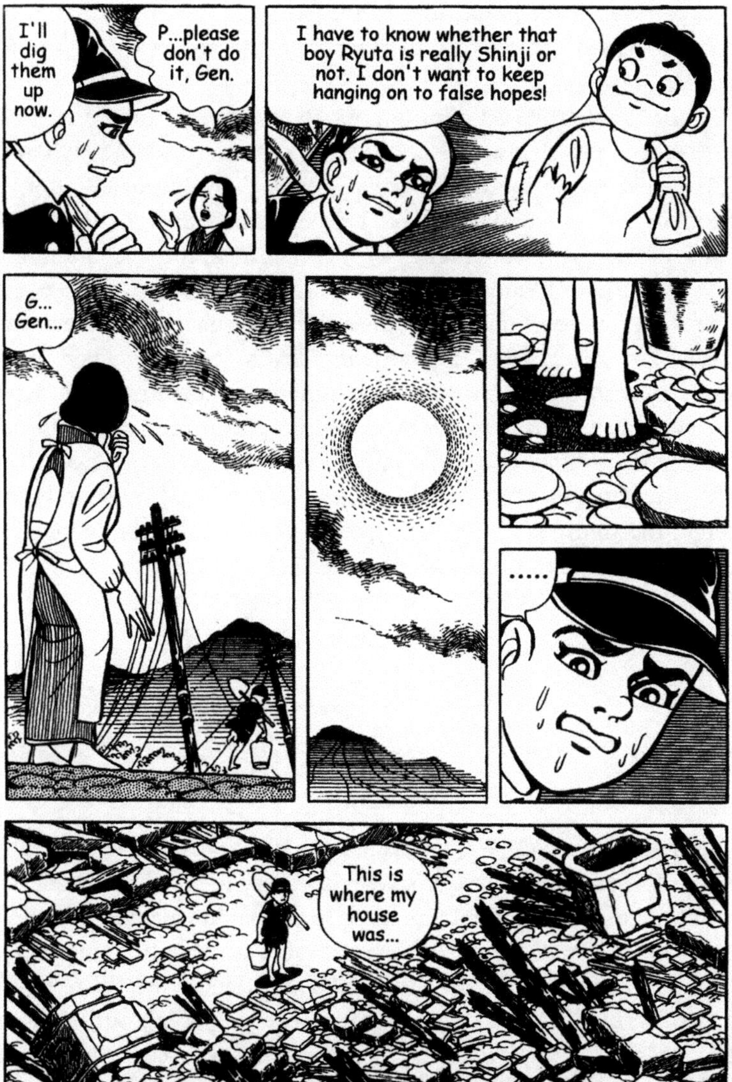

Figure 3.12. Nakazawa's use of the sun as metaphor in *Barefoot Gen* as Gen attempts to find his family's bones (*Volume 2, The Day After*, p.181). © Keiji Nakazawa 2005; translation Project Gen; reproduced with permission of Last Gasp of San Francisco.

Sound can only ever be present through text signifiers like the sound effects described above, with the important exception of the sound of pages being turned.[83]

Time is signified as duration, by its passage as the page is read, and also by spatial interval. This also applies to sound, where the length of the word/sound is usually signified by the convention of a horizontal line in katakana. The passage of time is especially important for the construction and layout of frames: the seminal moment in *Barefoot Gen* is when the bomb explodes, and time itself, especially concepts like 'before' and 'after', is a dominant theme in the narrative. Natsume's studies of eye movements across the page when reading manga (usually right to left, top to bottom in Japanese manga), demonstrate the way that frames provide a structure to render the narrative and text intelligible through the imposition of a time structure.[84] In this way the signifier for 'forward' becomes physically and psychologically linked to the signified 'future', as the subject is depicted moving across a page from frame to frame, all of which is tied to the idea of duration, orchestrated by the layout of frames on the page.

Spaces of Deprivation in *Jimmy Corrigan*

Time, and the psychological realism of children growing up in poverty, is developed in Chris Ware's *Jimmy Corrigan*, a fictional epic that jumps abruptly back and forth between generations. His protagonist exists in a continuous state of dissatisfaction and anxiety, and Ware makes social dysfunction a political issue rooted in the legacy of individualism and enterprise. This is played out in the past in the spaces of capitalist display, such as the vast *fin de siécle* exhibition halls of Chicago, or in the present within bland contemporary suburban interiors.

83 Natsume, "The Structure of Manga Expression."
84 Natsume, "The Structure of Manga Expression."

Like many of his contemporaries Ware exploits the distinctive features of the graphic novel medium to construct his narratives, utilising these with an adroitness borne of many years' labour and experience. The control that he exercises over time in his graphic work is great: moments that may be inferred as lasting seconds may be explored by spreading them over many frames for several pages; conversely days may be condensed into a single space between frames. [85] Ware is adept at pacing narratives by utilising this device, sometimes extending moments of reflection or even boredom with a sense of psychological time passing or arrested, all integrated into the virtual space of the page. He is also concerned with the relationship between text and image, the dynamic interplay between the virtual space of the image and the flatness of the text. Whereas this may have been formerly thought of as a disadvantage of the medium, with clumsy speech and thought balloons 'floating' over a character, Ware (like Sacco), turns this to his advantage by an *emphasis* on the distinctive illusionist anomalies to which it gives rise. The simultaneous creation of text and image enables him to posit ideas of space that refer to its political connotations and the way that children in domestic space may be represented as the site of solidarity, resistance or alienation.

Ware atomises time in some sections, devoting dozens of frames to his protagonists' emotional states as they are inflected through small moments of physical change. The boy Jimmy inhabits a variety of domestic and public spaces, many of which he is shown as knowing intimately, yet from which he is alienated by his psychological discomfort. Ware uses vivid colours, printed flat and entirely bereft of any modelling through shading or cross-hatching. This is not to say that Ware avoids depicting three-dimensional space; on the contrary, he deploys an extensive range of virtual spaces throughout the novel, including illusionist conventions such as linear and aerial perspective. The effect of using flat colour with regular, mechanical outlines is reminiscent of the techniques used for drawing utilitarian art forms, such as diagrams, posters or maps. Genealogical

85 McCloud, 100–103; Natsume, "The Structure of Manga Expression."

structures of the boy's family are displayed diagrammatically, for example, and inserted at intervals through the text along with bogus cut-out models of buildings and objects. Ware creates striking visual contrasts between the vast new architectural constructions of the late nineteenth-century exhibition spaces, and those of the cramped interiors of the suburban houses where the Corrigan family members interact and play out their fantasies. Such contrasts are emphasised by Ware in his creation of dreamlike spaces, where fantasy events are on equal terms with reality events, with no obvious distinction made between them. The anonymous and vacant spaces of contemporary offices and public housing are the spaces where present and past Corrigans struggle to come to terms with their perceptions of the errors and disappointments of their lives. The flat colour, the emphasis on outline and the overtly *printed* character of the pages all serve to reinforce the anonymity of the spaces.

It is sometimes in the space of a bed that important moments occur in Ware's narrative, bearing similarities with Georges Perec's interest in the topic.[86] Perec accords to beds and bedrooms significance for the invocation of domestic memory, discussing many rooms that he recalls from his past, and playfully muses on the possibility of making an inventory of all the beds that he has ever slept in.[87] He makes the important point that the act of recalling past beds and bedrooms spatially facilitates the recall of a myriad of related people and events, as if the space of the bed in our memory forms a significant link in a chain of spatial memory moments. Ware's bed events take place in a variety of bed types, including makeshift beds under tables, hospital beds, narrow single beds and vast double beds viewed from the ceiling. These beds become theatre platforms, where events like sickness, anxiety attacks and sexual liaisons are acted out, the rectangle of the bed giving yet another framing device for the staging of the performance. In one scene the small child Jimmy has to sleep under the table and endure the sounds of his father's

86 Georges Perec, *Species of Space and Other Pieces,* trans. by John Sturrock (London: Penguin, 1997).

87 Perec, 22–23.

sexual activities with temporary partners in the adjacent bed. Perec's recollections of the formative imaginings that occurred in his former beds have a more sinister parallel in Ware's bed scenes, where the beds signify the site of unresolved and traumatic psychic events.

The temporal transitions between sections of the novel, from present day to past, at first appear to acquire continuity by the reoccurrence of bed scenes. This sense of continuity is destabilised, however, by the underlying realism of psychic fracture, as each generation struggles to maintain its family or community identity. This labour is carried out in the largely unadorned apartments of public housing schemes for the low-waged, and by rendering them in a flat, hard-edged outlined geometry, they function as a metaphor for the minimised luxury of their underprivileged inhabitants. *Jimmy Corrigan* is delineated in his largely solitary existence, in the presence of a community to which he is unable to belong, inhabiting spaces akin to those described by Barbara Ehrenreich in her accounts of low-wage workers.[88]

Poverty and deprivation are themes to which a number of documentary graphic novelists attend, and Joe Sacco in particular pursues this, but under the very different circumstances of military occupation in his work *Palestine*, the subject of the following chapter.

88 Barbara Ehrenreich, *Nickel and Dimed: Undercover in Low-wage America* (USA: Granta Books, 2002).

Chapter 4: Documenting Oppression in Sacco's *Palestine*

A key work in terms of documenting oppression is Joe Sacco's *Palestine*; it is especially significant in terms of its political realism and its prescience, in view of the subsequent developments in the Middle East. Its political effectiveness in relationship to the graphic medium is discussed in detail in this chapter, as are its innovative visualisation methods, borne of direct and imagined experience of military oppression. Sacco's use of Palestinian narratives, and the ways he mediates and renders them graphically, is analysed in the following pages. Its combination of brutal political realism with entirely new methods of visual documentation represent an important moment in graphic novel production, establishing the medium's credentials for representations of momentous social events. In this respect it is comparable with Spiegelman's Holocaust accounts in *Maus*, discussed and analysed in following chapter.

Although not a huge commercial success, *Palestine* is nonetheless a seminal work of the documentary graphic novel genre, in terms of both its content, and its visual innovations. From the outset Sacco was determined to make *Palestine* a political work, one that ran contrary to the dominant political ideology of the US at the time of its writing, as he makes clear: '…I really wanted to do something to tell the other side. It was already in my mind to get the Palestinian point of view.'[1] This statement declares Sacco's intention to assume a position of opposition, indicating that prior to the inception of the work he was already making broad assumptions about the political culture of the US vis-à-vis the Middle East, and how *Palestine* would be located within it. The republication of *Palestine* in 2001 has a foreword by Edward Said, an important moment for Sacco since he

1 Thom Powers, "Joe Sacco Interview," *The Comics Journal* 176 (1995): 102.

had originally been inspired to write *Palestine* by reading Said's, Noam Chomsky's and Christopher Hitchens' books on the subject. The endorsement of the project by Said may be seen as a validation, in the context of the intellectual Arab-American political thinking on Palestine at this time.[2] Said was sufficiently impressed with the political potential of *Palestine* that he wrote:

> '[...]...the more I read compulsively in Sacco's Palestine comic books [...] the more convinced I was that here was a political and aesthetic work of extraordinary originality, quite unlike any other in the long, often turgid and hopelessly twisted debates that had occupied Palestinians, Israelis and their respective supporters.'[3]

The re-launch of *Palestine* with this academic, intellectually weighty foreword is evidence that the novel, despite its relatively poor sales, was seen by Said and other radicals as the kind of cultural material that represented a new strategy for effecting the 'imaginative' changes that he (and Sacco) had advocated.[4]

Sacco has, on more than one occasion, insisted that his theoretical and political reading informed his creation of *Palestine*:

> '... reading certain books turned things really upside down for me, in particular Noam Chomsky's *Fateful Triangle* and Edward Said's *The Question of Palestine*. [...] I started really reading about the issue [Israel and the Palestinians] in '89, when I got back from living in Germany. I went to the library. I was curious about this issue I'd been hearing about a lot in Europe. The intifada was pretty much in full force at the time. And I found the book by Chomsky. Reading it almost made me physically ill, because I realized how the media had manipulated my perception of Palestinians. I really had the impression that all Palestinians were terrorists.[...] I always thought of myself

2 Sacco was here referring to the following: Noam Chomsky, *The Fateful Triangle; The United States, Israel and the Palestinians* (London, Pluto Press,1983); Edward W. Said, *The Question of Palestine* (New York: Vintage Books, 1992); Christopher Hitchens and Edward Said, eds., *Blaming the victims: spurious scholarship and the Palestinian question* (London: Verso, 1987).

3 Said, foreword in *Palestine*, iii.

4 Said, foreword in *Palestine*, iii.

> as a relatively educated person. So it was news to me that I didn't know shit about this subject.'[5]

Sacco's distinctive style in *Palestine* partly drew on the many comic book innovations that had occurred in the late twentieth century, and also from much earlier models of political art and illustrated journalism, combined with stylistic characteristics and techniques that he had tried out in previous works.[6] Sacco is quite explicit about his visual models, and drew on a range of diverse sources, such as the early nineteenth-century political cartoons of George Cruikshank, and the work of contemporary comic book artists like Robert Crumb.[7] Sacco had also been exposed to the Palestinian cartoonist Najel Ali, and was aware of the precedents for political cartoons and comics in *Palestine*. He refers to the 'great respect for the power of the drawn image' that Palestinians have, an assumption based on the popularity of Ali's work.[8] Sacco's graphic novel was, however, fundamentally conceived for an American rather than a Middle East audience, and it may also be situated as a contemporary manifestation of the radical underground tradition of American comics.

The main narrative of *Palestine* takes the form of illustrated interviews with Palestinians in their homes in the occupied territories and in refugee camps. These are given a political dimension as Sacco pursues his theme of 'telling the other side'. The whole *Palestine* project is visually characterised by the repetition of the depiction of poverty and despair. Often this is overt, with images of deprivation, like Ammar's toilet in Nuseirat refugee camp; at others it is metaphorically suggested by, for example, the repetition of mud and rain as elements overwhelming domestic life.[9]

Palestine is conspicuously autobiographical, comprising many incidental sequences and asides that make constant reminders to the

5 Powers, 102.
6 Particularly his *Yahoo* (Seattle, Fantagraphics Books, 1991).
7 Sacco, interview with the author.
8 Powers, 107.
9 Sacco, *Palestine*, 16 and 218–219.

reader of Sacco's role as narrator and controller of the narrative. He is depicted as a constant presence throughout the novel, in a caricatured fashion reminiscent of the late eighteenth-/early nineteenth-century cartoonists like Cruikshank and James Gillray. Traditional print mediums such as etching or engraving are also referenced in the cross-hatching of his shading, used conspicuously in places. Both *Palestine* and his later work *Safe Area Gorazde* share fundamentally the same unrelenting realism of the day-by-day existence of people forced to endure a war situation, in the presence of Sacco as narrator. Sacco studied journalism at university, and believes that his work stems more from his journalistic background than it does from any of his visual training.[10]

Sacco has always claimed to have had 'total control' over the creation of *Palestine*, and encountered no attempt at political censorship at any point in the process of production.[11] Although the issues that he covered were as contentious as those Spiegelman dealt with in *Maus*, Sacco's relative anonymity was perhaps an advantage in both his research and production of *Palestine*. This 'low visibility' as he describes it, is true of many of these graphic novel authors when they were working on their respective graphic novels.[12] It was only post-publication that any of them (mostly Spiegelman and Satrapi) received media attention. Media prominence would almost certainly have brought pressure and political censorship in its wake. Consequently Sacco faced few of the objections that might have been expected from a work that may be vulnerable to interpretation as anti-Semitic.

Sacco's enduring interests have been to develop visual representations alongside textual ones, to express such revelatory experiences. He has had a long interest in developing war comics, and he embarked on a long comic book about the Vietnam War which became formative in his attempts to visualise a war ravaged country. Importantly, he eventually gave up this project because of his lack of

10 Sacco, interview with the author.
11 Sacco, interview with the author.
12 Powers, 102.

first hand experience of the location and its people. [13] This was to become a crucial factor in Sacco's practice, a concern with the primacy of the experience; later he made this authenticity of experience a defining characteristic of his working process in *Palestine*.

Methods of Visualisation and Documentation

Like many graphic novels, *Palestine* started out as a series of short comic books (nine in total), which were later compiled and bound together to form two large volume graphic novels: *Palestine: A Nation Occupied,* and *Palestine: In the Gaza Strip*.[14] In May 2001 Fantagraphics republished these again, but this time together as one volume entitled simply *Palestine*, with the foreword by Said.[15] *Palestine* was written and drawn from February 1993 to August 1995, and there are small dates on the bottom of each page to indicate the exact date of the production of that page. The pages were, however, usually drawn much later than the research, and often back in the US where Sacco lives, rather than on location in Palestine. He spent two months in Palestine and Israel, and his method of research was to carry out lengthy interviews with Palestinians living in the occupied territories and in refugee camps. These usually took place in the homes of the Palestinians, often during curfew hours. Sacco's journalistic background (he refers to the project as 'comics journal-

13 Powers, 95–96.

14 The first issues of the nine parts of *Palestine* in serial form sold about 2,500 copies each, but then sales slumped; they 'dipped below 2000 – very low', as Sacco remarked (interview with the author).

15 Prior to *Palestine* Sacco had worked on *Yahoo*, a series of comics that dealt in part with the Gulf War, and made reference to the Palestinian situation. The style of drawing and page layout in *Yahoo* was very similar to *Palestine*, and Sacco seemed to have used it consistently throughout both works.

ism') meant that he had been trained to take detailed written notes during his interviews with the Palestinians in their homes.[16]

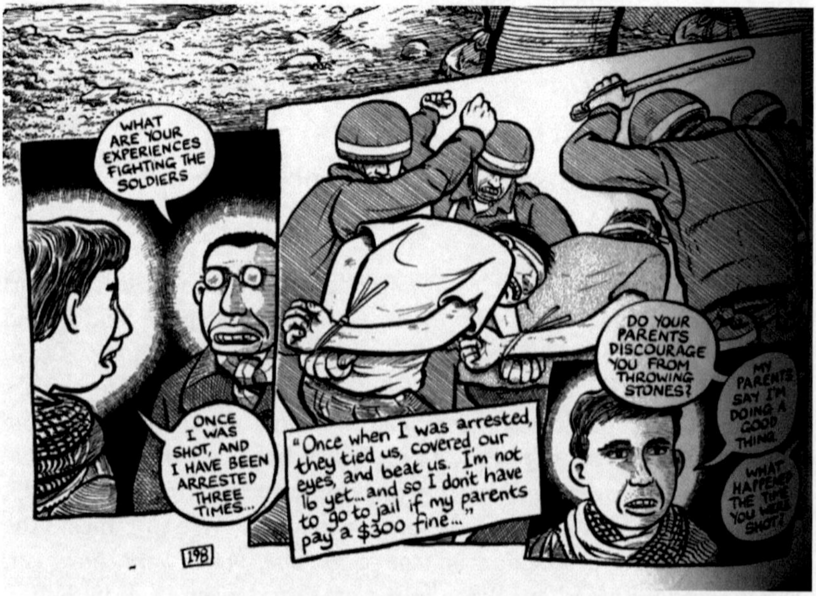

Figure 4.1. Sacco's technique for depicting his interviews with Palestinians, with overlapping sub-frames and a voice-over for the interviewee (*Palestine,* 2001, 198, detail). © Joe Sacco 2001; reproduced with permission of Fantagraphics Books Inc.

Sacco often depicts himself as an interviewer, sometimes in mini-portrait frames with the interviewee in close proximity (figure 4.1). As he explained, many photographs were taken after the talking was over – never before or during, to avoid the mistrust that might otherwise have been generated.[17] In the narrative itself Sacco's interviewees refer to their mistrust of Western journalists who took photographs but made no attempt to describe the real experience of life under occupation. It is important to note, and surprising, considering the

16 Sacco, interview with the author.
17 Sacco, interview with the author.

seemingly meticulous attention to observed detail of the graphic novel pages, that sketches and drawings were not used during any of the interviews, nor were any sketchbooks kept during the visits. Copious notes were made, however, and these would be written up rigorously each evening in Sacco's journal – often in far from comfortable surroundings.[18] Sacco developed his extensive use of these documentary techniques earlier in his career, working with a touring rock band (part of the subject of his earlier *Yahoo*). Although Sacco's use of the camera was methodical, painstakingly building up images from multiple camera shots from different viewpoints, the drawings themselves would not be created until he had returned from his research visits.

Topography

From his photographs Sacco would extrapolate further when making the drawings, constructing imaginary viewpoints – often aerial – from many photographs taken at ground level, his only visual access. The illustration of the surveillance tower in Jabalia refugee camp is an example of this practice, where the tower is drawn from an aerial viewpoint, showing its roof and the surrounding streets below, and is clearly an imaginary drawing, given that it is seen from 'forbidden' space above the tower.[19] Sacco explains that he had taken many photographs from ground level, and later developed from these sources the high-view depiction ('pulling the angle up', as he put it) that appears in the novel.[20] This was a common practice for Sacco, and one that he routinely carried out during his production of the novel. He also points out that this is an approach that he largely abandoned when working on his next project in Bosnia, *Safe Area Gorazde*, at least in so far as the interest in the variety of viewpoints is

18 Sacco, interview with the author.

19 Sacco, interview with the author; example referred to is *Palestine* 2001, 191.

20 Sacco, interview with the author.

concerned.[21] Sacco refers to these changes in viewpoint as being too visually complex – 'overdone', and at times distracting from the narrative events. He describes the Gorazde work as less technically experimental by comparison. When asked why he had used so many angles of viewpoint in *Palestine*, Sacco responded that he felt that it offered him a pictorial challenge, one that 'made it [the drawing of the books] more interesting'[22].

Sacco's method for constructing the topographical images of towns involved a similar operation. He would take numerous photographs of all of the main features of a place, such as buildings, streets, and fences, and from these create pictorial 'maps'. Jabalia refugee camp, for instance, is presented from an elevated viewpoint, a topographical view of the town with its inhabitants (figure 4.2). Sacco emphasises that he liked the idea of the spectator being able to 'navigate' between the buildings and streets as if familiar with the place. These 'roofscapes', as he describes them, often consist of depicting a place from a variety of viewpoints that it was impossible for him to obtain from his photographs. His drawing style is characterised by his use of this elevated viewing position throughout *Palestine*, to demonstrate the nature of the terrain, the landscapes and the buildings.

For the Jabalia pages Sacco delved into landscape European tradition for his viewpoint, the topographical layout of the town, and for the detailed grouping of the characters. Formally these scenes are reminiscent of the village landscapes of sixteenth-century Flemish painting, such as those of Pieter Bruegel (figure 4.3). Sacco was working with a large reservoir of art historical imagery to draw upon, including the well-known and established tradition of European painting. Bruegel frequently used an elevated viewpoint for his village scenes, of which *The Kermess of Hoboken* is typical. His landscapes are often populated with numerous groups of figures, each of which offers an anecdotal narrative.

21 Joe Sacco, *Safe Area Gorazde, The War in Eastern Bosnia 1992–95* (Seattle: Fantagraphics Books, 2000).

22 Sacco, interview with the author.

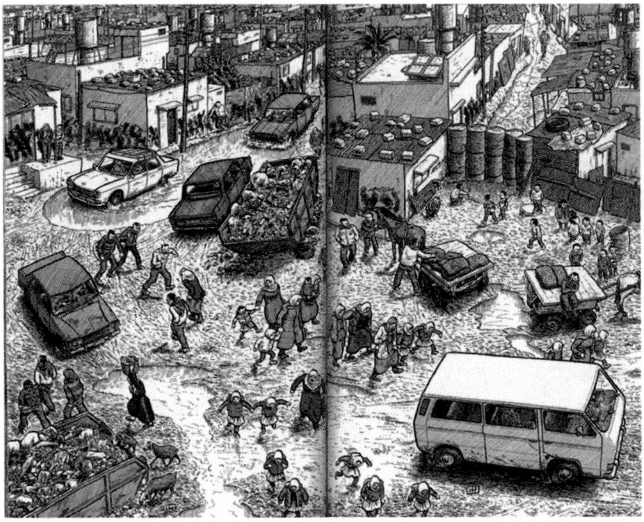

Figure 4.2. Jabalia refugee camp; an aerial view of the inhabitants going about their daily business. (*Palestine* 2001, p. 146–147). © Joe Sacco 2001; reproduced with permission of Fantagraphics Books Inc.

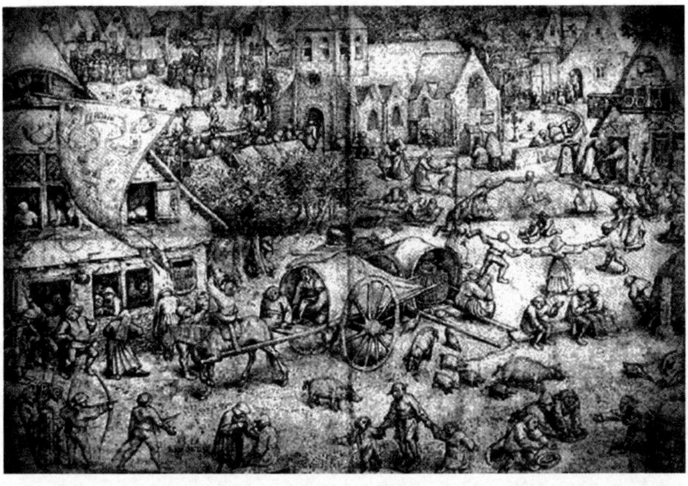

Figure 4.3. Features similar to Sacco's Jabalia refugee camp views are found in Pieter Bruegel's sixteenth-century drawings, such as *The Kermess of Hoboken* (1559). Reproduced with permission of the Courtauld Institute of Art, London.

The church festival theme of Bruegel's drawing appears almost secondary to the image, crowded as it is with seemingly extraneous detail. These informal groups of figures were known in Bruegel's time as 'naer het leven', meaning 'from life'.[23]

The stylistic similarities of Sacco's depictions of refugee camps to feudal landscape images, like those of the Flemish narratives of rural life, make a parallel with the almost feudal system of life imposed by the Israeli occupation. In places Sacco is more explicit about the feudal nature of social organisation in these camps, governed by the occupying military and the local militias. The disguised militia men who Sacco depicts stalking Nuseirat camp are described in the text boxes as beyond international or even national law, forming makeshift alliances and wielding unaccountable power:

> ...there's conventions made in Geneva for an occupying power to follow....there's UN resolutions calling for the occupying power to withdraw...But at the moment on a stretch of mire between Block 1 and Block 2 in Nuseirat camp, these are the guys in charge...it's their law now, whatever that might be.[24]

The regression from secular democracy that Sacco noted above is closely associated with his depictions of poverty and the resistance to these conditions that he had observed in the Palestinian refugee camps. John Barrell has discussed at length the representation of the poverty in the landscape painting of the eighteenth and nineteenth centuries.[25] He argues that what is *omitted* in representations is always of political significance. In what appeared to be pastoral idylls

23 Ludwig Münz, *Bruegel: The Drawings* (London: Phaidon, 1968), 21–23. Lionello Venturi explains in his study of Bruegel's work that this drew from humanist philosophies like those of Abraham Ortelius. He encouraged Bruegel to make a more secular depiction of events, with a focus on the specific characteristics of the figures and their environment. Lionello Venturi, *The Great Centuries of Painting: The Sixteenth Century; from Leonardo to El Greco* (Switzerland: Skira. 1956), 157.

24 Sacco, *Palestine*, 163.

25 John Barrell, *The Dark Side of the Landscape. The Rural Poor in English Painting 1730–1840* (Cambridge: Cambridge University Press, 1980).

peopled by contented or productive workers, the 'sensibilities' of the landscape painter were the product of a social structure that ensured that the artist would not depict workers the 'wrong' way. 'Wrong' being, as Barrell explains, depictions that showed signs of their distress or their discontent at their exploitation.[26] The role of the figure in the landscape is as complex in what is concealed as what is depicted:

> [...] in the mid-eighteenth century they work blithely, for work is then a pleasantly social activity; at the end of the century, cheerfully, to reassure us that they do not resent their condition, or blame us for it; in the work of Constable, automatically, and in the distance, for the resentments of the poor are now known to us all, and those resentments could not be concealed in any credible image of the poor except by hiding the poor in the middle ground, where we can see their labour but not their expressions.[27]

In Sacco's drawing of Jabalia the stylistic similarities to European landscape painting belied the radical shift of content, in Barrell's terms. Sacco's people are depicted as physically and spatially compromised, and quite clearly so. They are shown having to negotiate puddles, skips and barricades simply to move around their homes. They are depicted as cold, dejected and resigned, judging by Sacco's use of body language and facial expression. The physical obstructions of the environment may also be interpreted as an expression of the social obstructions the occupying forces imposed on Palestinians. Every building and feature in the Jabalia splash pages demonstrates the evidence of makeshift labour. The bricks placed on the roofs, the stains on the walls, the piled high skips, the footprints and muddy feet. Most of the environment has the gestures and traces of inhabitants inscribed upon it, which, in *Palestine*, offers evidence of oppression. Throughout *Palestine* Sacco refers to the impediments to individual ambition and to community aspirations, as well as the interference in, and control of, employment and production. This dystopic image is made all the more poignant by a likeness to the

26 Barrell, 19.
27 Barrell, 21.

scrupulously observed compositions of European artists, as well as to topographical traditions. Coming as it does in a graphic novel sequence it presents a vista between the sandwiched frames of the preceding and succeeding pages. The depiction of the opening out of a vista is paradoxical, since it primarily represents confinement.

Threatened Spaces

The topography of space is perhaps a primary site of intellectual and physiological competition in Palestine and Israel. Sacco's very act of mapping out the spaces that Palestinians occupy is itself a political act. Enraged by these conditions, Said expressed it as follows:

> [...] There has been no modification in the essential Zionist vision which condemns the Palestinian to a more precarious, less perceptible existence day by day. It is plainly there for everyone, Arab and Jew alike, to witness. No secret is made of this plan, no palliative or sugar coating seems to be required. We are taking the land detail by detail, inch by inch, house by house. [28]

Said's lament for the relentless land appropriation by Israel on an ethnically discriminatory basis was shared by Sacco, and both he and Said refer to United Nations resolutions that call for an end to the military occupation and the cessation of demolition of Palestinian homes for settlements on occupied territory.

Many prominent writers on the Middle East highlighted the continued building of Jewish settlements by Israel in contravention of these resolutions, Said and Chomsky included. Such criticism informed the work of Sacco, and the building of settlements is a topic to which he returns both in interview and as a subject for his drawing in *Palestine*.[29] The appropriation of space and land for Jews, and the consequent compression of space for Palestinians are represented in part by Sacco's depictions of space in *Palestine*. The perspective

28 Edward W. Said, *The End of the Peace Process; Oslo and After* (London: Granta, 2000), 290.

29 Sacco, interview with the author; Sacco, *Palestine*, 27, one example of several.

systems that he applied, and then distorted, from his photographic images is a key feature of his work. The variety of his viewpoints, the modifications to the perspective systems, and indeed the constant manipulation of pictorial space are striking. This Sacco sustained by the sequential nature of the medium, with its frames and the necessity of page turning during the reading process. The result is the imposition upon the reader of spatial awareness; whether it is the vistas of refugee camps or the confined interiors of the living rooms, or the raked views of military lookout towers. These act as salient metaphors for the contested spaces that the military occupied and into which the Palestinians were crammed. The issue was thus kept alive in the graphic novel and is a cornerstone of Sacco's realism.

The concept of 'domestic space' sited in the spaces of the refugee camp space creates a tension to which Sacco returns at stages through the narrative, and Sacco gives us a glimpse of how much worse these anxieties must be in the occupied territories of Palestine, in the extreme poverty that is exacerbated by the ever-present threat of violence. The contingencies of living in a condition that is, by definition, temporary and subject to the vagaries of a tempestuous political situation, bring a singularity to his portrayal of the Palestinians' plight. Sacco explores their domestic existence by means of stark juxtapositions, comparing, for instance, the appalling sewage flood stains on the walls of the houses in contrast with the delicately adorned interiors.[30] Sacco's repertoire of viewpoints in interior scenes is large, employed to depict the restricted spaces of the Palestinians into whose homes he is invited for his interviews. He lifts the viewpoint to give aerial views of his hosts and himself, or drops the angle to give floor views, or zooms-in for extreme close-ups of his interviewees' faces. All of this may occur within the space of a double page spread as he extrapolates an extensive virtual space from the confinements of a cramped room in a refugee camp.[31] Like Ware, the utilisation of these visual dynamics is directed towards the exploration of the psychic experience as much as that of the physical space. This

30 Sacco, *Palestine*, 218–19, 187.
31 Sacco, *Palestine*, 66–67.

becomes evident through comparison with Gaston Bachelard's experiments with space as representative of psychic conception.

Bachelard's concept of the oneric house is founded upon the idea of the house as protective, offering the physical and psychic manifestation of shelter: "[If] I were asked to name the chief benefit of the house I should say: the house shelters daydreaming, the house protects the dreamer, the house allows one to dream in peace".[32] The homes that Sacco depicts in *Palestine* are almost the antithesis of shelter, particularly in the sense of psychic security to which Bachelard refers to above. Instead they are susceptible to attack, the target for demolition, as well as the object of deterioration through poverty. Bachelard's shelter for the daydreamer becomes, in Sacco's hands, the site of anxiety and psychosis. These homes are often in camps like Jabalia, crammed together with makeshift doors, widows and roofs; camps which have, in some cases, existed for over fifty years.[33] The original tents have been replaced by brick structures with weighted metal roofs, yet the houses retain the appearance of the temporary, the contingent. This is a result of the poverty, overcrowding and lack of maintenance that prevails there. Sacco's friend Sameh has a home in Jabalia camp in which the roof leaks around its ill-fitting edges, and the room is depicted giving direct access to the cold night through a gap at the top of the wall.[34] The temporary nature of the room is evident in other signs of contingency in Sacco's drawing: the oil lamp on the arm of the sofa, the corrugated metal roof, the exposed wiring; all of this is amplified by white diagonal streaks representing hail stones entering the room and falling upon the occupants. The sense of incongruity between the temporary and the permanent is heightened by Sacco's depiction of the pictures on the walls, the potted plants on tiered stands, the rugs, bedspreads, blanket cupboard and patterned soft furnishings: 'He'd created as

32 Gaston Bachelard, *The Poetics of Space*, trans. by Maria Jolas (Boston, Massachusetts: Beacon Press, 1994), 6.

33 Sacco, *Palestine*, 184.

34 Sacco, *Palestine*, 181.

much of a refuge for himself as circumstances allowed...' (figure 4.4).[35]

Domesticity is, as Said points out, not merely evident in Palestinian homes but proclaimed therein by a variety of decorative means.[36] For Said these have come to represent solidarity, belonging to a Palestinian interior life, as well as a resistance to living in threatened accommodation under military occupation.[37] Said speaks of the term *min al-dakhil,* which he translates as "from the interior", as having a special resonance for Palestinians.[38] Originally designating Palestinians who lived within the 1948 boundary of the Israeli State, he discusses the way that the term acquired new meanings as Palestinian territory diminished, with the corresponding number of those living in appropriated territories or in exile increasing.[39] He goes on to argue that this term has further connotations that refer to specific social codes, such as those of recognition and the solidarity of shared experience, particularly that of loss. Said later ventures the idea that the interior decoration of Palestinian homes may be in some way representative of these ideas, a material expression of this sense of social interiority:

> The oddness of these excesses, and asymmetries, their constitutively anti-aesthetic effect, their communicated insecurity seem to symbolize exile - exile from a place, from a past, from the actuality of a home.[40]

These contradictory domestic Palestinian spaces, interiors that may be at once expressing exile as well as interiority, are an important feature of Sacco's work; key meetings in these interior spaces attenuate his narrative.

35 Sacco, *Palestine*, 187.
36 Edward W. Said, and Jean Mohr, *After the Dark Sky, Palestinian Lives* (London: Vintage. 1993).
37 Said and Mohr, 51–62.
38 Said and Mohr, 51.
39 Said and Mohr, 51–52.
40 Said and Mohr, 61.

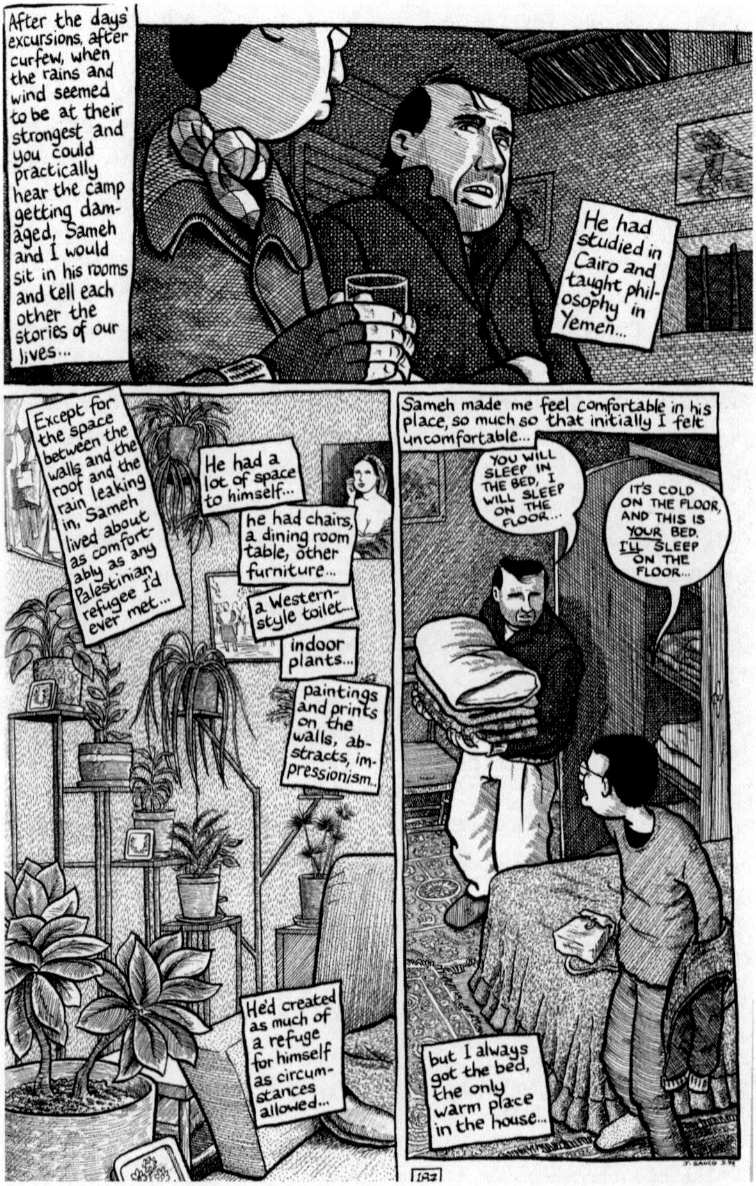

Figure 4.4. The decorated interior of Sameh's home. (*Palestine*, p.187). © Joe Sacco 2001; reproduced with permission of Fantagraphics Books Inc.

Each occasion is marked by the characteristics upon which Said commented: too much tea, offerings of comfort in excess of that available to the inhabitants, hospitality that is almost imposed as a mark of defiance.

In the tea sharing sequence at Nuseirat (figure 4.5) for instance, Sacco demonstrates his bewilderment at the repetition of ritual and anecdote that he encounters as they discuss their plight. Sacco also explores the idea, which Said articulated, that amongst many Palestinians who have been evicted there exists a condition of 'waiting': waiting to return.[41] This persists from generation to generation, and Said gives the example of the retention of deeds of houses reoccupied or destroyed by the original occupants long after all possibility of actual reclamation has gone.[42]

One of Sacco's methods for depicting their temporary homes includes layering text boxes to work to facilitate his depiction of space. Thus the interior of the Palestinian home in Nuseirat refugee camp, for instance, is plastered with text cartouches that dominate the image beneath.[43] Reminiscent of the confident displays of text in the European political cartoons of the eighteenth and nineteenth centuries (those of James Gillray, for example), this device has the effect of creating the equivalent of a window through which we peer. The picture plane is revealed and simultaneously the illusion of the space beyond is heightened; added to which is the occlusion of people and objects within the frame, brought about by the vertical line of the text cartouches. These are parcels of information that occupy the flat space of the picture plane and represent Sacco's private thoughts, which are also those of the guiding narrator. Simultaneously he develops the virtual space of the room, with the tea ritual and the anecdotes in full flow. Using shading by means of cross-hatching, he adds pictorial depth in the scene and allows us, the viewer/reader, to inhabit the space vicariously from this high vantage point. The exploration of the interior of the home is induced by these means, as the reader is

41 Said, "In Search of Palestine."
42 Sacco, *Palestine*, 152.
43 Sacco, *Palestine*, 152.

stimulated to imaginatively complete the missing parts of the space, thus corroborating the illusion created by the artist.

The idea of the refugee camp accords with the concept of the heterotopia, first mooted by Michael Foucault in 1967.[44] Foucault speculated on the existence of specific places common to all historical formations wherein particular kinds of social relation are expressed. The examples he gives are "crisis heterotopias" and "heterotopias of deviation".[45] The latter are those spaces created to accommodate groups considered deviant, as an expression of their relation to dominant accounts of normality: such spaces are prisons and psychiatric hospitals in Foucault's examples.[46] The social relations expressed in Sacco's representation of the refugee camp of Jabalia seem to comply with this heterotopic model, whereby the inhabitants' perceived status and culture runs contrary to the dominant social group, making them, de facto, deviant. The refugee camp contains and renders anodyne the threat of this deviance, and may be maintained indefinitely or relocated at the behest of the more powerful social group. One of Sacco's declared aims in writing *Palestine* was to resist the containment that such an ideological imposition implies, the privileging of one group and the impoverishment of another, resulting in the forced persistence of a huge and unwilling social configuration, the refugee camp.[47]

Sacco's resistance to the refugee camp heterotopia in the *Palestine* narrative is achieved partly through depictions of the domestic and interior life of Palestinians. At home in the camps the Palestinians are frequently depicted partaking in the ubiquitous tea ritual of hospitality. Their detailed anecdotes are interpolated as short sequences within the larger sequence of the autobiographical narrative. This often has the effect of creating imagined space inserted

44 Michael Foucault, "Different Spaces," in *Aesthetics, Method and Epistemology: Essential Works of Foucault, Volume Two,* ed. James D. Faubion, 175–85 (Allen Lane: Penguin, 1998).

45 Foucault, 179–80.

46 Foucault, 179–80.

47 Sacco, interview with the author.

into the domestic space: the virtual boundary of the interiors are disrupted by the intensity of the inserted tales of desperation and crises, as they relive their experiences, depicted as if taking place at the moment of interview. Thus the domestic space is invaded by vicarious experience, just as the transient space of the refugee camp is susceptible to violation by the occupying soldiers or the local militias that rule in the absence of effective civil institutions protecting human rights.

The domestic spaces represented by Sacco, like Ware, are often rendered in a state of unsettled transience, ranging from the sterile to the dilapidated, and often these sites of disquiet and unease are in keeping with the theories of ideological space put forward by Said and Foucault. Bachelard's daydreams are replaced by anxieties and psychoses in these spaces, and the irreconcilable ambiguities of illusionism act as a metaphor for the uncertainties of lived experience, offering us a bleak concept of domestic space.

The reality of discrimination is illustrated through the concept of pictorial space in other ways in *Palestine*. Even incidental narrative events, like the movement of cars along a road as Sacco travelled between West Bank towns, is illustrated by the unequal division of space.[48] In one example, numerous cars are shown queuing and, by virtue of the aerial viewpoint, are contained within the left third of a frame. The only car depicted on the right two-thirds of the same frame space is a settler's car, moving unhindered, although its movement is shown with minimal marks. More important than depicting its movement is the space that it had been allowed to occupy, a visual reference to the discriminatory rules that Sacco discusses in his text; a practice where Palestinians' cars are marked with blue number plates, enabling the curtailing of movement of one ethnic group, to the advantage of another.

48 Sacco, *Palestine*, 274.

Technical Characteristics of Palestine

Sacco's use of frames is particularly varied, with floating panels, pages without frames at all, frames that are absent but implied by groupings of characters (even where figures were partly occluded) and overlapping frames. In one series of pages the frames are shaded black and begin to contract page by page, as the narrative deals with imprisonment and interrogation.[49] The frames 'imprison' the characters as the drama is played out, a straightforward adaptation of the diminishing frame convention that normally 'speeds up' the assimilation of the visual and textual information. This contrasts with the opening out of the frames upon the release of the interrogated into a busy Jerusalem street, where the passers-by have no idea what has been happening behind the nearby walls.

The pages of *Palestine* vary in format, a technique Sacco had also deployed in *Yahoo*. Some pages are only partly image, with large areas of text, whilst others, like the 'splash' (double) page of the view of Jabalia (figure 4.2), are the opposite: almost entirely image, without frames and with little or no text. Some have the text presented as a newspaper column down one side of a series of frames that have no text balloons.[50] These departures from the usual conventions of comic book drawing give the book the appearance of illustrated text, or text captions to illustrations, especially where pages have no frames as such.

An important, defining function of the comic frame device is to provide a sequence that underpins the flow of the narrative as the story is 'read'. One of the problems of illustrated text, where one or two pictures give visual aid to extensive text, is that the coherency of the sequence might be lost. Sequence may still be impaired by a run of frames that jump in time, or location, or both. If 'action to action' sequence is one of McCloud's simplest and most common modes in a series of frames, then loss of continuity, even temporally, is disruptive

49 Sacco, *Palestine*, 102–113.

50 For example: Sacco, *Palestine*, 94–95.

to this mode.[51] Sacco tends to use these different modes, effectively making some parts of the book less comic-like and more concerned with epic narrative, referring to large sweeps of history. Aware of the pejorative use of the term 'illustration' in the discourse of fine art, Sacco insists that the novel is illustrative in a journalistic sense, linked to the idea of documentary.[52] It seems that his idea of illustration, as both concept and style, is fundamental to the project, in particular to the value that he gave to specificity. Specificity in this sense can be seen as a mode of resistance to the generalising tendencies of large media corporations, with the likely collapse of the 'general' into myth. The tendency, for example, of the term 'Palestinian' to be associated with the hostile and equally general concept of 'terrorist', is the signifying chain reaction that Sacco attempts to resist with specificity – in this case his detailed characterisation, in figure 4.5 for instance. The reader 'meets' Masud and Ibrahim in their front room in Nuseirat on a wet and muddy January afternoon, and 'hears' their discussion while 'drinking' tea – the flavour of which is considered in some detail.[53]

The strong sense of a specific location brought about by a detailed image like that of Jabalia, creates some pictorial problems in *Palestine*, particularly in terms of graphic novel sequencing. Sacco explains that occasionally such images are counterproductive in the reading of a sequence, where the reader might dwell upon an image too long and find it too interesting, at the cost of the smooth flow of the narrative.[54] Comparing *Palestine* to *Safe Area Gorazde* it is easy to see how the more regular and consistent framing of the sequences in the latter gave less of sense of a diversion.

51 McCloud, 74.
52 Sacco, interview with the author.
53 Sacco, *Palestine*, 8–12.
54 Sacco, interview with the author.

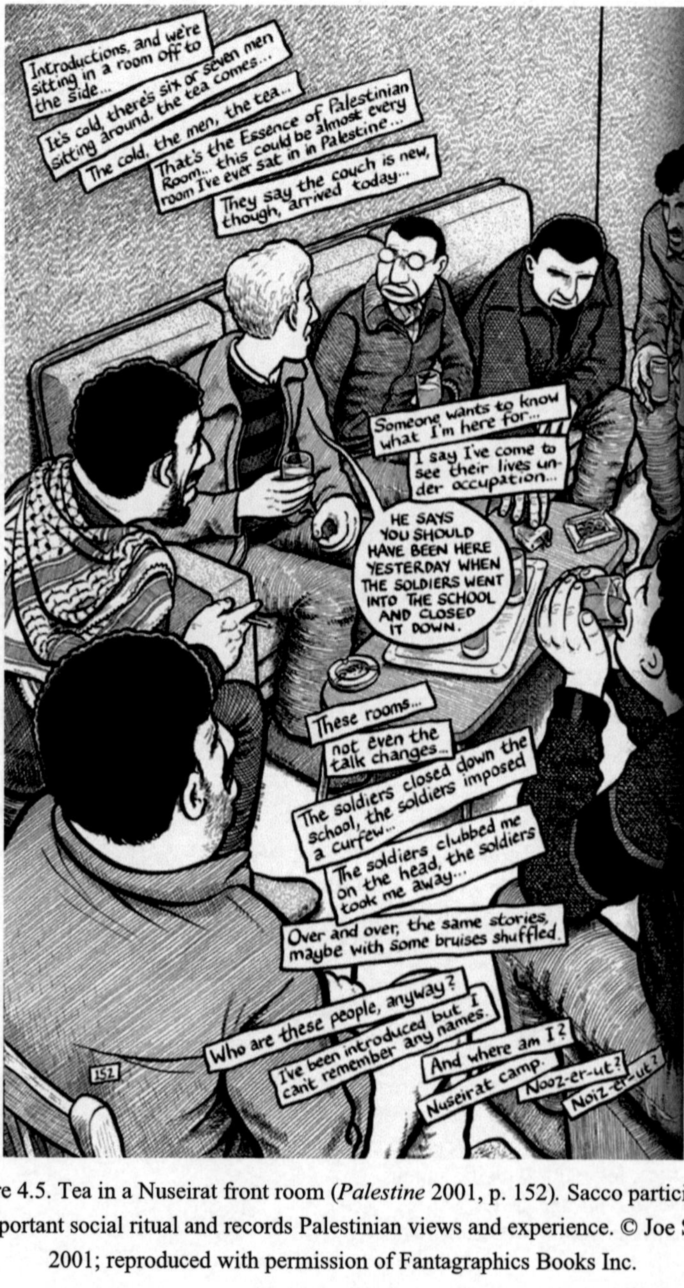

Figure 4.5. Tea in a Nuseirat front room (*Palestine* 2001, p. 152). Sacco participates in important social ritual and records Palestinian views and experience. © Joe Sacco 2001; reproduced with permission of Fantagraphics Books Inc.

In this respect *Gorazde* is more like *Maus*, which overall has a remarkable consistency of frame size and uniformity of text and shading. The more dynamic, varied approach of Sacco in *Palestine* does, however, give a pictorial excitement that is as compelling as it is distracting. Importantly, it allows for a higher level of visualisation of the locations. The evidence of painstaking labour in the images enhances this, with cross-hatching that is also reminiscent of pre-lithographic printing processes, like etching or engraving. These signify as labour and assiduousness on the part of the artist, with his painstaking method of production acting as a metaphor for the content, also laboriously researched.

Text

Sacco favours narrated text in a caption or cartouche (rectangular text boxes overlaying the image) type of format, rather than speech balloons, where the text 'floats' over the image, without a tail directed at any figure in particular, even at himself as narrator (figure 4.5). The occasions where he does use standard speech bubbles are in the minority. The text boxes, in their cartouche/caption format, have an additional visual function, which is to 'anchor' vision in places across the page, a feature that he is inclined to use in moments of narrative tension.[55] Figure 4.6 for example, is of Palestinians in close physical contact as protesters are arrested.[56] This demonstrates the structure of the text binding together the looseness of the unframed images. Sacco comments that he had been criticised for using too much text, and at times the pages are blanketed with dozens of cartouches.[57] In this protest scene the boxes of text are 'scattered' across the page; melodrama is conveyed, not by a sequence of action-to-action frames, but by a sequence of text boxes. These guide the reading and

55 Sacco, interview with the author.
56 Sacco, *Palestine*, 56.
57 Sacco, interview with the author.

visualisation of the image, and assist with the choreographic theme of the textual narrative at this point.

The device of text boxes also enables the frames to become panel-like, lacking any particular sequence. When this device is used the text boxes are often not attributed to any single character, in such a way that 'the words hold together the clumps of panels [frames]', as Sacco puts it.[58] Sacco's repertoire of image and text strategies is very full, and the visual strategies, that he later deliberately reined in when working on *Gorazde*, are plentiful in *Palestine*. [59] As with the Situationists' comic books, Sacco recognises the power of the text and the opportunities that it provides for radical reinterpretation of images, through the imposition of meaning specific to the text. Irrespective of the image, the text conventions enable a set of meanings to be generated. When in conjunction with an image these meanings are immediately modified, but still retain at least the residue of their former meanings, albeit in unpredictable ways.

Radical practices: Cinematic Devices

Sacco, like many graphic novelists, was keen to appropriate the visual language of the cinema in so far as it could be adapted for a graphic novel. Manga artists like Katsuhiro Otomo, in works like *Akira* and *Domu,* pursue styles with characteristics that are clearly intended to reference the cinema[60]. Otomo's repertoire includes attempts at rapidly changing frame angles like those of a camera operator trying to create a sense of vertigo, and different print techniques (e.g. half-tone) to different parts of the same picture to imitate filters that are applied to a camera lens. Sacco uses cinematic techniques throughout the pages of *Palestine*, one of which is the frequently repeated device of changing the viewpoint on a page several times, typically from high to low and back again. Similarly, either between pages or on the same

58 Sacco, interview with the author.
59 Sacco, interview with the author.
60 Katsuhiro Otomo, *Domu*, (Mandarin, 1994).

page, Sacco uses a variety of 'focal' distances for his viewpoint.[61] These imitate the camera's ability to 'zoom', and to pan across a view. Mixing these together increases the references to film and enhances the cinematic feel of the work, in common with many contemporary graphic novelists that have sought to develop their work in this way, Chris Ware being a prominent example.[62]

Dziga Vertov's 1920s' film *Man with the Movie Camera* is a seminal piece of film-making that established the declared use – as opposed to disguised use – of the camera and lens. According to Malcolm Turvey, [63] who discusses in some depth the relationship between the mechanical camera and sight, Vertov thought that the film camera's 'seeing' was superior to human sight. Enthralled as he was with this technology, Vertov believed that it posed the possibilities of revolutionary social change: enlightened 'seeing' being commensurate with the goals of political revolution. The key feature that distinguish Vertov's films are his awareness of the camera as machine, with images mediated through the physical properties of the lens. The mediation of vision by the camera is always explicit, and the audience is not permitted to forget or suspend disbelief about the act of watching a film. Such techniques, which militate against the mystifying power of narrative and illusion, are characteristics of film production later championed by critics like Laura Mulvey.[64]

Lens-based media are referenced throughout *Palestine*, in a kind of simulation of the techniques of camera and lens awareness that Vertov championed. This has the effect of increasing the documentary aspects of the work, in that it references film and TV, which are the most familiar media forms of the genre.

61 Sacco, *Palestine*, 56–57 and 125.

62 Ware, *Jimmy Corrigan*.

63 Malcolm Turvey, "Can the Camera See? Mimesis in 'Man with the Movie Camera,'" *October* 89 (Summer 1999): 25–50.

64 Laura Mulvey, "Visual Pleasure and Narrative Cinema," *Screen* 16.3, (1975): 6–18.

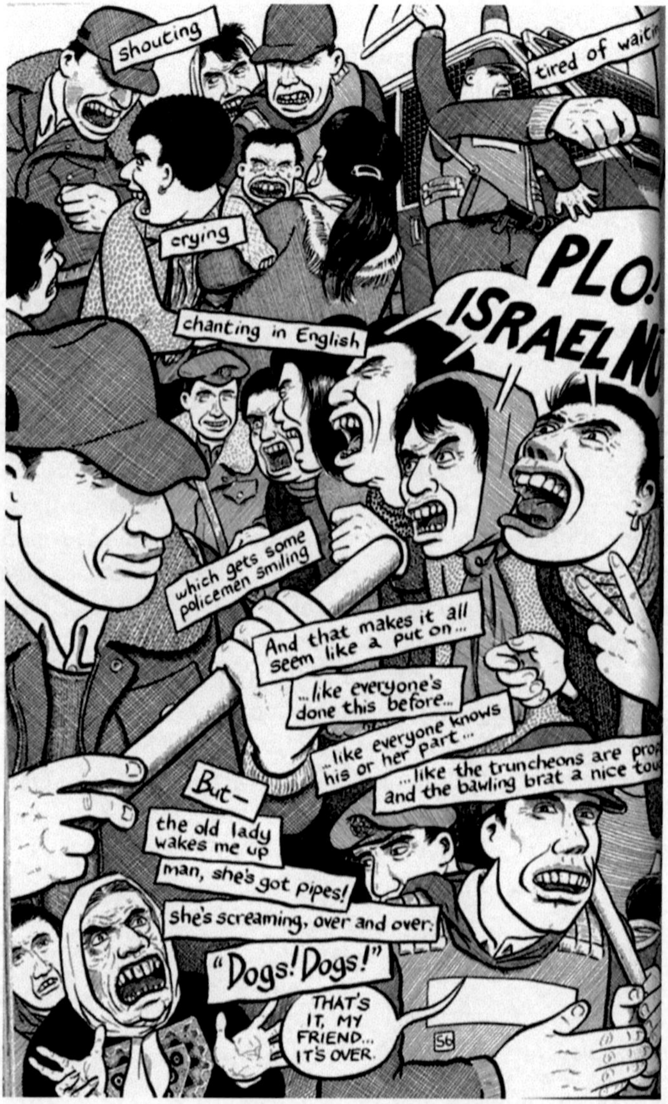

Figure 4.6. Cinematic viewpoints and text boxes choreograph a protest scene (*Palestine,* 2001, p.56). © Joe Sacco 2001; reproduced with permission of Fantagraphics Books Inc.

In figure 4.6, for instance, Sacco deploys a number of cinema-referencing devices; these occur alongside a number of forms and techniques that were comparatively new and unfamiliar at the time, in graphic novel terms. The close-ups of the protesters and soldiers are divided into four viewpoint sections. The top band is also subdivided in terms of viewpoint, into two overlapping sections; the page is thus divided into compartments governed by viewpoints, despite the absence of the traditional comic frames or cells. This may be seen to correspond to the 'split screen' of the cinema, where several scenes or narratives are played concurrently, a device that Vertov used. Each of the horizontal sections is drawn from a different viewpoint, and exhibit distortions of space characteristic of a camera lens distortion, but not of unassisted sight. The largest soldier on the middle left of this section appears closer and lower than the other figures in that section. Reading these images in their complex space and temporal variability – the order of events is determined more by the text than by the visual sequence – follow conventions that are established through the context of the cinema as well as the context of graphic novel production.

Both Sacco and Vertov make the act of learning new conventions of representation apparent; the reader, once comprehending the innovation in the convention, can now read the medium as life-like. As Williams explains, the concept of mimesis (or 'life-like') is determined entirely by our familiarity with the codes that are employed in the medium. He insists that there is actually no such thing as life-like:

> Realist art... is seen as simply one convention among others, a set of formal representations, in a particular medium to which we have become accustomed. The object is not really lifelike but by convention and repetition has been made to appear so.[65]

65 Raymond Williams, *Keywords* (London: Flamingo, 1983), 'Realism' entry.

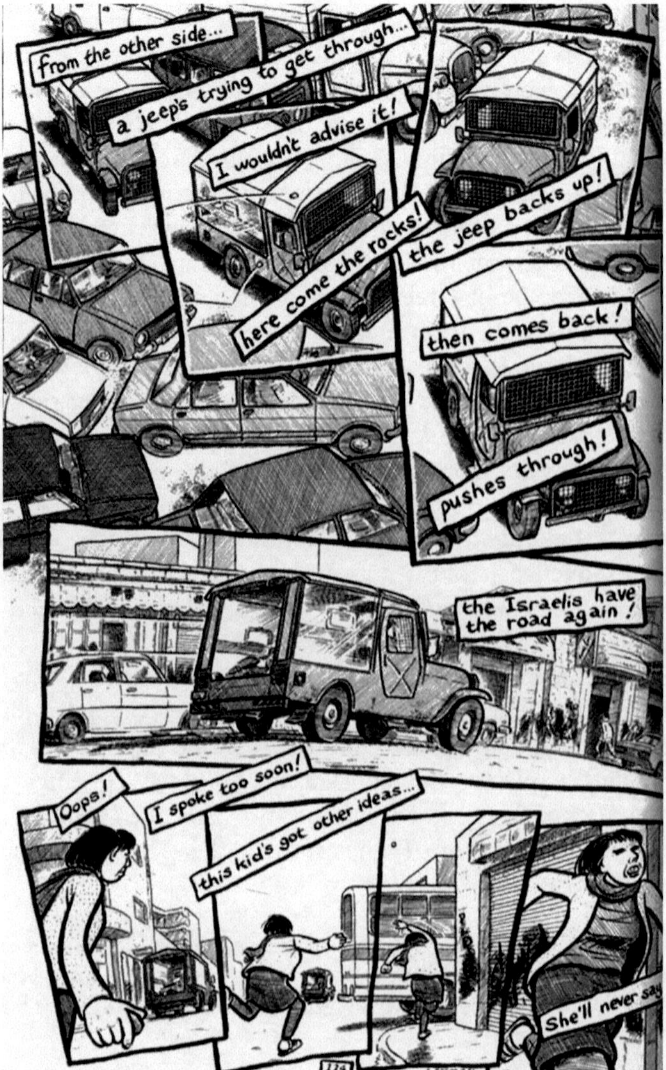

Figure 4.7. Sacco's use of clusters of panels with text boxes to help navigate the page, with overlaid transparent temporal zones to emphasise the tension and drama of the scene. (*Palestine* 2001, p.124). © Joe Sacco 2001; reproduced with permission of Fantagraphics Books Inc.

Occasionally Sacco is particularly ambitious with the conventions that ordinarily denote time and sequence. In figure 4.7 he employs clustered frames representing different moments in quick succession occurring in the same space across the page. In this case the frames represent temporal intervals detached from the usual signifying of physical space. The picture remains coherent and unified underneath the frames as the jeep image 'crosses' over it, 'carrying' the frames with it. Similarly the woman in the sequence at the base of the page is hurrying along within her own frame (like a camera frame) over a single large image. Like Vertov's camera lens in the *Man with the Movie Camera*, the spectator is constantly reminded of the medium, the act of watching and interpreting the representation.

For the new reader, Sacco's graphic novels instil unfamiliarity, a state of pre-learnedness, which seems to be a crucial stage in the reception and interpretation of graphic codes. This is the stage where the novelty of the new visual experience unexpectedly enhances the effectiveness of the political meaning. As with Vertov's insistence on the presence of the camera lens through focusing, reflection and distortion, so too with Sacco's predilection for pushing the conventions for graphic mark-making to the boundaries of the prevailing signifying process. Like Vertov's call for 'revolutionary' ways of seeing to be allied to political radicalism, so Sacco applied his devices in situations where the graphic marks are synonymous with a metaphor of 'seeing' anew. The realism of his work is a political radicalism integrated into a technical radicalism, located in the broad traditions of comic book production and political cartooning.

The Iconography of Protest

The iconography of textual and visual relationships has a long history within the field of political cartooning, of which Sacco is well aware. He was particularly influenced by Cruikshank's prints of the *Peterloo* atrocity (figure 4.8), a depiction of the violent suppression by cavalry charge of a political reformists' rally in Manchester in 1819. It is an important example of the historical, political cartooning that was to inform his practice in *Palestine.*[66] As Sacco explains, he was sufficiently interested and informed about the massacre, and the images of Cruikshank in particular, that he visited Manchester to see the location and to research the event locally.[67] Cruikshank, as John Wardroper has pointed out, was well aware of the class basis of the event, with middle class anxiety at the organisation of the poor and working classes depicted through both the text and the composition of his wood engraving.[68]

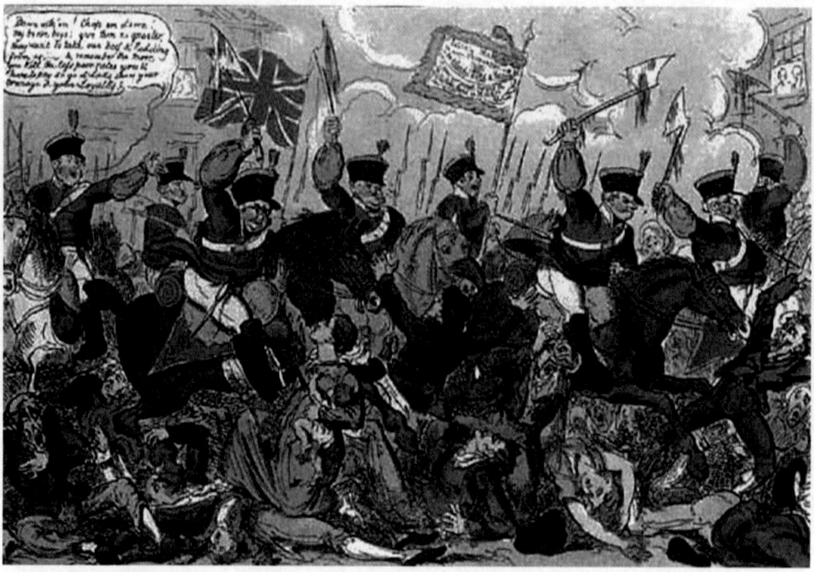

Figure 4.8. George Cruikshank's wood engraving of the Peterloo atrocity, *Massacre at St. Peter's* (1819).

Compositionally the *Peterloo* print has a horizontal division into upper and lower sections, which divide it into social class categories

66 Sacco, interview with the author.

67 Sacco, interview with the author.

68 John Wardroper, *The Caricatures of George Cruikshank* (London: Gordon Fraser, 1977), 79.

as well as visual groups; the troops, comprising 'small shopkeepers or farmers' are arranged in the upper half above the trampled poor and dispossessed in the lower half.[69] The class difference is also signified in Cruikshank's print by his caricaturing of the figures as fat (well fed) above and thin (underfed) below. A subtler signifier of oppression is achieved through Cruikshank's application of classical motifs to the lower half – the kneeling woman and the dead woman both reference heroic figures from classical and romantic history painting. The horse riders, however, were given bloated and grotesque caricatured figures, devoid of such references.

When Sacco came to depict scenes of conflict in *Palestine* he used similar techniques. In the page where troops and civilians meet head on in conflict (figure 4.6) Sacco, like Cruikshank, accentuates the oppressive and violent actions of the soldiers through the claustrophobic use of space – he has removed the frames and squashed many characters into the page. The squeezing is emphasised by the overlapping of the 'scenes', the enlarged scale of some figures, and the occlusions that occur at the page edges and between the tableaux he has created. Just as Cruikshank had depicted suffering by condensing images of people contained within the spaces delineated by the horse's legs, so Sacco adopts a similar compression between groups of people that emphasises the visceral nature of the encounter.

Documenting Palestine

In Sacco's work visual memory, as with Nakazawa, Satrapi, and Spiegelman, plays an important and contentious part in the documentary process. As Sacco explains:

> […] memory has a lot to do with it. But the photographic reference has been pretty helpful. And there are a few times where I draw almost exactly what I've photographed. But very few times. Usually I'll change the angle or something like that. But often the photographs, like the ones I took in the Gaza Strip, give me a real good feel for what the place looks like. But now, at this point [1995],

69 Sacco, interview with the author.

> I pretty much draw things from memory because I've been drawing it for two and a half years now. It's not really a problem to come up with what a water tower looks like or whatever.[...] I think time takes its toll. Especially at my age. There's been a little greying of what things look like, but I don't think enough to make a noticeable effect at this point.[70]

From this we can see that despite his extensive note taking and photographs, he was working through his ideas from internalised visual experience. For Sacco the documentary process does not necessitate fidelity to written or photographic records. Instead the visual recording of experience is subordinate to a process of orchestration, transforming his records to the specific technical demands of the graphic novel medium. The changing viewpoints, grouping of figures, caricatures and text arrangements are all post-experience modifications made in the application of his material to this medium. Sacco makes no bones about this, openly declaring the subjectivity of the process. A subjectivity, moreover, that was structured politically.

Memory plays a major role in the content of the anecdotal narratives that he uses in reconstructing the Palestinian's experience of occupation. It is the recall of the Palestinians themselves that he relies upon and he reproduces these recollections by adhering to the storyteller's narrative, further modified and mediated by his control as producer and manager of the visualisation process. The tale he relates about the prison camp Ansar III, for instance, with the prisoners sending a 'fax' (throwing messages tied to stones over the fence to fellow prisoners), is organised with adjoining text boxes giving verbatim accounts of the activity.[71] This is a sequence reminiscent of Spiegelman's account in *Maus* of his father, Vladek, passing messages over the fences in Auschwitz.[72]

In conjunction with imagined drawings of the camp, Sacco depicts a Palestinian relating the narrative thread. This is accomplished by Sacco's use of quote marks in the text, and the

70 Powers, 107.

71 Sacco, *Palestine*, 86.

72 Spiegelman, *Maus*, 65.

addition of a small thumbnail portrait – similar to a TV documentary 'talking heads' format. This emphasises the mediated nature of *Palestine*, a mediation that is compounded by several significant factors: firstly, it is largely based on secondary information given in the form of accounts made in interview, often long after the events themselves; secondly, the interviews were recorded as written notes and consequently subject to the vagaries of interpretation through verbal language and then through written language, as well as memory – it may have been weeks before the notes were transformed into graphic novel pages. This final transformation involved mediation at the technical level of the medium, since the construction of the image with text necessitated extensive – perhaps total – manipulation of information. Contemporary news reporting is similarly fraught, however, as Chomsky has been quick to point out.[73]

Sacco's work forces a rethink of the politics of visual documentary. Hitchens, in the foreword to *Safe Area Gorazde*, said that Sacco's work had the unsettling effect of forcing a reconsideration of a political and social situation.[74] Hitchens observes that Sacco deploys a strategy, refined in *Palestine*, of applying close scrutiny to people's experiences on the 'far side' of the media's attention, and a willingness to deliberately offer narratives that contradict official, institutional accounts. In both *Palestine* and *Safe Area Gorazde* Sacco's realism is to constantly retell and supplant orthodox myths with political accounts. Sacco's contribution to the conflict in Palestine is to demonstrate the possibility of visualising Palestine and Palestinians in a new, untypical way. Said's own work, in his film for BBC television *In Search of Palestine*, has this objective. By repeatedly showing particular domestic scenes of loss and deprivation, Said is able to reveal the oppressive structures of the Israeli State at work in the occupied territories.[75]

73 Chomsky, *Necessary Illusions*.

74 Christopher Hitchens, foreword in Sacco, *Safe Area Gorazde*.

75 Edward W. Said, "In Search of Palestine," BBC TV, screened in the UK on BBC 2, May 17, 1998, 8pm, 50 min.

Both Sacco and Said were agreed that the one of the greatest obstacles to Israeli and Palestinian peace was the mutual absence of information about, or an understanding of, each other's culture and history. This absence is all the more remarkable considering the geographic proximity of these cultures, co-existing as they have in the same relatively small territories. As violence has worsened so such discrepancies have become more common and more entrenched. They led, as David Grossman notes, to wider gaps between cultural practices, and to greater mutual ignorance of social factors on both sides. [76] The suffering of non-military civilians has been a case in point, and Grossman makes this poignant observation:

> Two years have gone by and there is no hope. […] according to data provided by UN agencies, more than a quarter of Palestinian children now suffer malnutrition as a result of the military situation. The second: Israeli school children will soon be receiving special lessons in early identification of suicide bombers. Israelis and Palestinians who refuse to see the connection between these two facts ensure that for many years to come we will all be each other's hostages, agents of gratuitous and pointless death.[77]

For Grossman the fate of children in the conflict is of special concern, since the next generation's ideological adherence and prejudices would be determined by such suffering and anxiety. Sacco shares these concerns, and the construction of ideology in children became a theme to which he returns throughout *Palestine*, often focusing on their attitudes during his interviews. It is in the conclusion to the *Palestine* series, however, that he pays most direct and sustained attention to this, and, given the support and participation by young people in suicide bombing several years later, it is this part that

76 David Grossman, "Any winners?" *The Guardian*, September 30, 2002, Manchester edition, G' section, 2. Others would acknowledge the first Intifada as the starting point, 1987–92.

77 Grossman, 3.

has proved to be most prescient (figure 4.9).[78] Sacco depicts a young boy forced to stand in the rain while soldiers, standing undercover, taunt him.

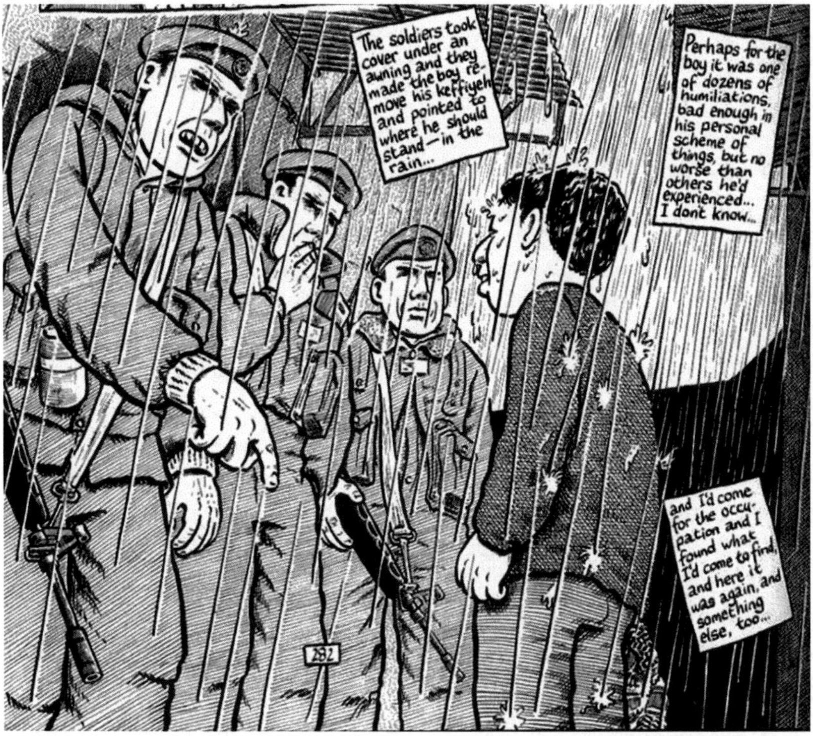

Figure 4.9. A boy is made to stand in the rain as he is questioned by sheltering soldiers (*Palestine* 2001, p. 282, detail). © Joe Sacco 2001; reproduced with permission of Fantagraphics Books Inc.

The viewpoint is shifted from frame to frame, alternating like camera shots between the low viewpoint of the boy looking up and the high one of soldiers as they are made to seem to tower over him. The rain is drawn as a deluge upon the boy using white rods of lines

78 Sacco, *Palestine*, 279–285.

against the blacked-out background. The boy's face is drawn filling the frame and alternately closing one or other eye as his face fills with rain. Sacco uses this combination of cinematic framing with high contrast ink drawing conventions to create a sequence that principally represents abuse and humiliation. In a graphic version of Grossman's concern for the future consequences of such abuses, Sacco uses the text boxes to offer his bleak conception of this boy's fate. He acts as a symbol of Palestinian despair and hopelessness for Sacco.

Sacco argues that this specificity stemmed from his background as a journalist, and he goes further by describing the whole project as a journalistic one.[79] One of the fundamental purposes of the *Palestine* project is to create a sense of specificity: that events take place in a particular way, in a defined space, and involve visually identifiable individuals. The philosophy for this is outlined in chapter one of *Palestine*, where Sacco objects to his experience of the Palestine situation as mediated (in a pejorative sense) by the American and European press and TV.[80] This cultural dominance, particularly as it manifests itself in the news media, may be analysed as an agency in the crisis rather than a conduit of information. The persistent, highly politicised control of language results in euphemistic use of terms like 'crossfire', 'terrorist', 'refugee' and 'settler' to describe ideologically driven military and political events.

This tight control of language enables myth development, as these and other terms interlock with older discourses. 'Settler', for instance, has romantic frontier connotations that were readily assimilated into a receptive North American consciousness primed by Hollywood myth manufacture, rather than the belligerent armed militias that are more commonly the Palestinians' view of such groups. Sacco painstakingly explores and defines these categories, demonstrating the instability of such terms from a Palestinian perspective, and in doing so illustrates the fundamental way in which language and media are inseparable from the ethnic crisis on the ground. Said argued that Sacco's work is

79 Sacco, interview with the author.

80 Sacco, *Palestine*, 1–10.

remarkable because it does not conform to orthodox models of comic book narrative, where 'good triumphs over evil'.[81]

Sacco also explores the ideological myth-making on the part of Palestinian militias, discussing the intimidation of suspected collaborators and the manipulation of Islam to ideological ends, for example. These are examined in the course of detailed interviews and conversations visualised in domestic settings. The reaction of the Palestinians is usually set in the context of received dogmas with which Sacco (as interviewer and narrator) sometimes challenges the interviewees. Later, this time referring to Bosnia, Sacco spoke of the slaughter of civilians being mythologized and sanitised by the media: 'It [the brain] rationalises it, or any explanation of it, or any lie about it will be embraced. It's easier to believe a lie than to look at the truth. Even if the truth is in front of your eyes. I have many examples of that. Many examples.'[82] His work in both Bosnia and Palestine can be seen as a determined effort to counter media myths. Clearly the documentary is dramatised and subjective, yet paradoxically gives access to a truth that is verified by its medium. As with the other graphic novels studied here, the medium itself may be used to signify truthfulness negatively; by *not* being television or digital photo-journalism. Presumably the whole wealth of material that Sacco collected, all the photographs and the notes, could have been presented in their original form. The major, and very laborious, intervention of the graphic novel medium – the transformation into drawings and graphic novel pages – distances the material from connotations of corporate, institutional control and manipulation, and aligns them within comic book traditions.

81 Said, foreword in *Palestine*.

82 Gary Groth, "Joe Sacco, Frontline Jounalist: Why Sacco went to Gorazde," *Comics Journal* online www.tjc.com/2 ws/1 sacco.html (accessed January 11, 2002).

Sacco explains the purpose of *Palestine* in the following terms:

> The hope is that you raise the awareness of the average American person, so he or she knows to consider other than the Israeli point of view.[…] Through the comic, the idea was to show the Palestinian point of view, to give human faces to the Palestinians. They're not just terrorists. They are people who are struggling, who are striving for something…who are victims too. Most of the people I met were very strong people. And their stories are moving. I just want to show that.[83]

These statements, made whilst working on the second volume of *Palestine*, demonstrate that Sacco was defining his practice as a negation of such interests of power in the media. He cites Chomsky as a model for this:

> 'I read Noam Chomsky's *The Fateful Triangle*, which really outlines in detail America's relationship to Israel, and how that affects the Palestinians. And what he does is take newspaper accounts – he uses the New York Times, and he kind of lets people hang themselves. He doesn't do any of his own interviews or anything like that, he just takes the newspaper accounts and just builds up this case to show the untruths and the lies, basically.'[84]

The key point here is that truth is, for Sacco, defined in the context of the larger picture of US foreign policy and the media coverage of it. 'Untruths' here are measured by Sacco's journalistic knowledge of people's experience and the discrepancies that appear in the manufacture of news.

> I don't really know what 'objectivity' means, I mean, 'cause basically I think that a real historical injustice is being perpetrated on the Palestinian people. There's no doubt in my mind about that. But as far as 'telling the truth' as far as

83 Powers, 109.

84 Bennett, Kathleen. "Joe Sacco's Palestine: Where Comics Meet Journalism." Interview in *Subliminal Tatoos* 5, (summer 1995): 12–19.

> what you saw or how people reacted when you were there, that's something you have to be objective about, and you have to be very truthful about.[85]

The conception of injustice preceded the documentary truth for Sacco, and is his condition for measuring that truth. The evidence he collected and presented corroborated this conception, and the myth making he perceived in the US media for him maintained this injustice.

According to Said, the mythologies that had prevented social progress in Palestine were deeply embedded in political history, particularly British history. He used the British Lord Balfour's 1919 speech as the starting point for the establishment of the proposed State of Israel in Palestine, and made the point that even as early as this the state would be segregationist and require the forced displacement of masses of Palestinians:

> […] … a memorandum written by Balfour in August 1919 in which he said: 'In Palestine we do not propose even to go through the form of consulting the wishes of the present inhabitants of the country…. The four great powers are completely committed to Zionism and Zionism, be it right or wrong, good or bad, is rooted in age-long tradition, in present needs, in future hopes, of far profounder import than the desire and prejudices of the 700,000 Arabs who now inhabit that ancient land.[86]

For Said, Balfour's concept of knowledge is an example of 'knowing', an imperialist notion that underpins military conquest and occupation. Thus, Balfour 'knows' what is right and necessary and is willing to establish the civil and military structures to support this knowing.[87] Sacco, informed in part by Said, felt sufficiently strongly about the injustice declared in Balfour's speech that he reiterates it, using selected passages, in *Palestine*. To do this he uses an 'epic' frame technique. These sections are more conservative in style, with immense passages in time represented between each frame. The narration is depicted like a voice-over, contained within separate

85 Bennett.

86 Said, *The End of the Peace Process*, 216.

87 Edward W. Said, *Orientalism*, (London: Penguin, 1991), 31–38.

boxes at the edge of the page. The political message tends towards the dogmatic here, since a political position is taken through the selection of certain passages and the absence of others.[88] As a strategy, it is more overt and uncharacteristic of those used elsewhere in *Palestine*, where the political language and imagery is generated by the condition of a lived experience of oppression.

Sacco's search for truths outside of the dominant media discourse is a raison d'etre for his *Palestine* project, with the impediments of Palestinian domestic life central to his realism. He focuses on the plight of businesses that cannot market or sell their produce, the obstacles imposed upon travelling to work, upon health and education, and the restrictions upon the training of social service workers.[89] Sacco represents the geographic and demographic limitations upon Palestinian existence through the specific details of people's life; this specificity is a characteristic of Sacco's realism throughout *Palestine*.

88 Sacco, *Palestine*, 13.
89 Sacco, *Palestine,* 207.

Chapter 5: Visualising Discrimination and Persecution

A Pedagogy of Exile: Sebald's *Emigrants*

For Sebald authentic learning, or relearning, of traumatic events can be derived from images and text phrases, which have locked within them the potential for the illumination of the barbarism of the Holocaust, and its enduring social effects. His method, the derivation of narratives from a sequence of black and white photographs, creates a provenance for the images that may be partially or entirely fabricated. Sebald's fictionalised biographies, like that of his Paul Bereyter in *Emigrants*, continually play on the ambiguous boundaries of fiction, especially where he uses the method of extensive proxy 'first-hand' accounts – assuming the position of witness by feigning a lived experience. Sebald's novels *Emigrants* and *Austerlitz* are examples of prose inundated with image-text juxtaposition.

The series of images of Bereyter (figure 5.1) imply a chronological autobiography to complement the narrative, which tell of his displacement from his profession as a teacher, and also from his nationality because of his partly Jewish parentage. The sequences initially take the form of a photographic contact sheet, and then develop through individual photographs dispersed at intervals through the following pages (figure 5.2). Together with the text, these read as a coherent visual biography of displacement, despite the lack of visual evidence that they are even photographs of the same individual. The powerful visual effect of a sequence imposes a narrative even in the absence of the normal cues for visual consistency.

The story of Bereyter is driven by Sebald's idea of the 'discovery' of unknown stories, biographies of people that had been forcibly removed from society, particularly the absences of Jewish communities in his native Germany. As he explains:

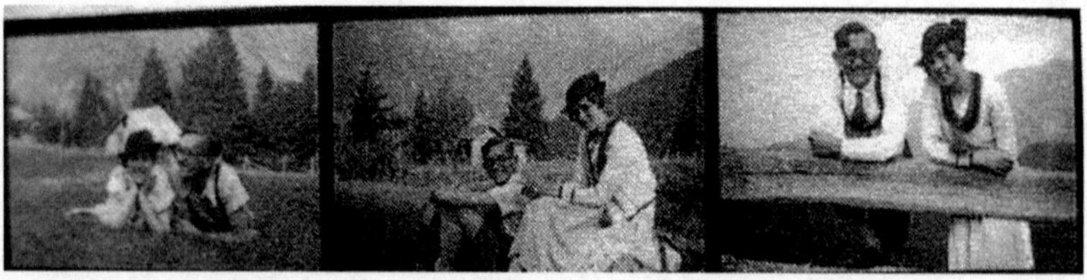

Figure 5.1. Initial sequence of images that Sebald uses for Paul Bereyter. © W.G. Sebald from *The Emigrants* (2002, Vintage, p.48), first published in Germany under the original title *Die Ausgewanderten* by Eichborn AG, Frankfurt/Main 1993.

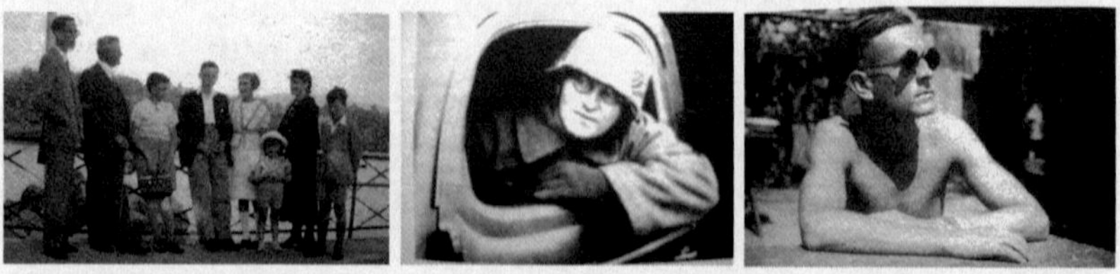

Figure 5.2. Sebald's sequence of images representing the teacher Paul Bereyter in different phases of his life and exile. These three photographs, and those in figure 5.1, are distributed over several pages, and are possibly images of different, unrelated people. © W.G. Sebald from *The Emigrants* (2002, Vintage, p. 49, 55, 56), first published in Germany under the original title *Die Ausgewanderten* by Eichborn AG, Frankfurt/Main 1993.

> [...] You could grow up in Germany in the post-war years without ever meeting a Jewish person. There were small communities in Frankfurt or Berlin, but in a provincial town in south Germany Jewish people didn't exist. The subsequent realisation was that they had been in all those places, as doctors, cinema ushers, owners of garages, but they had disappeared – or had been disappeared. So it was a process of successive phases of realisation.[1]

Bereyter is one such person, a teacher, and Sebald's concern with the disappeared inhabitants of his hometown is evident in his introductory remarks in the text itself, where Sebald is shocked at the discovery of the teacher's exile and later suicide under a train.[2] Bereyter's case is particularly poignant since he is cast as Sebald's own childhood teacher, one who greatly enriched his life. Sebald's model of a teacher in Bereyter is as an idealist, a person driven to teach, so much so that he undergoes hardship and personal suffering in order to maintain this vocation, after being driven out by National Socialist laws that forbade him to teach on account of his less than Aryan ancestry.

Sebald does not confine himself solely to photographs, often using a significant proportion of images that cannot be considered to be photographs in any straightforward sense[3]. The frequent insertions of images that are drawn from different modes of visual media (postcards, calling cards, handwritten diary entries, etc) seem to be part of Sebald's visual method, the effect of which is to emphasise the artifice of the narrative construction process. Sebald uses a diagram of the railway that Bereyter has drawn at the conclusion of the story in conjunction with the narrative of his suicide. He kills himself on the railway tracks, an event which is coupled with the ironic prophecy from Bereyter's uncle that he will 'end up on the railways'.[4] It would seem fitting that Sebald's teacher uses the pedagogical tool of the diagram; the studious avoidance of any pictures of horror or

1 Jaggi, "The Last Word: Interview with W.G. Sebald."

2 Sebald, *Emigrants*, 22–23.

3 In the translated version of Sebald's *Emigrants*, for instance, 14 of the c.74 images fall into this category, and comprise diagrams, prints (engravings, etchings, lithographs), and six reproductions of text (diaries, newspapers, calling card and ticket).

4 Sebald, *Emigrants*, 62.

mutilation serves to add to the bleakness of the imagery at this point, and the mechanistic plan view offers a reference to the tragedy. This is similar to the way that Spiegelman utilises diagrams at pivotal moments in the text, often points of high dramatic tension, thereby helping to offset melodrama and demonstrate the methods by which Jews attempted to resist Nazi oppression. Spiegelman uses diagrammatic inserts that give, with his father's narrative, instruction on such matters as hiding in coal cellars, boot repairs and uniform fitting, in situations where life literally depended on practical adaptation.

This mixture of applied drawing methods – illustration, diagram, map – provides an iconography that forces the reader to re-conceptualise the reading of certain frames. Diagrams and maps, with their particular conventions, signify the authority derived from empiricism, investing the image with connotations of 'accuracy' and 'truthfulness'. These changes in form, at intervals throughout the narrative, help signify documentary truth. Spiegelman, like Sebald, enables a seemingly authoritative visualisation of people subject to the desperate ordeals of exile, labour camps and ghettos, with the humiliation that accompanied them.

The Encounter: Photographs in Graphic Novels

Sebald's photographs of Bereyter (figure 5.1 and 5.2) are visual interventions in the text, which act like coded palimpsests, layers and erasures of interpretations overlain with Sebald's narratives. Each image in the sequence here is like a Lacanian *point du capiton*, an anchor point in the text which gives a momentary illusion of fixing meaning, although this is quickly lost as their inherent instability as bearers of meaning is realised.[5] The photograph, as an authentic verification of an account, is both questioned and utilised in Sebald's work. Sebald was familiar with Barthes' theories, particularly his

5 Dennis Atkinson explains Lacan's theory concisely in his book *Art in Education: Identity and Practice* (Dordrecht/Boston/London: Kluwer, 2002).

concept of the camera operative as an 'agent of death'.[6] Sebald likens photographs to the 'residue of a life perpetually perishing', as the biographical decay of Bereyter demonstrates.[7] The attempt to preserve this interminable process of decay is, for Sebald, at the root of the desire and fascination for studying aging photographs, and also accounts for the intimidation and revulsion that arises as we are reminded of death in the face of such images; the old photograph as a memento mori.

The function of reproduced photographs in these narratives may be seen as reminiscent of Barthes' theory of the 'punctum'; Barthes contendes that the punctum is an elusive quality that serves to make photographs certify and authenticate the reality of an event, or more properly a phenomenon. This entirely subjective perception of a punctum is bound up with the relationship between contingency and photograph. According to Barthes the 'absolute Particular, the sovereign Contingency' of a photograph enables a viewer's perception to rupture the studium (the realm of aesthetics, composition, artistry etc.) and force a brutal awareness of the actuality of a past moment.[8] Where the subject is a person then this may induce what Barthes (from Lacan) refers to as the Encounter (with the Real).[9]

Many graphic novelists (Spiegelman, for example) reproduce photographs, including drawn 'photographic reproductions', which appear to refer to the Encounter as a means of imbuing the image texts with authenticity. This is an effect that, as Barthes theorised, simply could not be reproduced other than through its intrinsic medium, a photograph; yet the use of drawings as surrogate photographs – seemingly without diminution of an overwhelming, vicarious Encounter, calls this into question. Photographs, drawn or otherwise, act to condition the receptivity of the reader to the possibility of a

6 Arthur Williams, "Sebald, W. G. (1944–2001)," entry in *The Literary Encyclopedia.* http://www.litencyc.com/php/speople.php?rec=true&UID=4961 (accessed October 16, 2006).

7 Sebald, W.G. and Jan Peter Tripp, *Unrecounted*, trans. Michael Hamburger (London: Penguin, 2005), 84.

8 Barthes, *Camera Lucida*, 4.

9 Barthes, *Camera Lucida.*

continuity with a traumatic history, existing outside of the narrative of past and present, and yet belonging to both of them. The effectiveness of photography in signifying terms is, Barthes claimed, because of its perceived close relationship to the referent.[10] The signifier, the photograph itself, could be overlooked (invisible), or *seen through* to the referent – in this case straight through to the person, suggesting a direct link by virtue of the (perceived) authenticity of the chemical impression, enabling its reception as a means of learning and knowing of past traumas.

A seminal moment in *Austerlitz* illuminates Sebald's visual historical pedagogy.[11] He has the character Vera explain to us the experiential nature of learning of the past through photographs:

> […] I heard Vera again, speaking of the mysterious quality peculiar to such photographs when they surface from oblivion. One had the impression, she said, of something stirring in them, as if one caught small sighs of despair […] as if the pictures had a memory of their own and remembered us, remembered the roles that we, the survivors, and those no longer among us had played in our former lives.[12]

This reflexive process, of experiencing the image, and the idea that the image experiences us, is important to the idea of learning of the past – in the sense of the act of 'becoming to know'. One of Sebald's visualisation techniques is to conjure the idea of the return of the gaze, imbuing the subject (even where this is an inanimate object) of a photograph with the ability to look back out of the image. He develops this idea perhaps most strikingly when Austerlitz, a childhood Holocaust refugee, steps out of his train at Pilsen station to take photographs of the capital of a pillar:

> … the idea, ridiculous in itself, that this cast iron column, which with its scaly surface seemed almost to approach the nature of a living being, might

10 Barthes, *Camera Lucida*, 5.

11 Noted in Mark McCulloh, *Understanding W.G. Sebald* (Carolina: University of Carolina Press, 2003), 8–9.

12 Sebald, *Austerlitz*, 258.

remember me and was, if I may so put it, said Austerlitz, a witness to what I could no longer recollect for myself.[13]

At this point the particular photograph to which he refers is *not* reproduced in the text, however, and he appears to rely solely on the textual recounting of the event at this point. This demonstrates Sebald's highly variable strategies with the relationship between text and image. He confounds reader expectations by an absence of an image, the void generated by the previous sequence of image encounters. The reader is thus forced into a dilemma; the application of Sebald's interpretation is followed by an ambivalence of verification: should one accept the given narrative or question it? A reader of Sebald's text is levered out of the 'flow' of the prose, enhanced by the excessive length of his sentences (which may run to several pages), into what seems to be a confrontation with the image. The images behave like nodes in the text, and the confrontation occurs because the textual meaning is not fixed by the image, but rather opens up a contest of interpretation. This technique raises awareness of the artifice of a narrative and the way that it is in embedded in the medium. One is constantly unsettled by the verification imperative that the insertion of the image demands. The occasional absence of an image, where the reader anticipates finding one in accordance with the image-text pattern, disrupts the sequence that Sebald has initiated. When this technique is combined with the grave subject matter of displacement, there ensues an unsettling effect upon the reader engaged in learning of these events.

Perhaps the last word on the veracity of photographs for enabling the reader to learn of the disasters of social history should perhaps be left to Sebald: asked about his interest in photography, he responded:

> I've always been interested in photographs, collecting them not systematically but randomly. They get lost, then turn up again. [...] These old photographs always seem to have this appeal written into them, that you should tell a story behind them. In The Emigrants there is a group photograph of a large Jewish

13 Sebald, *Austerlitz*, 311.

family, all wearing Bavarian costume. That one image tells you more about the history of German-Jewish aspiration than a whole monograph would do.[14]

Documenting the Holocaust: Spiegelman's *Maus*

The narrative structure of *Maus* comprises an extended exchange between Spiegelman and his father Vladek about his and Anja's (Spiegelman's mother, who committed suicide) experiences as Jews in prison camps in Germany and Poland. Spiegelman builds the narrative around his own contemporary experience of discovering the Holocaust as the offspring of a survivor. Thus *Maus* is also a narrative representing contemporary anxieties about the Holocaust for the subsequent generation of American Jews.[15]

Maus is profoundly unsettling, through its sequences of laboured drawings, with the very occasional insertion of a photograph. This unease is intensified by the ambiguity of the allegorical characterisation. Like George Orwell's *Animal Farm*,[16] Spiegelman uses animal species to represent national, ethnic or religious groups. He cast the Jews as mice, the Nazis as cats and the Poles as pigs, but each of these equivalents is relatively unstable, with elisions between them. These correspondences are deliberately kept loose and interchangeable throughout the narrative, in order to emphasise the instability and contingency of these ethnic and nationalistic social

14 Maya Jaggi, "The Last Word: Interview with W.G. Sebald," *The Guardian*, December 21, 2001, http://books.guardian.co.uk/departments/generalfiction/story/0,,624750,00.html (accessed October 16, 2006), 3.

15 *Maus* has appeared in various forms prior to this, including a serial in Spiegelman's and Françoise Mouly's *Raw* comics (between 1980 and 1991 in the US), and in an earlier and much shorter version, *Funny Aminals* [sic] 1 in 1972.

16 George Orwell, *Animal Farm* (London: Secker and Warburg, 1945).

categories; this relationship of animal type to social group is fundamental to Spiegelman's conception of his Holocaust narrative.

The narrative structure of *Maus* comprises an extended exchange between Art Spiegelman and his father, Vladek, about his and Anja's (Spiegelman's mother) experiences during the war. Both Anja and Vladek were Jews in prison camps in Germany and Poland, and Vladek's tales about surviving the Holocaust were recorded by Spiegelman at their homes in New York. Spiegelman built the narrative around his own contemporary experience of discovering the Holocaust as an offspring of a survivor, as well as around his father's and other survivor's accounts. Thus *Maus* also became a narrative representing contemporary anxieties about what the Holocaust had come to represent in the minds of the following generation of American Jews.

These two narratives are integrated throughout *Maus* with Spiegelman's debates with his father interspersed between scenes from the Holocaust. Often frames of Vladek recounting lead directly to frames of the prison camps, where his voice continues as a narrator in captions. Throughout *Maus* Spiegelman maintains the narrative of the interview itself, revealing the difficulties of his personal relationship with his parents and between his father and his second wife, Mala. The psychological scarring of the Holocaust in the form of dysfunctional present day relationships underpins the horrors expressed in the wartime narrative. The balance of the two in the animal allegory is one of the major achievements of Spiegelman's work, and of his critical realism. Early reviewers of *Maus* pointed out that the interplay of the personal with the historical was important for Spiegelman's success in *Maus*: '[*Maus*] pulls the narrative out of the private sphere and places it in the context of world history; the interplay between the two is what makes the book so real.'[17] The publication of *Maus* received a great deal of mainstream and comic press attention, winning awards for Spiegelman, including a Guggenheim Fellowship and the Pulitzer Prize for literature in the

17 Richard Gehr, "Richard Gehr on Art Spiegelman," review of *Maus*, *Art Forum* 25 (1987): 10.

USA, as well as prominent exhibitions, including one at the Museum of Modern Art in New York.

It took Spiegelman thirteen years to complete the *Maus* project, including forty hours of interviews with his father. *Maus*, like *Barefoot Gen* and most manga, but unlike most Western comic books, was drawn entirely in black and white.[18] Its formal properties, especially the strong contrasts of tone, were designed by Spiegelman to visually exploit such visual characteristics as the stripes of the Holocaust victims' prison uniforms. These formal decisions, like the small scale on which it was drawn, are distinguishing characteristics of *Maus* as a graphic novel.

Working Methods

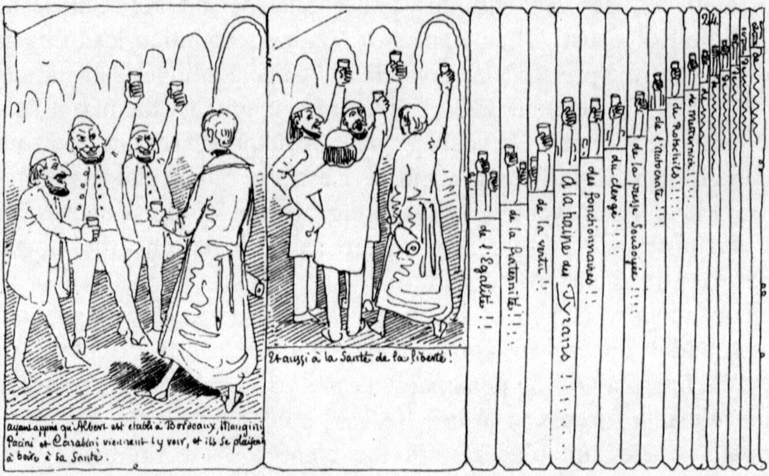

Figure 5.3. Töpffer's compressed frames from his *Histoire d'Albert* (1845).

18 Information from Avis Berman, "The Maus That Roared," *Art News* 92, (May 1993): 64; also Lawrence Langer, "A Fable of the Holocaust," review of Art Spiegelman's *Maus II*, *New York Times*, November 3, 1991.

Spiegelman was well aware that the abbreviations of the comic strip form that Rudolphe Töpffer discovered in the nineteenth century could be extremely effective for the organisation of sequential frames in a narrative. Töpffer demonstrated that the reduction of drawn marks to minimal signs in a sequence can be extreme, especially if there are enough repetitions.[19] As with much of Töpffer's work, there is a political dimension to his drawing; in the case of figure 5.3 they are drinking to Republican chants of liberty, fraternity etc., and he makes fun of the event by extending the toast using compressed frames and sign repetition. Like Töpffer, Spiegelman uses a minimum of extraneous detail, working on a deliberately small scale and with a reduced vocabulary of graphic signs in *Maus*. This economic and minimal approach has, for Spiegelman:

> some of the precision that mapmaking has.[…] I didn't want too much room for bullshit, so by working really small, there's less room to decorate. So what's there has to be important, or get left out – which is what cartoons are about anyway.[20]

Spiegelman worked on the pages of *Maus* at the 260x180mm size typical of final print size for US comic books. This was an unusual practice, since comic book artists generally work on double that size, to facilitate the sharpening up of the lines and to obscure re-workings when the page is shrunken for publication. As the pages were reduced to half-size ready for printing this practice ensured that the images appeared cleaner and sharper. Spiegelman, however, decided to retain the traces of his labour in the images, and the heavy lines and shading is a result of working at this confined scale.[21] The resultant murkiness acts as a metaphor for the hopelessness and brutality of the Holocaust, but as Spiegelman explains, this was problematic, for it was in danger

19 Töpffer in Wiese. Rudolphe Töpffer's *The Story of Albert* (1845, figure 5.3) was chosen for reproduction and comment by Spiegelman himself. Art Spiegelman, "Commix: An Idiosyncratic Historical and Aesthetic Overview," 62.

20 Barry Schwabsky, "Art Spiegelman: an exquisite sense of balance," *Art Press* 194 (1994): 30.

21 Berman, 64.

of collapsing into chaotic marks signifying expressive subjectivity, rather than accuracy and truth:

> I needed two contradictory things [...] I needed the intimacy, directness, unselfconsciousness, and humbleness of a direct sketch. To get that I worked very small – to scale. I also needed a kind of precision to bring my father's story into focus for myself, which was the opposite of those other qualities. That precision was essential because without it one would be lost in my personality in a sense, in the gesture and the mark.[22]

The shading throughout *Maus* is generally of high contrast, with large areas of black in most frames, usually set against the areas of white, with few gradations of grey. This gives an impression of heavy, laboured working, which serves as a visual metaphor of the forced labour of the subjects. The white frame borders tended to be slightly wider than generally used in graphic novels of this size (another result of working at a small scale perhaps), and this enhances the sense of confinement. Each frame contains its images with thick borders 'heavy' with ink in the almost excessive use of shading. Consequently *Maus* has a grubby appearance, the latency of its horror rendered through scratchy drawings of the black and murky uniformed animals (figure 5.4). The dark, heavily etched pages, in which the figures almost vanish into smudges of inky black, a simile of the soot (itself a constituent of ink) which pervaded Dachau and Auschwitz, into which those imprisoned literally disappeared.

The page illustrated in figure 5.4 is one the more visceral pages of *Maus*, where his father is contracting typhus.[23] Spiegelman organised this page in such a way that the heavy shading dominates; he uses white lettering for the exclamation 'typhus' over the top left, set against the darkness within the frame. The organisation of the sequence is such that the room-view of the third frame gives way to a close-up in the final frame, coinciding with the narrative moment when Vladek decides to make his horrific walk.

22 Spiegelman, quoted in Berman, 64.
23 Spiegelman, *Maus,* 255.

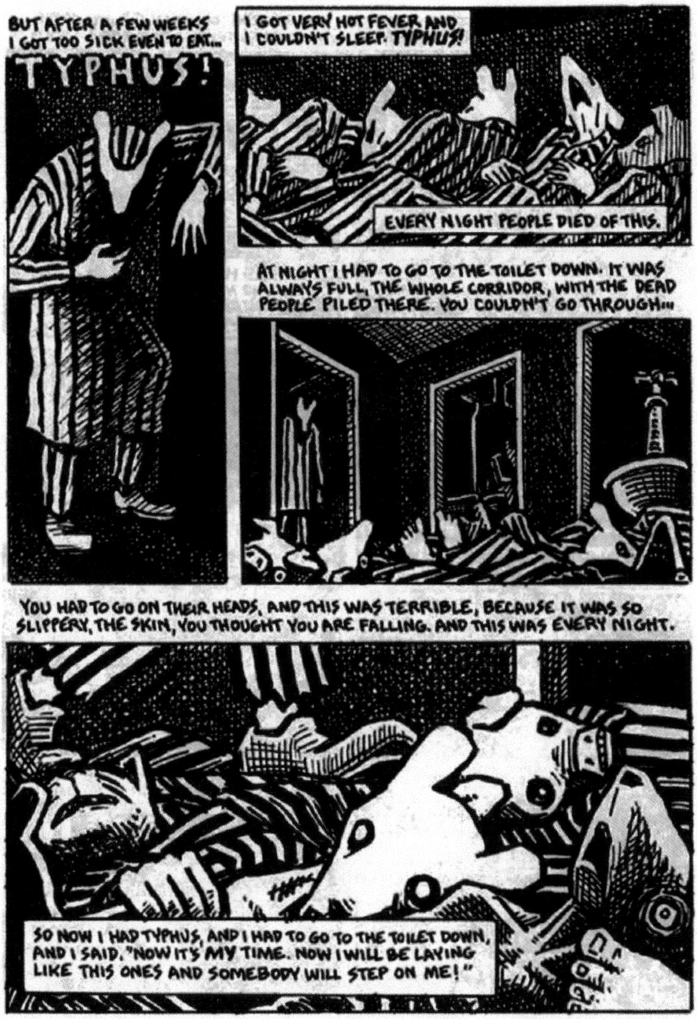

Figure 5.4. Vladek is stricken with typhus and forced to walk over the dead bodies of other victims in Auschwitz.

To take these steps, which he has to do every night, he is forced to walk over the decaying corpses of fellow prisoners, and envisages the moment when he will succumb to the disease and be trodden upon himself. In the final horizontal frame at the base of the page the dead faces of the prisoner/animals are made more striking by their whiteness. The orderly stripes of their prison uniforms become chaotic zigzags in this final frame, signifying the corporeal disintegration that coincides with the narrative horror.

Diagrams and Maps

To represent the psychological aspects of the horror of this oppression Spiegelman, like Sebald, often uses the device of the diagram. They are frequently inserted into the text of *Maus*, and serve to demonstrate the methods by which the Nazis oppressed the Jews, or the techniques of survival and resistance used by prisoners and those evading capture (figure 5.5). Spiegelman uses diagrammatic inserts that give guidance on such matters as hiding in coal cellars, boot repairs and uniform fitting, in situations when life literally depended on practical adaptation. As with *Emigrants*, this mixture of applied drawing methods provides an iconography that encourages the reader to re-conceptualise their assimilation of the narrative at these points. Diagrams and maps, with their particular conventions and codes, signify an authority derived from scientific empiricism; the reader, familiar with this iconography from other contexts, invests the image with connotations of 'accuracy' and 'truthfulness'. Spiegelman thus enables a seemingly authoritative visualisation of people subjected to the desperate ordeals of the labour camps and the ghettos, and the humiliation that accompanied them.

These technical graphic devices allow for different modes of event description, as he works through seemingly prosaic incidents such as the fitting of uniforms, with the oppressive connotations of nationalism, intimidation and oppression imbued therein. On one page there is a diagram of how to stitch a boot, for instance, and is an example of what appears to be an explanatory diagram imbued with oppressive signification; in this case, the failure to complete the procedure correctly at the first attempt may result in execution.[24] The step-by-step conventional simplicity of the diagram offers a stark contrast to the extreme emotion that must have accompanied its implementation. Similarly, his bunker elevation diagram (figure 5.5) demonstrates the specifics of desperation, showing how to conceal people below floors in secret compartments, and through his father's narrative one learns not only the factual but also the highly emotive details of such a structure.[25] The fitting of the removable wood panels, the location of floor bolts, serve to amplify the enormity of a situation where such measures required full attention for a person's very existence.

Spiegelman articulates his narrative methods in different terms from Sacco. Where the latter is almost defiant in his defence of graphic novels as 'illustration', Spiegelman has denied the use of this term to describe *Maus*, perhaps because of its pejorative connotations of superficiality, of its subordination to text.[26] Instead, he prefers a more pragmatic, technical definition:

> Understand that comics aren't illustrations, [...]. It's a kind of picture writing and diagramming. Somehow for me cartography and diagramming have the same root.[27]

Spiegelman's preference for cartography and the diagrammatic is significant, since these features are commonplace in *Maus*. Occasionally he inserts maps into the pages, and these orientate the reader by providing geographical reference points for each section of the narrative. Often these are pictorial maps containing out-of-scale figures to facilitate the imagining of the event actually taking place in that location.

24 Spiegelman, *Maus*, 60.
25 Spiegelman, *Maus*, 112.
26 Sacco, interview with the author.
27 Spiegelman, quoted in Berman, 63–64.

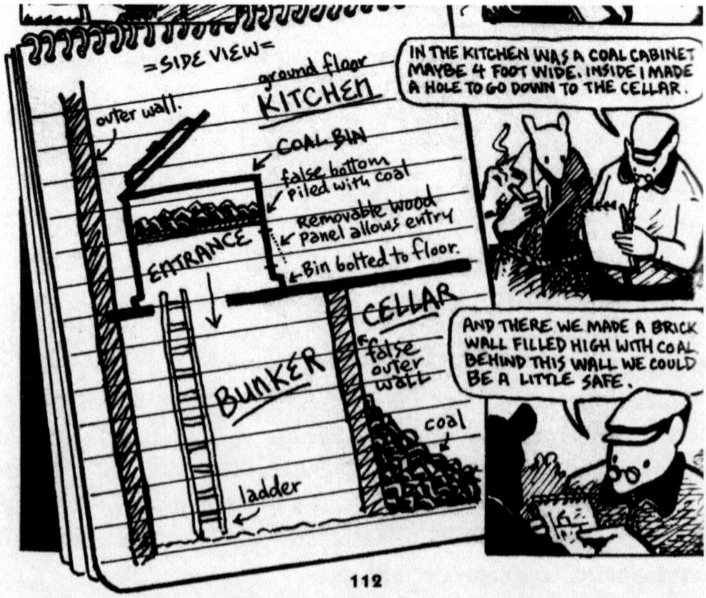

Figure 5.5. Diagram of secret bunker design in *Maus*.

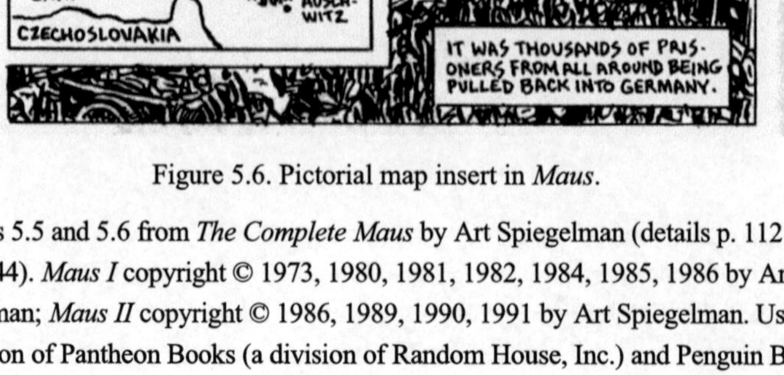

Figure 5.6. Pictorial map insert in *Maus*.

This is similar to the practice of Italian Renaissance painters depicting (relatively) large-scale figures in a landscape to indicate the full panoramic qualities of the site while still preserving the narrative.[28] In Spiegelman's map of prisoner movement (figure 5.6) the small figures that troop diagonally across the frame are exhausted inmates made to march across Poland to a German concentration camp as the Nazis are driven back near the end of the war.[29]

Spiegelman readily intersperses geographical references through his maps, temporally organised between the place in the past (his father's experience in the war) and in the present (as he interviews his father at various locations), giving scale, place names and features as a tourist map would. The multiple time sequences often occur simultaneously, as in the instance he describes here:

> The palimpsest of past and present is a natural in comics because you see all these various times at once, so sometimes I make that more manifest, [...] For instance, in the second volume, Vladek and I are talking at a table in the Catskills – that series of panels is inserted into a map of Auschwitz and Birkenau. We're in the present, and would usually be in a grid. But several divisions have been removed from the middle of the page to create a chasm of the past. It's something that happens in comics.[30]

Animals and Ethnicity

One of the key characteristics of *Maus* is Spiegelman's use of animals to represent ethnicity. There are several important precedents for this, including Orwell's *Animal Farm* and Walt Disney's animal cartoons like *Mickey Mouse* and *Donald Duck.* Joseph Witek compares the current version of *Maus* with an earlier version, where the animal metaphor was less developed:

28 For example, Giovanni di Paolo's fifteenth-century painting *St. John the Baptist retiring to the Desert* in the National Gallery, London.

29 Spiegelman, *Maus*, 244.

30 Spiegelman, quoted in Berman, 63.

Spiegelman was able to tell the story without referring to Jews and Nazis at all (the oppressors of the mice are simply 'die Katzen'), but such indirection was awkward and artificial in the full-length telling of the Holocaust story.[31]

Witek's goes on to describe how Spiegelman refined the animal metaphor until it became less inclined towards the characteristics of animals and more towards human reactions to the effects of the Holocaust.

Spiegelman's preoccupation with ethnic conflict and discrimination is central to the concerns of *Maus*. His belief that a comic book could effectively air and disseminate these concerns predated *Maus*; he had already been alerted to the possibilities of animals representing people in comic stories about prejudice, and was thinking of creating a book about racism and African-Americans.[32] Spiegelman's decision in *Maus* to introduce animal species to represent ethnicity, with its deliberate confusion with nationality, appeared to stem from this earlier interest in ethnic incongruities. This added another, primarily visual, layer of complexity to the issue. The animal disguises – sometimes as worn animal masks, sometimes as complete animal heads – function in the same way as the prison uniform. In both cases the relationship between signifier and signified is confounded within the visual sign construction. This tension is intentionally never resolved, maintaining deliberate signification incongruities throughout the work.

The politics of Disney's Donald Duck is especially important for the study of Maus, as it is the subject of a seminal political critique by Dorfman and Mattelart.[33] In *How to Read Donald Duck* they made a careful analysis of the way that the Donald Duck character has been used for political purposes, especially in countries where the US wished to establish political influence and control, in particular the

31 Joseph Witek, *Comic Books as History: The Narrative Art of Jack Jackson, Art Spiegelman and Harvey Peckar* (Mississippi: University Press of Mississippi, 1989), 103.

32 Berman, 63.

33 As Leonard Rifas pointed out, correspondence to the author, December 21, 2001.

case of Chile in the 1970s prior to the overthrow of its democratic government.[34] They argue from the outset that Disney's cartoon animal was a representation of a set of ideological values that were fundamental to the imperial character of US foreign policy. They further postulate that the colonial aspirations of the US in central and southern America were aggressively represented by the Donald Duck character, and that ideologically it was an important instrument of cultural transformation and control. As Dorfman and Mattelart put it, in relation to a Donald Duck comic strip where the duck leads the navy of the 'Republic of San Bananador' into a counter revolutionary battle:

> 'The political drift of Disney is blatant in these few comics where he is impelled to reveal his intentions openly. It is also inescapable in the bulk of them, where he uses animal symbolism, infantilism, and 'noble savagery' to cover over the network of interests arising from a concrete and historically determined system: US imperialism.'[35]

They also argue that the imperialism represented by the Donald Duck character had a class base, and that this representation of class is mythological, serving to undermine the workers and producers in society to the advantage of the bourgeoisie. Such is the strident critique that Dorfman and Mattelart put forward to unmask the ideological roots of *Donald Duck.* Their analysis reveals the representations of class and imperialism underlying colonialism in central and southern America.

On September 11, 1973, the Chilean government was overthrown in a coup d'état. Dorfman and Mattelart recognised that the media-enforced popularity of Donald Duck was instrumental in establishing cultural hegemony; they argue that the ideological appropriation of the Disney character had the important effect of disguising and misrepresenting the underlying political, economic and

34 Ariel Dorfman, and Armand Mattelart, *How to Read Donald Duck: Imperialist Ideology in the Disney Comic*, New York: I.G. Editions, Inc., English trans., 1984, originally published 1971 in Chile as *Para Leer al Pato Donald.*

35 Dorfman and Mattelart, 58.

military struggle, creating myths favourable to the military and hostile to any resistance. As Chomsky has made clear, to successfully carry out destabilising military interventions and proxy wars it is necessary to establish the ideological ground through populist illusions.[36] The mechanisms for ideological disguise are an essential component of the strategy for cultural hegemony, where it is what is *not* spoken of, and *not* represented, the strategies of omission in the popular media, that carry as much significance as that which is. In what ways do Spiegelman's animal characters conform to, or resist, these ideological models of representation?

Firstly, the device of mice substituting for Jews is a deliberately temporary visualisation of a social construct. Unlike the ideological consistency of Disney's characters, Spiegelman's animal identities are periodically exchanged in accordance with nationality, utility or social function. Mice (Jews, fascist scapegoats) are metamorphosed visually to dogs (American), pigs (German/Polish) cats (Nazi military), according to the way that others perceive them, or the way they perceive themselves.[37] To add to the realism of ethnic complexity, the ambiguities of animals as representatives of ethnicity became part of the story itself. Consequently the mouse-as-author Spiegelman is depicted discussing the difficulties of the attribution of animal-type with his French-Jewish partner, Françoise Mouly. She is depicted questioning whether she should become a mouse (Jewish), or be representative of France – where no animal had been determined.[38] This questioning of identity is completely absent from the discourses of their Disney animal counterparts. Donald Duck could not question the nature of his own role as a counter revolutionary, or even refer to any issues of identity that might reveal his character's political interests.

Secondly, the class basis of the animal characterisation in *Maus* has a completely different function to that employed in *Donald Duck*.

36 Noam Chomsky, *Necessary Illusions.*

37 Art Spiegelman, correspondence published under the title "A problem of Taxonomy," *New York Times*, December 29, 1991, 50.

38 Spiegelman, *Maus*, 171–172.

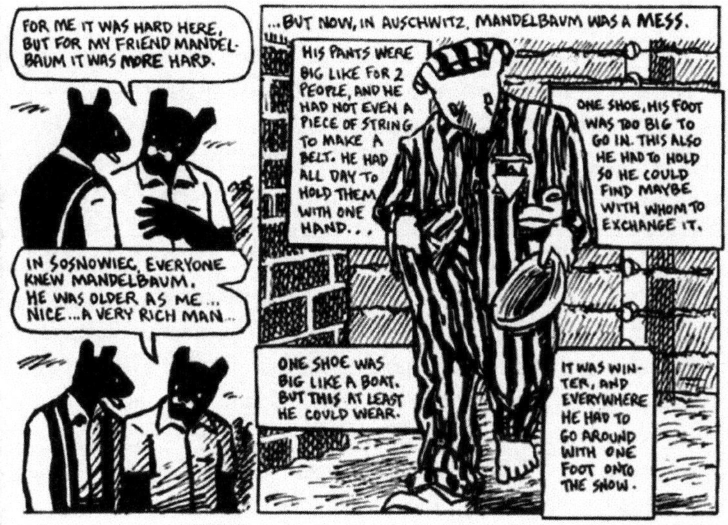

Figure 5.7. The ridicule of Mandelbaum in Auschwitz.

From *The Complete Maus* by Art Spiegelman (detail p. 29). *Maus I* copyright © 1973, 1980, 1981, 1982, 1984, 1985, 1986 by Art Spiegelman; *Maus II* copyright © 1986, 1989, 1990, 1991 by Art Spiegelman. Used by permission of Pantheon Books (a division of Random House, Inc.) and Penguin Books.

Spiegelman is at pains to declare the range of classes that were overridden by the racism of the National Socialist policies in operation in Germany and Poland, and in the concentration camps. Consequently, in *Maus* the Jewish prisoner Mandelbaum is ridiculed for his former wealth and privilege (figure 5.7) by the camp 'kapo' – a prisoner-supervisor who is himself forced to wear the striped uniform. The ridicule consists of forcing Mandelbaum to wear a uniform that is too large for him, with trousers that are falling down without a belt of any kind, with only one wearable shoe, so that he must hop. The ridicule is delivered by the kapo, enforcing Nazi discrimination that would, in time, also be applied to himself. Spiegelman is keen to maintain this awareness of the anxieties of social status that are mixed up with ethnic discrimination throughout *Maus*.

The text in his father's speech balloons retains the 'authenticity' of his second language speech patterns. Interestingly, and perhaps deliberately, it is these very inconsistencies in language that can mark out minority ethnic groups, helping the agents of an oppressive state to identify them. This type of attention to detail has been characteristic of the many incarnations of realism, and just as the images retain their specificity, so too does the text. This specificity is consistent with a social realism that elucidated, in this case, some social anxieties of ethnic identity. The instability of ethnic identity is given an additional airing in *Maus* through the transitory role of animal identity. For example, there is a sequence where a German-Jewish prisoner protests his ethnicity as 'German' (figure 5.8). His animal identity oscillates from mouse to cat and back, as he is identified as Jewish by the Nazi soldiers, despite his conviction of himself as ethnically German and non-Jewish. The frame with the prisoner-as-cat on the right hand side is otherwise identical to the prisoner-as-mouse frame on the left, inviting direct comparison. The partly shaded cat figure literally suggests the obscurity and uncertainty of his ethnic identity in Vladek's memory. This is in contrast to the clearly defined mouse, who is seen simplistically by his oppressors as unequivocally Jewish.

The wearing of masks, with its long literary and dramatic traditions for varying the representation of identity of the protagonists in a work, is a strategy Spiegelman employs in those parts of the story that are set in the present.[39] The mask, as in the theatre, also signifies identity as potentially transferable, which is exactly how Spiegelman uses it, keeping alive the potential for ethnic switches, the opposite of the mythic dogmas that declare ethnicity as fixed.

39 Spiegelman, *Maus*, 201–207.

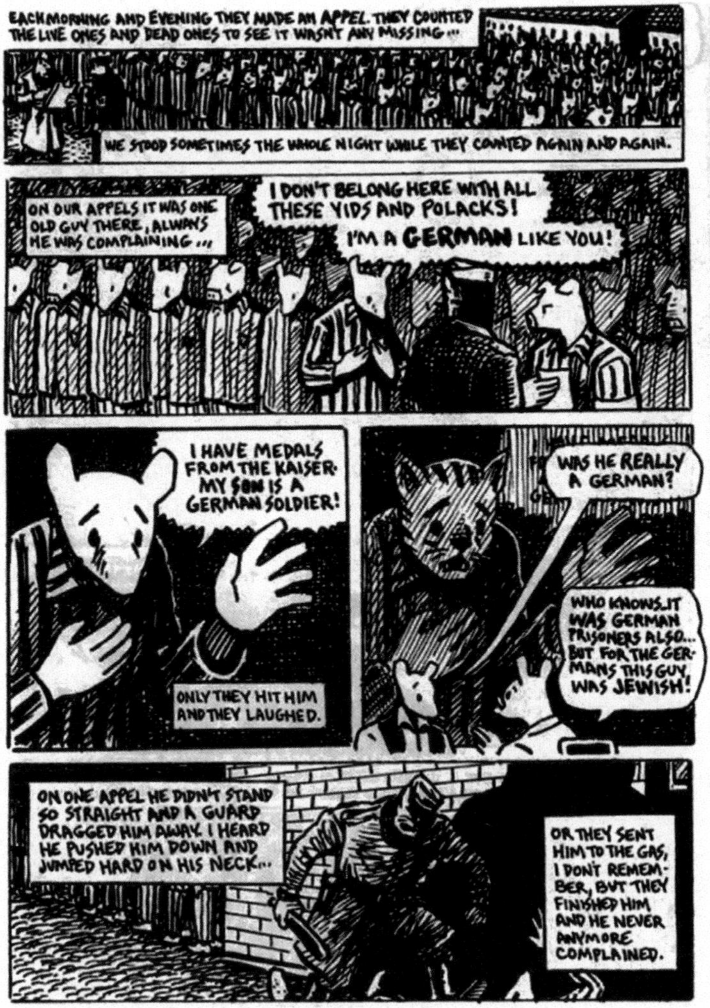

Figure 5.8. Shifting ethnicity as a prisoner protests his innocence.

From *The Complete Maus* by Art Spiegelman (p. 50). *Maus I* copyright © 1973, 1980, 1981, 1982, 1984, 1985, 1986 by Art Spiegelman; *Maus II* copyright © 1986, 1989, 1990, 1991 by Art Spiegelman. Used by permission of Pantheon Books (a division of Random House, Inc.) and Penguin Books.

For Spiegelman the difficulties of representing the subject-as-animal was paralleled by the problems inherent with *representing* the Holocaust at all. The enormity of the atrocity is such that the very act of representing it risked trivialising or over-dramatising it. Yet the ideological conditions in the US in the late twentieth century seem to have been increasingly favourable for such a representation. The positive critical reception for *Maus* and the willingness of critics and reviewers in the US to accept its unorthodox forms were partly to do with the reception of Holocaust itself. Peter Novick argues that the concept of the Holocaust has undergone transformations within US 'collective memory', as he describes it. [40] The essential case that he makes is that US Jews, as well as non-Jews, largely suppressed accounts of the persecution of the Jews during the Second World War, in the first decades afterwards. This enabled the assimilation and acceptance of Jews into US culture and society, and resisted the constructions of 'victim' that might otherwise have been imposed by lingering anti-Semitism.

> The few survivors who staggered out of the Nazi death camps faced a stunned, sometimes indifferent world [...] In the late 1940s refugees who arrived in Israel were greeted with embarrassment and scorn for their victim status, and tagged with the epithet sabon, soap.[41]

The extensive cultural changes in the US and Israel that brought about the shift in status, from Jewish victims shunning the past, to the declaration of the Holocaust that *Maus* represents, are complex. Novick's thesis is that the success of cultural productions about the Holocaust only became acceptable in the last decades of the twentieth century, in stark contrast to the immediate post-war years, where it was almost taboo in the US. He links the 'rediscovery' of the Holocaust to the developments in US foreign policies on Middle East.

40 Novick.

41 Lore Dickstein, "Inside the Grey Zone," review of *Pre-empting the Holocaust* by Lawrence L. Langer, *New York Times,* February 7, 1999.

In contrast to this, the destruction of Hiroshima and the embryonic nuclear Cold War was more deeply embedded in the US psyche in the early years after the war than was the Holocaust.[42]

> If it was only a minority of Americans who saw the United States as the perpetrator of a ghastly atrocity, the overwhelming majority had little doubt that they might themselves share the fate of the people of Hiroshima. The press drove home this prospect. Local newspapers ran graphics of the Hiroshima circle of devastation superimposed on their communities; *Life* devoted nine pages to descriptions of a future nuclear war, culminating with a technician testing the rubble of New York City for radioactivity under the blank eyes of the (surviving) lions in front of the public library on Fifth Avenue.[43]

The vivid place of Hiroshima and atomic destruction in US visual culture waned with the Cold War. Nonetheless, there was still sufficient anxiety for *Barefoot Gen* to be received enthusiastically by the Peace movement even in the 1990s. With the developments in Palestine and Israel the establishment of the Holocaust as the defining moment for Jews in the twentieth century grew more definite:

> The fears of a renewed Holocaust on the eve of that [Six-Day] war left their mark on American Jewish consciousness. Also important was the way the image of Jews as military heroes worked to efface the stereotype of weak and passive victims, which, as we've seen, had previously inhibited Jewish discussion of the Holocaust.[44]

Spiegelman's portrayal of his father as resourceful and robust in the face of the extremes of adversity, despite circumstances where chance played a large part in determining who survived, resourceful or not. Nonetheless, Vladek's resilience is an enduring theme of hope and resistance throughout the novel, that serves to ameliorate the idea of Jewish vulnerability, and helps resist the slippage into the classification of Jews as 'victims'.

42 Novick, 110–112.
43 Novick, 111.
44 Novick, 149.

Maus is a stark reminder in a popular culture medium of extreme suffering, acceptable to Jews who wished for a warning of the consequences of anti-Semitism, and readily consumed by non-Jews keen to demonstrate solidarity; for those wishing to see *Maus* as representing prejudice and racism more generically it also works well, partly through its format as an animal fable.

Photographs in Maus

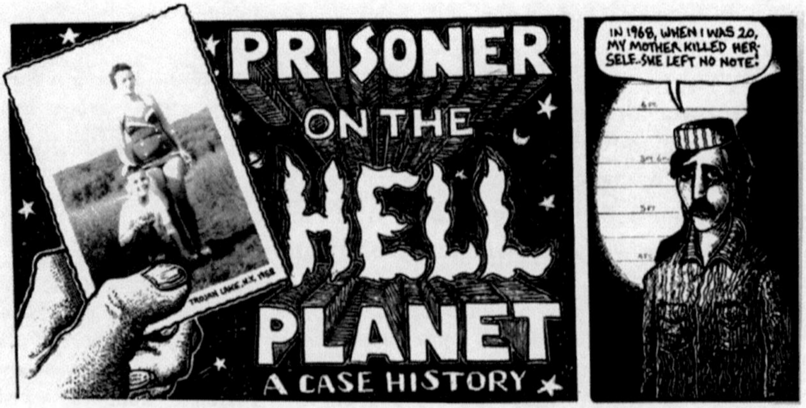

Figure 5.9. Spiegelman's use of a reproduced photograph of his mother.

From *The Complete Maus* by Art Spiegelman (p.100). *Maus I* copyright © 1973, 1980, 1981, 1982, 1984, 1985, 1986 by Art Spiegelman; *Maus II* copyright © 1986, 1989, 1990, 1991 by Art Spiegelman. Used by permission of Pantheon Books (a division of Random House, Inc.) and Penguin Books.

The problem of the representation of the Holocaust is, as Andrea Liss explains, complicated by the 'sheer horror of the events', and reveals the inadequacy of documentary photographs:

> The events themselves as traumatic history resist simple understanding, accessibility and representation. [...]. For some historians, understanding the unfathomable cruelty and hatred of Hitler's regime, its calculated policies to exterminate the Jews of Europe and to decimate millions of Communists, Catholics, Romas (Gypsies), homosexuals, political dissenters, the handicapped and the mentally retarded is impossible. As Holocaust historian Saul

Friedlander has characterized it, an opaqueness remains at the very core of the historical understanding of what happened. [...] The traditional mandate of the documentary photograph to 'bear witness' can thus no longer go unquestioned. Its precious if uneasy burden to 'never forget' reigns over its unarticulated occlusions.'[45]

Spiegelman routinely uses archival Holocaust photographs on which he based his drawings, but, in contrast to Sebald, actual photographs as such are placed conspicuously in the text in only three places.[46] The reproduced photograph of Spiegelman's mother in the suicide story section (figure 5.9) may be seen as analogous to Roland Barthes' unpublished 'Winter Garden' photograph of his dead mother.[47] Much of Barthes' *Camera Lucida* is devoted to answering the question of what is unique to photographs, and dealing with the 'invisibility' of the (chemical aspect) of the medium. The poignancy of an 'Encounter' with the photograph overwhelms Barthes, when he discovers an old photograph of his dead mother. Spiegelman's photograph, given the context of his own mother's suicide and the guilt that it presaged, may have had a similar affect upon him. Choosing to reproduce a photograph at this point, rather than the drawn copies of photographs he had favoured until this moment in the *Maus* narrative, appears to refer to such an Encounter. This is an effect that, as Barthes had theorised, simply could not be reproduced other than by its intrinsic medium, a photograph. The effectiveness of a photograph in signifying terms is, Barthes claims, because of its perceived close relationship to the referent.[48] The signifier, the photograph itself, could be overlooked (invisible), or *seen through* to the referent – in this case straight through to the person, suggesting a direct link by virtue of the (perceived) authenticity of the chemical impression.

45 Andrea Liss, "Distant Witnessing," *Afterimage,* February 26, 1998, 3. In particular she is referring to the installation *Tower of Faces* at the US Holocaust Memorial Museum.

46 As Liss notes, 3.

47 Roland Barthes, *Camera Lucida* (Vintage: London, 2000)

48 Barthes, *Camera Lucida,* 5.

Barthes also theorised that photographs are fundamentally linked to the concept of death, since a subject is transformed to an object by a photograph. This objectification is for Barthes an insistence on corporeal existence and the fear of time passing, as the seeming present-ness of the moment is revealed as always a past moment, a history. The illusion of the remoteness of death is thus re-presented as immediate, through Barthes' inability to 'transform' the subject of his photograph of his mother; the horror of death and helplessness in the face of the fact, is insisted upon by the photograph.[49] If Spiegelman is able to access the presence of his mother and her death through his use of her photograph, then the question of why he didn't use photographs more frequently in *Maus* arises?

The effect of few photographs amongst many drawn frames clearly accentuates the presence of the few. It is possible, however, that the dearth of photographs in many documentary graphic novels, despite the common referencing of the lens and photography's means, may suggest a deeper distrust of the photographic medium. In the hand-drawn, sequenced and narrated documentary graphic novel, a new set of conditions has transformed the photograph as Barthes defined it. Spiegelman's painstakingly drawn copies of photographs question Barthes' fundamental concept of a photograph's function; paradoxically it is as if the secondary labour of drawing necessary to corroborate the 'certificate of presence' provided by a photograph.[50] In one striking example (figure 5.10), Spiegelman uses photographs as frames, with the whole page design collapsing into an avalanche of photographs. This structure is presaged on the previous page, with drawn copies of photographs occasionally being substituted for frames, and also acting themselves as frames.

49 Barthes, *Camera Lucida*, 93.
50 Barthes, *Camera Lucida*, 87.

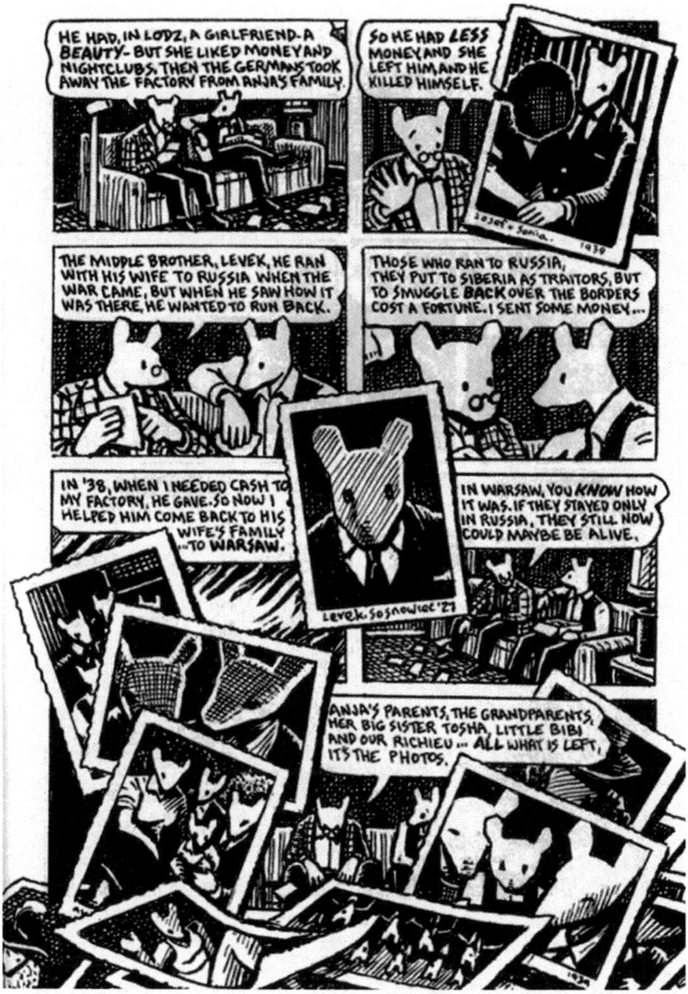

Figure 5.10. Spiegelman's use of drawn copies of photographs as frames; his father is overwhelmed by loss.

The depicted moment occurs when Spiegelman meets with his father to discus his photograph collection; as Vladek despairs at the loss to the Holocaust of so many of his friends and relatives recorded in the photograph album, so the photograph frames visually overwhelm the ordinary rectangular frames of the page. Yet the sequential framing structure is preserved, maintaining the continuity of the narrative.
The intrusion of frames as photographs acts as a means of alternating between times – the present with the burgeoning past – as well as a metaphor for memory; the combined graphic structure of the collapsing page signifies the grief that this represents for Vladek.

The hand drawn copies of photos appear to have a pedagogical function, bestowing authenticity to the representation for the inexperienced audience, despite seeming to distance the events through drawn mediation, they create the space for at least a semblance of assimilation of these unutterable events.

Taxonomy and Critical Reception

For Spiegelman, and for many of the reviewers of *Maus*, defining and classifying the work became a substantive issue. As long as it remained an 'underground' work all this was of little consequence to the established mainstream media. The work acquired commercial status as soon as it rose to prominence, mainly by way of broadsheet newspaper literature reviews, charts and prizes, and then through the gallery system, notably its New York exhibitions. Within this cultural landscape *Maus* had to be considered, evaluated and analysed as part of the process of cultural assimilation, just as with any other artefact. What marked *Maus* out at this time was Spiegelman's use of the graphic novel medium for the Holocaust, in combination with the realism of his autobiographic and contemporary narrative.

The historiography of the Holocaust is already a hotly contested issue of major proportions, even within works by Jews, without all of the issues of anti-Semitism that surrounded the topic. The appearance of such a history in a medium associated (in the US) either with light entertainment for children or anti-establishment 'alternative' culture, was likely to touch a cultural nerve. Given this context, the first strategy that the media, represented mainly by newspaper journalists, developed to manage this political and ethnic problem was assimilation by classification. As some post-structuralists have observed, Barthes amongst them, the naming and classifying of seemingly aberrant social phenomena can be a powerful means of control.[51] By resolving the taxonomy question the work could be located within orthodox structures. In the case of *Maus* it was no longer presented directly as a comic book, or comix, with its potentially disruptive and subversive connotations, but rather as 'history' and 'biography'. These were safer categories for the process of assimilation, leading further to 'normalisation', the rendering of a political work anodyne.

Spiegelman himself was acutely aware of the problem, although his own response may have served to play a significant part in this assimilation process. After *Maus II* was published in the US in 1991 it achieved sufficient sales to make the best-seller lists in the broadsheet newspapers, including the *New York Times*. The difficulty for Spiegelman was classification, with *Maus* appearing in the fiction best seller list. He wrote to the paper at the end of December 1991 in a letter that was published by the editor:

> 'I'd like to thank The Times for its recognition and support of my book 'Maus II.' I was delighted to see it surface on your best-seller list (Dec. 8). I never expected my work to reach such heights [...] If your list were divided into literature and non-literature, I could gracefully accept the compliment as intended, but to the extent that 'fiction' indicates that a work isn't factual, I feel a bit queasy. [...] I know that by delineating people with animal heads I've raised problems of taxonomy for you. [...]'[52]

The editor's reply was published simultaneously, stating that Maus had been reclassified as non-fiction. [53] Clearly Spiegelman's letter had his desired effect, and his battle is important, in that it established the historical veracity of *Maus*, especially in the eyes of Jews, many of

51 Roland Barthes, *Mythologies* (London: Paladin, 1973), 158–159.

52 Art Spiegelman, correspondence published under the title "A Problem of Taxonomy", *New York Times*, December 29, 1991.

53 Spiegelman, "A Problem of Taxonomy".

whom had assisted by offering their own accounts as survivors. Spiegelman sought to classify *Maus* as non-fiction in order to stamp authenticity on the work, to ensure its status as documentary truth.

This classification had significance in terms of its relation to its audience, emerging into the wider culture through its institutions – as Spiegelman recognised in the letter to the *New York Times* editor. In terms of description, of defining the work, however, it may have been less important than Spiegelman suggested. It would have made little difference to the accuracy of the reconstruction of racism and oppression if much of the book were fictional, as Sebald's work demonstrates; it is the perceived authenticity of the recollections (to his particular US audience) and the evidently researched conditions of the Holocaust victims that give the piece its realism. Spiegelman's opening 'prologue' is a case in point, where its parable-like narrative would work just as effectively if it were perceived as fiction.[54] Spiegelman himself alluded to this ambiguous possibility when he referred to his father as a 'fictional character' in *Maus*, an assessment made when he discussed his relationship with Vladek, in an article headed, ironically, 'fiction writers'.[55] Later, Spiegelman's description of his own practice as that of making 'commix' is probably a more significant remark, and this is a theme to which he returned several times, usually as an objection to the sanitising effect of the term graphic novel being applied to his work.[56] Nevertheless, *Maus*' standing as a graphic novel was a novelty for the mainstream media, and one that may have increased the scope of its readership. As one reviewer put it: 'Perhaps no Holocaust narrative will ever contain the whole experience. But Art Spiegelman has found an original and authentic form to draw us closer to its bleak heart.'[57]

54 Spiegelman, *Maus*, 5–6.

55 *New York Times,* "Summer Reading: Who Created Whom? Characters that talk back," Book Review Desk, May 31, 1987.

56 Art Spiegelman, "Commix: An Idiosyncratic Historical and Aesthetic Overview," 192; also, Alan Gleason, interview with the author, December 20, 2001.

57 Lawrence Langer is quoted in Laurel Graeber, "New and Noteworthy," book reviews in the *New York Times*, September 13, 1992.

Spiegelman's device of juxtaposing domesticity and concentration camp horror, with the revelation (for the reviewers) of comics being reinvented, seemed to be a key configuration in its success. Neither of these devices was particularly new, and comic books had previously dealt with equally appalling human suffering – *Barefoot Gen* being a case in point. For the Holocaust, however, this was a new practice and Spiegelman published at a time when the political and cultural conditions were favourable for exploring the Holocaust in innovative ways: 'The comic is as much a depiction of the artist's survival as it is the story of his father's'[58].

Overall the reception of *Maus* should be seen in the context of the changing reception of the Holocaust in US culture in the post war period. It was published for an audience that seemed willing to accept Spiegelman's narrative despite its explicit harshness, and it became celebrated in to an extent that was unusual for a graphic novel. In contrast, the equally explicit realism of Sacco's *Palestine* struggled in commercial terms, which may also be partly explained by its much less secure position in relation to the prevailing ideological conditions.

58 William Hamilton, "Revelation Rays and Pain Stars," review of *Maus I* by Art Spiegelman, *New York Times*, December 7, 1986, p.71.

Conclusion: Graphic Novels as Realism

The success of Spiegelman in aligning the graphic novel medium with the idea of realist documentary, all within a wider forum of the mainstream book market, is a significant contribution to the present and future effectiveness of radical graphic novel production. Spiegelman's realisation of the nuances of human reaction to events of such appalling magnitude offered a method that was readily exploited by others like Sacco and Satrapi, keen to apply the model to contemporary events. The potential of the comics book medium as a vehicle for extended narratives with an overt political content, developed by the Situationists and underground artists, was brought to a stage of sophistication in the lens-based media culture of the 1980s and '90s. This is well beyond the artificial notion of comics as light entertainment for children, which is still prevalent in some countries. The increase in the visual sophistication of graphic novels and with a corresponding increase in the volume of production, does not, however, necessarily result in more radical, realist or documentary works.

There are still serious problems with this specific form of graphic art, not least in the anachronistic stereotyping harboured in the narratives of numerous 'adult' comic plots. It is still the case that in most countries the majority of readers are male, which producers interpret as a demand for particular types of graphic novels that fall into the category of that peculiarly pejorative use of the term 'adult'.[1] These comics and graphic novels tend to conform to a model that is characterised by patriarchal narratives, packed with gratuitous violence and pornography. The conspicuous absence of women in significant numbers from mainstream comic consumption and production is indicative of the current state of affairs. The prevalence

1 Rod Shaile described the composition of the UK audience for manga in these terms. Interview with the author.

of a large body of graphic novels, which either perpetrate unthinking misogyny and discrimination or lapse into anodyne narratives, tends to stigmatise those offering a serious documentary social analysis, like those discussed here. Ware's *Jimmy Corrigan*, for instance, was sufficiently unfamiliar in its formal innovations to make its critical reception beyond the means critical analysis for some reviewers. Despite winning the *Guardian* First Book Award in 2001, initially reviews were infrequent. In the UK the novel encountered difficulties with retailers, with one major high street bookseller insisting on classifying the book as 'science fiction' on the basis of its medium, rather than its subject matter. This illustrates some of the enduring problems that authors making realist documentaries in the graphic novel medium are likely to encounter, irrespective of their subject matter.

Graphic novel authors' strategies for resistance to assimilation into the myth-making process has been discussed at length above. Each of those studied here attempt to portray a political view of reality as experienced by themselves or their subjects. These narratives incorporate a questioning of many of the ideological absolutes that constitute orthodox myths, prevailing in the cultural context within which the work was produced. The media illusions that Chomsky deplores, for instance, with their concealments, their political 'absences' discussed above, are challenged by these authors through their novels.[2] Chomsky demands greater openness in mainstream politics and the media, referring to the necessity for open debate about the way that national governments conduct themselves globally. Through their documentaries Sacco, Satrapi, Sebald, Spiegelman and Nakazawa all reveal the deprivation and the suffering caused by the disregard or manipulation of laws and social responsibilities.

The graphic novel format is, of itself, important as a relatively new way to re-present radical thinking about major issues such as that of the anti-atomic bomb movement. As Chomsky put it: 'It is necessary, somehow, to find ways to reach an audience that isn't

2 Noam Chomsky, *The Fateful Triangle; The United States, Israel and the Palestinians* (London: Pluto Press, 1983), 45.

attuned to elaborate analysis and documentation.'[3] Independent publishers and documentary graphic novelists have to find ways to circumnavigate the control of the mainstream media, as Sacco points out; for Sacco it is precisely because graphic novels can be a medium that is able to reach its audience with minimum intervention from the controlling interests of media corporations.[4] The serious disadvantage with this strategy, as Sacco also discovered, is the problem of relatively poor sales, and the difficulty of barely breaking even financially.[5]

The extent to which the graphic novels considered conform to a social, political realism has much to do with the type of concept of realism being applied as it does with the culture within which the novel was produced. Despite all of the graphic novels having challenged, in one sense or another, dominant and orthodox political positions, their realism is manifest in different ways. *Palestine* is the strongest contender for a Brechtian realisation of the theory, premised upon Brecht's definition of realism as fundamentally concerned with politics, demystifying and resisting ruling class orthodoxy. Sacco's *Palestine* is designed from the very start to challenge the orthodox mythology of Arab culture as hostile, contrary, inferior and of less consequence to the dominant culture of the western culture, particularly in the US where it was created. Brecht's test for this realist practice is to ask whether the work of art in question brought comfort to a ruling class, whether it disrupts or supports the 'prevailing view of things as the view of those in power'.[6] By this test *Palestine* is a work most in opposition to the 'prevailing' view; Sacco's work is as radical as a graphic novel could be and still hope to be published with a semblance of global distribution. Even within Sacco's own oeuvre, with his penchant for inhabiting war zones, the

3 Noam Chomsky, correspondence to Leonard Rifas, April 4, 1983, with reference to the publication of Nakazawa, *I Saw It*.

4 Sacco, interview with the author.

5 Sacco, interview with the author.

6 Brecht, "Popularity and Realism," 491.

work stands apart for the risk that he took in attempting to portray the realism of the everyday existence of the Palestinians.

Spiegelman's *Maus,* on the other hand, is conspicuously innovative in literary and graphic terms, and transformed the literary category of the comic book into a graphic novel. This was of great significance to the other authors, by providing an intellectual platform for a radical documentary realism in graphic novels, from which Sacco and Satrapi have benefited. The realism of depiction, with its oscillation between survival in the Nazi death camps and domestic survival as on offspring of a survivor, is unsurpassed. Spiegelman's visceral description of the conditions in the forced labour camps exposes prejudice and bigotry even amongst the victims, and scrupulously analyses the psychological impact upon subsequent generations. Where it is powerful as a work of realism is in its exposure of the social structures that provide the conditions for discrimination.

When not lapsing into idealism, Nakazawa's political work is subversive in relation to the dominant Japanese ideology of bomb victimisation, primarily because it distributes blame for aggression and militarism between Japan and the US, and resists the orthodox concept of 'victim' by having Gen and the other children actively controlling their social environment. The context of its translation and publication in the West, made it a powerful a realist production in the latter stages of the nuclear threat of the Cold War, when it first appeared outside of Japan. The concept of the US military having responsibility for the atomic bombing of Hiroshima and Nagasaki, and the colossal scale of the suffering that resulted, is a direct challenge to US bomb ideology.

Satrapi's realism lies in the specific, gendered position that its narrative takes. Marjane's perspective on the seismic societal changes with which she is surrounded is imbued on the one hand by her seeming naivety, and on the other by her knowing understanding of the wider political context within which she was growing up. The politics of gender are in the foreground of her narrative as she offers accounts of the impact of prejudicial and discriminatory government, a rare view of the oppression endured by secular women. The highly simplified drawing style enhances the directness of the message, and surprisingly, perhaps, even underpins its documentary realism; its idealism is kept in check either by its humour or by its pathos.

Sebald's work offers an unrelentingly bleak realism within its apparently fictional structure. His scathing analysis of the catastrophic social consequences that arise from petty domestic prejudice and racism are characterised by his innovative juxtaposition of image and text. Sebald's image generated narratives raise profound questions of authenticity, veracity and the concept of documentary.

In his, and each of these cases, the methods of manipulation of the graphic medium is essential to the effectiveness of the political narrative that the author is able to generate in relation to the prevailing conditions of their existing culture. All of these works have been celebrated, rejected, or assimilated in the context of a global comic book culture in transition. The emergence of the graphic novel genre during this period affected their production and reception, enhancing their potential for registering in wider political forums.

Specificity is a fundamental ingredient of documentary realism of the kind presented by the authors in this book. Consequently soldiers or violent state agents are often depicted questioning or troubled by their actions, or alternatively, where they are unthinking, the consequences of their actions are revealed as resulting in suffering, often of innocent people. Domestic events are integrated into social crises, and narratives are developed around highly specific and personal responses, emphasising the authenticity of the accounts given. These highlight the importance of the role that these authors play in both disseminating cultural information hitherto unknown, and at the same time offering alternative ways of thinking of seemingly intractable social problems. In each case these documentary graphic novelists were speaking, through their innovations of the medium, of profound social experiences that might otherwise have remained obscured.

Bibliography

Adams, Jeff. "The Pedagogy of the Image Text: Nakazawa, Sebald and Spiegelman Recount Social Traumas." *Discourse: Studies in the Cultural Politics of Education* 29.1 (2008): 37–52.

——"Troubled Places: Domestic Space in Graphic Novels." In *Our House: The Representation of Domestic Space in Modern Culture*, edited by Joanne Croft and Gerry Smyth, 161–174. Amsterdam: Rodopi Press, 2006.

—— "Working Out Comics." In *International Journal of Art and Design Education* 19.3 (2000): 304–312.

Althusser, Louis. "Ideology and the Ideological State Apparatuses." In *Cultural Theory and Popular Culture,* edited by John Storey, 151–162. New York and London: Harvester/Wheatsheaf, 1994.

Atkinson, Dennis. *Art in Education: Identity and Practice.* Dordrecht/ Boston/London: Kluwer, 2002.

Atwood, Margaret. *The Handmaid's Tale*. London: Virago Press, 1986.

Bachelard, Gaston. *The Poetics of Space*. Translated by Maria Jolas. Boston, Massachusetts: Beacon Press, 1994.

Banerjee, Sarnath. *Corridor*. New Delhi, India: Penguin, 2004.

Barker, Martin. *Comics: Ideology, Power and The Critics*. Manchester: Manchester University Press, 1989.

—— *A Haunt of Fears, The Strange History of the Horror Comics Campaign*. London: Pluto Press, 1984.

Barrell, John. *The Dark Side of the Landscape: The Rural Poor in English Painting 1730–1840.* Cambridge: Cambridge University Press, 1980.

Barthes, Roland. *Camera Lucida*. London: Vintage, 2000.

—— *Image, Music, Text.* Glasgow: Fontana. 1990.

—— *Mythologies*. London: Paladin, 1973.

Berman, Avis. "The Maus That Roared." *Art News* 92 (May 1993): 63–64.

Berndt, Jaqueline. "What's art got to do with it? Observations on recent inter-relationships between manga and visual art." Paper presented at the Chelsea College of Art and the Japan Foundation symposium 'Manga and Art: Visual Culture in Contemporary Japan', London College of Fashion, London, February 1, 2002.

—— "The Time of Comics: Reading a Post-historical Art Form from the Perspective of Manga." Paper presented at the 15th International Congress of Aesthetics, Makuhari, Japan, August, 2001.

Boime, Albert. "The Comic Stripped and Ash Canned: A Review Essay," review of *The Art of the Comic Strip* by Judith O'Sullivan, *The Art Journal,* 32/1, Fall 1972, 21–30.

Brecht, Bertolt. "On the Formalist Character of the Theory of Realism" In *Aesthetics and Politics: The Key Texts of the Debate Within German Marxism*, edited by Fredric Jameson, 72–76. London: Verso, 1998.

—— "Popularity and Realism." In *Art in Theory*, edited by Charles Harrison and Paul Wood, 489–493. Oxford: Blackwell, 1993.

Bruzzi, Stella. *New Documentary: A Critical Introduction.* London: Routledge, 2000.

Butler, Judith. *Precarious Life: The Power of Mourning and Violence.* New York: Verso, 2004.

—— *The Psychic Life of Power*. Stanford: Stanford University Press, 1997.

—— Paper presented as guest lecture at Senate House, University of London, September 29, 2005.

Carnoy, Martin. *The State and Political Theory.* New Jersey, USA, and Guildford, Surrey: Princeton University Press, 1984.

Carrier, David. *The Aesthetics of Comics.* USA: Pennsylvania State University Press, 2000.

Chomsky, Noam. "The New War on Terror." In *The Spokesman*: *War is Peace,* 73, edited by Ken Coates, 25–45. UK: Bertrand Russell Peace Foundation, 2001.

—— *Necessary Illusions: Thought Control in Democratic Societies.* London: Pluto Press, 1993.

—— *The Fateful Triangle; The United States, Israel and the Palestinians.* London: Pluto Press, 1983.

Clark, Timothy J. *Image of the People: Gustave Courbet and the 1848 Revolution.* London: Thames and Hudson, 1999.

——*The Absolute Bourgeois: Artists and Politics in France 1848–1851.* London: Thames and Hudson, 1999.

Clements, Jonathan. Interview with the author, unpublished. September 13, 1996.

—— "Otomatic Exposure." Interview with Kutsuhiro Otomo. *Manga Mania* 37, August, 1996.

Constitution of Japan. In *The Constitution of Japan – Its First Twenty Years 1947–1967* edited by Dan Fenno Henderson. Seattle and London: University of Washington Press, 1968. Originally published in English in Japan, 1947.

Cooper, David Edward. *Authenticity and Learning: Nietzsche's Educational Philosophy.* London: Routledge and Kegan Paul, 1983.

Courbet, Gustave. Letter to Champfleury from "Gustave Courbet 1819–1877." Exhibition catalogue, Grand Palais, Paris, 246–250. Translated by Francis Frascina. Reproduced in *Modern Art Practices and Debates,* A316, 'Texts A', 17–18. Milton Keynes: Open University, 1993. Originally written in 1854.

Cruse, Howard. *Stuck Rubber Baby.* USA: Paradox Press/DC Comics. 1995.

Davidson, Steef. *The Penguin Book of Political Comics.* Middlesex: Penguin, 1982.

DC Comics. *9–11 The World's Finest Comic Book Writers and Artists Tell Stories To Remember*, 2. New York: DC Comics, 2002.

Dorfman, Ariel and Armand Mattelart. *How to Read Donald Duck: Imperialist Ideology in the Disney Comic*. New York and Hungary: I.G. Editions, Inc., 1984. Originally published 1971 in Chile as *Para Leer al Pato Donald.*

Douglas, Allen, and Fedwa, Malti-Douglas. *Arab Comic Strips, Politics of an Emerging Mass Culture.* Bloomington and Indianapolis: Indiana University State Press, 1994.

Duttlinger, Carolin. "Traumatic Photographs: Remembrance and the Technical Media in W.G. Sebald's Austerlitz." In *W.G. Sebald: A Critical Companion*, edited by J.J. Long and Anne Whitehead, 155–171. Edinburgh: Edinburgh University Press, 2004.

E.C. Comics. *Comics Shock SuspenStories* 1.18. West Plains, Mo: Gemstone Publishing, Tiny Tot Comics, 1996. Originally published by EC Comics, 1954.

Eisner, Will. *Comics and Sequential Art.* Florida: Poorhouse Press, 1985.

Fenwick, Geoff. "Comics: An Alternative View." *Reading* 2.2 (July 1977): 3–11.

Fernie, Eric. *Art History and its Methods.* London, Phaidon, 1995.

Flaubert, Gustave. *Madame Bovary*. New York: Bantam Books, 1962. Originally published in France in 1856.

Foucault, Michael. "Different Spaces." In *Aesthetics, Method and Epistemology: Essential Works of Foucault, Volume Two,* edited by James D. Faubion, 175–85. Allen Lane: Penguin, 1998.

Gaines, William M, Jnr. editorial in *Shock Suspend Stories,* EC Comics, No. 18 1954; Facsimile reproduced December 1996, USA, EC Comics, Gemstone Publishing.

Gehr, Richard. "Richard Gehr on Art Spiegelman." *Art Forum* 25 (1987): 10–11.

Gleason, Alan. "The Keiji Nakazawa Interview." *The Comics Journal* 256 (2003): 38–52.

—— Interview 2 with the author, unpublished. December 20, 2001.

—— Gleason, Alan. Interview 1 with the author, unpublished. September 20, 1998.

—— 'Manga Honco', interview with Art Spiegelman in Japanese, transcript 19.10.01.

Golomstock, Igor. *Totalitarian Art*. London: Harper Collins, 1990.

Gravett, Paul. *Graphic Novels: Stories to Change your Life*. London: Aurum, 2005.

—— *Manga: Sixty Years of Japanese Comics*. London: Laurence King Publishing, 2004.

Groth, Gary. "Art Spiegelman Interview." *The Comics Journal* online www.tjc.com/2 archives/i spiegelman.html (accessed January 11, 2002).

—— "Joe Sacco, Frontline Journalist: Why Sacco went to Gorazde." *The Comics Journal* online www.tjc.com/2 ws/i sacco.html (accessed January 11, 2002).

—— "Grown up comics: breakout from the underground." *Print*, vol. 42 (1988): 98–111.

Hajdu, David. *The Ten-Cent Plague: The Great Comic Book Scare and How It Changed America*. New York, Farrar, Straus and Giroux, 2008.

Harris, Jonathan. *The New Art History: A Critical Introduction.* London and New York, Routledge, 2001.

Harrison, Charles and Paul Wood. *Art in Theory*. Blackwells: Oxford, 1993.

Hatfield, Charles. "Heartbreak Soup: The Interdependence of Theme and Form." *Inks: Cartoon and Comic Art Studies* (May 1997): 3–17.

Heath, Shirley Bryce. *Ways With Words: Language Life and Work in Communities and Classrooms*. Oxford: Oxford University Press, 1983.

Henderson, Dan Fenno, ed. *The Constitution of Japan – Its First Twenty Years 1947–1967*. Seattle and London: University of Washington Press, 1968, appendix for Constitution of Japan.

Hergé, *The Adventures of Tintin in the Land of the Soviets*. San Francisco: Last Gasp, 2003.

Hernandez, Gilbert and Jaime. *Love and Rockets*. Seattle, USA: Fantagraphics Books. 1981–1995, series.

Herries, Merion and Susie Herries. *Sheathing the Sword, The Demilitarisation of Japan*. London: Heineman, 1987.

Hitchens, Christopher, foreword in *Safe Area Gorazde, The War in Eastern Bosnia 1992–95* by Joe Sacco. Seattle: Fantagraphics Books, 2000.

—— and Said, Edward W., eds. *Blaming the victims: spurious scholarship and the Palestinian question*. London: Verso, 1987.

Hobsbawm, Eric. *Age of Extremes: The Short Twentieth Century* UK, Penguin, 1994.

—— *Age of Empire 1875–14*. London: Penguin, 2001.

Hogan, Michael J., ed. *Hiroshima in History and Memory*. Cambridge University Press: NewYork, 1996.

Huyssen, Andreas. *Present Pasts: Urban Palimpsests and the Politics of Memory*. Stanford, California: Stanford University Press, (2003).

Ishiguro, Kazuo. *An Artist of the Floating World*. London, Faber and Faber, 1986.

Ivy, Marilyn. "Formations of Mass Culture", reproduced in *Postwar Japan as History,* ed. Andrew Gordon. Berkeley, Los Angeles and Oxford: University of California Press, 1993.

Jacobson, Sid and Ernie Colon. "Story of a Momentous Day." Extracted from *The Illustrated 9/11Commission Report*. UK: Viking & The Times, timesonline.co.uk/books, 2006.

Jameson, Fredric, ed. *Aesthetics and Politics: The Key Texts of the Debate Within German Marxism* , London: Verso, 1998.

Kinsella, Sharon (2000) *Adult Manga: Culture and Power in Contemporary Japanese Society*, ConsumAsiaN.

—— 'Change in Social Status, Form and Content of Manga 1986–1996' from *Japan Forum* 8.1 (1996): 104–112.

Kondo, Yukio. "The Agony of Astro Boy: curating the first Osamu Tezuka exhibition at the Tokyo Museum of Modern Art," symposium paper presented at *Manga and Art: Visual Culture in Contemporary Japan*, London College of Fashion, London, February 1, 2002, organised by Chelsea College of Art and the Japan Foundation.

Kubert, Joe. *Fax from Sarajevo, A Story of Survival*. Dark Horse Books, 1998.

La Breque, Eric. "In Search of the Graphic Novel" *Print* 47 (1993): 21–35.

Liss, Andrea. "Distant Witnessing." *Afterimage* 26.2 (1998): 3.

Mack, Gerstle. *Gustave Courbet*. New York: Da Capo, 1951.

Maki, J.M. "Direction and Theory in Constitutional Developments." In *The Constitution of Japan – Its First Twenty Years 1947–1967*, ed. Dan Fenno Henderson. Seattle and London: Uni. of Washington Press. 1968.

Martin, Stewart. "W.G. Sebald and the modern art of memory" in *Radical Philosophy* 32 (2005): 18–30.

McAllister, Matthew P., Sewell (Jr), Edward H., and Gordon, Ian. *Comics and Ideology*. New York: Peter Lang, 2001.

McCloud, Scott. *Understanding Comics*. New York: Harper Collins. 1994.

McCulloh, M. *Understanding W.G. Sebald*. Carolina: University of Carolina Press, 2003.

McLennan, Gregor, David Held, and Stuart and Hall, eds. *The Idea of the Modern State*. London. 1984.

Meecham, Pam and Julie Sheldon. *Modern Art: A Critical Introduction*. London: Routledge, 2004.

Mitchell, William J. T. *Iconology. Image, Text, Ideology*. Chicago: University of Chicago Press, 1987.

Munz, Ludwig. *Bruegel The Drawings*. London: Phaidon, 1961.

Nakazawa, Keiji. *Barefoot Gen: Volume IV, Out of the Ashes*. San Francisco: Last Gasp, 2005.

—— *Barefoot Gen: Volume III, Life After the Bomb*. San Francisco: Last Gasp, 2005.

—— *Barefoot Gen: Volume II, The Day After*. San Francisco: Last Gasp, 2004.

—— *Barefoot Gen: Volume I, A Cartoon Story of Hiroshima*. San Francisco: Last Gasp, 2004. Originally published as *Hadashi no Gen*. Project Gen: Tokyo, 1972–73. Republished as *Gen of Hiroshima #1*, and *Gen of*

Hiroshima #2, translated by Project Gen. San Francisco CA: EduComics, 1980 and 1981.
—— *I Saw It*, San Francisco, CA: EduComics. 1982. Originally published as *Ore wa Mita.* Translated by Project Gen, Tokyo, 1972–73.
Natsume, Fusanosuke. "The Structure of Manga Expression." Paper presented at the symposium "Manga and Art: Visual Culture in Contemporary Japan," Chelsea College of Art and the Japan Foundation, London College of Fashion, London, February 1, 2002.
Nichols, Bill. *Introduction to Documentary.* Indiana, USA: Indiana University Press, 2001.
Nochlin, Linda. *Realism.* London: Penguin, 1990.
Novick, Peter. *The Holocaust and Collective Memory.* London: Bloomsbury, 2001.
Nyberg, Amy Kiste. "William Gaines and the Battle Over EC Comics." *Inks: Cartoon and Comic Art Studies* 3.1 (1996): 3–15.
Orwell, George. *Animal Farm*. London: Secker and Warburg, 1945.
Otomo, Katsuhiro. *Akira: The Beginning*. London: Mandarin Paperbacks, 1994. Graphically reversed English translation, originally published in Tokyo, 1983.
—— *Domu*. London: Mandarin Paperbacks, 1994. Graphically reversed English translation, originally published in Tokyo.
Perec, Georges. *Species of Space and Other Pieces.* Trans. by John Sturrock. London: Penguin, 1997.
Powers, Thom. "Joe Sacco Interview." *The Comics Journal* 176 (1995): 88–109.
Ricoeur, Paul. *Memory, History, Forgetting.* Chicago and London: The University of Chicago Press, 2006.
Rifas, Leonard. "Globalizing Comic Books from Below: How Manga Came to America." Paper presented at *Big Apple Anime Fest*, USA, December, 21, 2001. Conference paper with minor additions by Rifas, sent to the author.
—— 'Procedures and Dismissals' (review of 'Seal of Approval: the History of the Comics' Code' by Amy Kiste Nyberg) in *The Comics Journal* #209, 1998, pp. 36–37.
—— 'Fredric Wertham: Scientist'. Conference paper from 1st Comic Arts Scholars' Conference in San Diego in 1992, Unpublished.

Sabin, Roger. 'Reflections on the status of manga in the US and the UK', symposium paper at *Manga and Art: Visual Culture in Contemporary Japan*, London College of Fashion, London W1, 1.2.02; organised by Chelsea College of Art and the Japan Foundation.

—— *Comics, Comix and Graphic Novels.* London: Phaidon, 1996.

—— *Adult Comics: An Introduction.* London: Routledge, 1993.

Sacco, Joe. *Palestine.* London: Jonathan Cape, Random House Group Limited, 2003. Originally published 1993, and again by Seattle, Fantagraphics Books. 2001).

—— Interview with the author, unpublished, September 11, 2000.

—— *Safe Area Gorazde, The War in Eastern Bosnia 1992–95.* Seattle: Fantagraphics Books. 2000.

—— *Yahoo.* Volumes 1 and 2. Seattle: Fantagraphics Books, 1991.

Said, Edward. 2003. Foreword in *Palestine* by Joe Sacco, i–v. London: Jonathan Cape, Random House Group Limited, 2003.

—— *The End of the Peace Process; Oslo and After* London: Granta, 2000.

—— "In Search of Palestine." Film for BBC television, screened in the UK, May 17, 1998, 8pm, BBC 2.

—— and Jean Mohr. *After the Dark Sky, Palestinian Lives.* London: Vintage, 1993.

—— *Culture and Imperialism.* London: Chatto and Windus: 1993.

—— *The Question of Palestine.* New York: Vintage Books, 1992.

—— *Orientalism.* Penguin: London, 1991.

—— and Christopher Hitchens. *Blaming the victims: spurious scholarship and the Palestinian question.* London: Verso, 1987.

—— *Covering Islam; How the Media and Experts Determine How We See the Rest of the World.* London: Routledge and Keegan Paul, 1985.

Saito, S. *Japan at the Summit: Japan's Role in the Western Alliance and Asian Pacific Co-Operation.* London and New York: Routledge, 1991 (for the Royal Institute of International Affairs).

Satrapi, Marjane. *Persepolis 2: The Story of a Return.* New York: Pantheon. 2004.

—— *Persepolis: The Story of a Childhood.* London: Jonathan Cape. 2003.

Savage, William W. Jr. *Comic Books and America 1945–1954.* USA: University of Oklahoma Press, 1990.

Schodt, Frederik L. Interview with the author, unpublished, February 7, 2002.

—— *Dreamland Japan; Writings on Modern Manga.* California: Stonebridge Press, 1996.
—— *Manga, Manga, The World of Japanese Comics.* New York: Kodansha International, 1983.
Schwabsky, Barry. "Art Spiegelman: an exquisite sense of balance." *Art Press* 194 (1994): 27–32.
Sebald, W.G. and Jan P. Tripp, *Unrecounted.* Translation Michael Hamburger. London: Penguin, 2005.
Sebald, W.G. *On the Natural History of Destruction.* Translation Anthea Bell. London: Hamish Hamilton, 2003.
—— *Austerlitz.* Translation Anthea Bell. London: Penguin, 2002.
—— *Vertigo.* Translation Michael Hulse. London: Vintage, 2002.
—— *The Emigrants.* London: Vintage. Translation Michael Hulse, 2002.
Shaile, Rod. Interview with the author, unpublished, February 22, 1996.
Spiegelman, Art. *The Complete Maus.* London: Penguin, 2003. Originally published as *Maus: A Survivors Tale Volume I: My Father Bleeds History*, and *Maus: A Survivors Tale Volume II: And Here My Troubles Began.* London: Penguin, 1987 and 1991.
—— "Commix: An Idiosyncratic Historical and Aesthetic Overview." *Print* 42 (1988): 61–73.
Spielberg, Steven and S. Zaillian, *Schindler's List.* (Film). USA: Universal, Amblin Entertainment, 1993.
Stendhal. *Le Rouge et Le Noir.* London: Penguin, 1953. Originally published in France, 1829.
Swales, Martin. "Theoretical Reflections on the Work of W.G. Sebald." In *W.G. Sebald – A Critical Companion*, edited by J.J. Long, and Anne Whitehead, 23–28. Edinburgh: Edinburgh University Press, 2006.
Tezuka, Osamu. *Adolf: An Exile in Japan*; Canada, Cadence Books, 1996.
Tsurumi, Shunsuke. *A Cultural History of Postwar Japan 1945–1980.* London and New York: Kegan Paul International, 1994.
Turvey, Malcolm. "Can the Camera See? Mimesis in 'Man with the Movie Camera.'" *October* 89 (Summer 1999): 25–50.
Venturi, Linoello. *The Great Centuries of Painting: The Sixteenth Century From Leonardo to El Greco.* Switzerland: Skira, 1956.
Wardroper, John. *The Caricatures of George Cruikshank.* London: Gordon Fraser, 1977

Ware, Chris. *Jimmy Corrigan: The Smartest Kid on Earth*. London: Jonathan Cape, Random House Group Limited, 2001.

Wertham, Frederic. *Seduction of the Innocent*. New York: Holt, Rinehart and Winston, 1954.

Wiese, Ellen. ed. *Enter the Comics: Rudolphe Töpffer's Essay on Physiognomy and the True Story of Monsieur Crépin*. Lincoln: University of Nebraska Press, 1965.

Williams, Raymond. "The Works of Art Themselves?" In *Art in Modern Culture: An Anthology of Critical Texts,* edited by Francis Frascina and Jonathan Harris, 315–318. London: Open University Press and Phaidon, 1992.

—— *The Politics of Modernism: Against the New Conformists*. London: Verso, 1990.

—— *Keywords*. London: Fontana, 1984.

—— *The Long Revolution*. London: Pelican, 1961.

Wilms, Wifried. "Tabbo and Repression in W.G. Sebald's 'On the Natural History of Destruction.'" In *W.G. Sebald – A Critical Companion*, edited by J.J. Long, and Anne Whitehead, 175–189. Edinburgh: Edinburgh University Press, 2006.

Wiltz, John E. *From Isolation to War 1931–1941*. London: Routledge and Keegan Paul, 1968.

Witek, Joseph. *Comic Books as History: The Narrative Art of Jack Jackson, Art Spiegelman and Harvey Peckar*. University Press of Mississippi, 1989.

Wood, Paul. "Realisms and Realities" in (1993) *Realism, Rationalism and Surrealism, Art Between the Wars,* edited by Bryony Fer, David Batchelor, and Paul Wood, 250–332. London, Yale, Open University, 1993.

Wright, Bradford G. *Comic Book Nation: The Transformation of Youth Culture in America*. John Hopkins University Press, 2001.

Zola, Émile. *La Debacle*. London: Penguin, 1980. Originally published in France, 1892.

Index

Cultural Interactions
Studies in the Relationship between the Arts

Edited by J.B. Bullen

Interdisciplinary activity is now a major feature of academic work in all fields. The traditional borders between the arts have been eroded to reveal new connections and create new links between art forms. Cultural Interactions is intended to provide a forum for this activity. It will publish monographs, edited collections and volumes of primary material on points of crossover such as those between literature and the visual arts or photography and fiction, music and theatre, sculpture and historiography. It will engage with book illustration, the manipulation of typography as an art form, or the 'double work' of poetry and painting and will offer the opportunity to broaden the field into wider and less charted areas. It will deal with modes of representation that cross the physiological boundaries of sight, hearing and touch and examine the placing of these modes within their representative cultures. It will offer an opportunity to publish on the crosscurrents of nationality and the transformations brought about by foreign art forms impinging upon others. The interface between the arts knows no boundaries of time or geography, history or theory.

Vol. 1 Laura Colombino: Ford Madox Ford: Vision, Visuality, and Writing
Forthcoming. ISBN 978-3-03911-396-5

Vol. 2 Graham Smith: 'Light that Dances in the Mind': Photographs and Memory in the Writings of E. M. Forster and his Contemporaries
257 pages. 2007. ISBN 978-3-03911-117-6

Vol. 3 G.F. Mitrano and Eric Jarosinski (eds): The Hand of the Interpreter: Essays on Meaning After Theory
Forthcoming. ISBN 978-3-03911-118-3

Vol. 4 Grace Brockington (ed.): Internationalism and the Arts in Britain and Europe at the *Fin de Siècle*
Forthcoming. ISBN 978-3-03911-128-0

Vol. 5 Gabrielle Townsend: Proust's Imaginary Museum: Reproductions and Reproduction in *À la Recherche du temps perdu*
232 pages. 2008. ISBN 978-3-03911-124-4

Vol. 6 Lennart Nyberg: Bodies of Poems: Graphic Poetics in a Historical Perspective
Forthcoming. ISBN 978-3-03911-343-9

Vol. 7 Jeff Adams: Documentary Graphic Novels and Social Realism
214 pages. 2008. ISBN 978-3-03911-362-0

Vol. 8 Caroline Patey and Laura Scuriatti (eds): The Exhibit in the Text: The Museological Practices of Literature
Forthcoming. ISBN 978-3-03911-377-4

Vol. 9 Francesca Orestano and Francesca Frigerio (eds): Strange Sisters: Literature and Aesthetics in the Nineteenth Century
Forthcoming. ISBN 978-3-03911-840-3

Vol. 10 Carole Bourne-Taylor and Ariane Mildenberg (eds): Phenomenology and Modernism
Forthcoming. ISBN 978-3-03911-409-2

Vol. 11 Gillian Pye (ed.): Trash Culture
Forthcoming. ISBN 978-3-03911-553-2

Vol. 12 Carol Adlam and Juliet Simpson (eds): Critical Exchange: Art Criticism of the Eighteenth and Nineteenth Centuries in Russia and Europe
Forthcoming. ISBN 978-3-03911-556-3

Vol. 13 Kyriaki Hadjiafxendi and Patricia Zakreski (eds): What is a Woman to Do? A Reader on Female Artistic Occupations c. 1830–1900
Forthcoming. ISBN 978-3-03911-116-7

Vol. 14 Emma Wagstaff: Writing Art: French Literary Responses to the Work of Alberto Giacometti
Forthcoming. ISBN 978-3-03911-871-7

Vol. 15 Linda Goddard: Aesthetic Rivalries: Word and Image in France, 1880–1926
Forthcoming. ISBN 978-3-03911-879-3

Vol. 16 Kim Knowles: A Cinematic Artist: The Films of Man Ray
Forthcoming. ISBN 978-3-03911-884-7